american idyll

american idyll

academic antielitism as cultural critique

catherine liu

university of iowa press, iowa city

University of Iowa Press, Iowa City 52242
Copyright © 2011 by the University of Iowa Press
www.uiowapress.org

Printed in the United States of America

Design by Omega Clay

The University of Iowa Press is a member of Green Press
Initiative and is committed to preserving natural resources.

Printed on acid-free paper

Library of Congress Cataloging-in-Publication Data
Liu, Catherine.
American idyll : academic antielitism as cultural critique /
Catherine Liu.
p.   cm.
Includes bibliographical references and index.
ISBN-13: 978-1-60938-050-2 (pbk.)
ISBN-10: 1-60938-050-9 (pbk.)
ISBN-13: 978-1-60938-051-9 (e-book)
ISBN-10: 1-60938-051-7 (e-book)
1. Elite (Social Sciences)—United States. 2.
Intellectuals—United States. 3. Education, Higher—
United States. 4. United States—Social conditions—
20th century. I. Title.
HN90.E4L58 2011
305.5′52097309045—dc22
2011013864

This book is dedicated to the teachers and students of Pennington Elementary School in Mt. Vernon, New York, and Greenvale Elementary School in Eastchester, New York. I would like to single out Ms. Levine, Ms. Hartnett, and Ms. Von Conta as well as my math teacher Mr. Hunecke. They not only taught me academic skills, but also, in the best traditions of democratic education, they demonstrated what it meant to be an American. To them I want to offer very belated thanks.

This book is also dedicated to the Seward/Longfellow neighborhood of Minneapolis, the precinct caucus where I caucused during the presidential elections of 2004. The voters in this Minneapolis precinct showed me local democratic politics in action, and it was both messy and moving.

contents

acknowledgments

I would like to thank Joseph Parsons at the University of Iowa Press and everyone there involved in the production and editing of this book. Their support and commitment have been critical to my belief that writing and publishing a book like this could be possible. I would like to thank the University of Minnesota Grant-in-Aid Program, which supported the beginning of my research. Thanks to the UC Irvine International Center for Writing and Translation for funding travel to the Warburg Archives in London. A seminar I gave at Queensland University of Technology allowed me to test these ideas very early on. I want to thank Ian Hunter, Andrew McNamara, Jerome Christensen, Richard Godden, and Michael Szalay, who read parts of this work at various stages of its evolution and gave me invaluable advice and criticism. Peng-yi Tai helped with critical aspects of research. She must be thanked for being a true collaborator. Victoria Hsieh and Brian Thompson were critical to cleaning up a manuscript that was a sprawling mess. I would like to thank my colleague Jeff Wasserstrom for his commitment to clear, precise, accessible writing. Special thanks should go to Russell Berman, who introduced me to Joseph Parsons and encouraged me to submit the manuscript to the University of Iowa Press. Two anonymous reviewers offered extremely helpful and challenging criticism. All mistakes and omissions are my responsibility alone.

Special thanks to Beverly Semmes and Henry Schwartz for being the very best friends that one could hope for. Finally, thank you to Peter and Leo Krapp, my family, who never humored me in my darkest moments and were always ready to distract me with lots of loving subversion.

american idyll

introduction

populist idylls, cultural politics

During the past two or three decades, antielitism has played a vital role within the most progressive segments of American academia. Here, antielitist cultural critique saw itself as a powerful, eminently political form of self-critique for intellectuals: in addressing political and social exclusion and injustice, it aspired to debunk the oppressive myths of normativity and nation as well as curriculum and canon. The American political imagination has long been shaped by a seductive myth of antielitist agrarian righteousness and rustic vigor. If People's Party Populists had imagined their idyll as a place where the money power had been brought low so that an egalitarian world of farmers and small towns could finally prosper, academic populists imagined a world of ordinary people with popular tastes and deep passions who, as fans and amateurs, could finally create a culture of their own that eluded the experts.[1] In academia, populist yearnings fueled a troubling critique of modernity, reason, and universalism. In both cases, the intellectual and the critic stood aloof as mere observers, unable to enjoy or produce anything truly new or useful.

In 1989 academic populism found a charismatic and articulate spokesman in the figure of Andrew Ross. In his book *No Respect: Intellectuals and Popular Culture*, Ross urged cultural critics and intellectuals to stop preaching and start "rearticulating" a "popular politics" in the face of the overwhelming appeal of right-wing populism. Intellectuals, Ross argued, were going to have a hard time grasping "popular politics" since, as eggheads, they were invested in reason and the new politics was grounded in "the body." Popular politics "trades on pleasures which training in political rationality encourages us to devalue."[2] By the late 1980s, the Anglo-American Left desperately needed a new political and cultural strategy. Considering its failure in both the United States and the United Kingdom to win the people's favor through the popular vote, Ross suggested that the Left would henceforth have to reimagine a newly configured politics of hedonism and irrationality. He pleaded with intellectuals to give up "preaching" about popular pleasures: he asked them to renounce their expertise and to seek out a "common ground" with the people in order to build a real "popular-democratic culture."[3]

In 2005 Ernesto Laclau, in his work *On Populist Reason*, echoed Ross's denunciation of political rationality in favor of an affirmative theory of populist politics.[4] Laclau admired the way in which populism divided the political field into two starkly opposed camps, "the people" and a "power bloc." Instead of organization, populist political activity affirmed creativity, spontaneity, and improvisation in hitherto denigrated forms of popular resistance. They could participate in linked but not cohesive collectives, each with its own distinctive set of demands: the people were finding ways to articulate a series of more and more radical demands, some economic, some infrastructural, some cultural, some psychosexual. The populist chain of demands kept the power bloc off balance and set the terms for reaction from the elites.[5] According to Laclau, only "theory" could adequately explain what the people wanted and who the people were. With the rise of global populism as a completely new form of politics, the people and their desires could only be deciphered through an esoteric form of poststructuralist linguistics: "the people" were hailed as the emptiest of signifiers. Laclau's protean populism resembled the potentialities attributed by Michael Hardt and Antonio Negri to the creative multitudes.[6] The "people," like the "multitude," escaped the old, battered Marxist concept of class struggle as easily as it eluded traditional forms of referentiality.[7] Laclau's explanations of populism seemed at times to be earnestly addressed to former Communist Party apparatchiks who clung stubbornly to the working class as an agent of history. They were now urged to believe that the new political actuality could only be grasped through careful study of Lacanian position papers explaining populist agency. Laclau was in an intense struggle with his erstwhile ally, Slavoj Žižek, who had "come out" against "the populist temptation" in an article addressing popular hostility toward the European Union.[8]

If Laclau made elaborate arguments against reason, Andrew Ross, John Fiske, and Lawrence Grossberg found in popular culture's carnivalesque pleasure a negation of the power of intellectual dissent. Reason, not tyranny, had become the people's true oppressor. The Enlightenment philosophers were now greeted by Left vanguardists as the perpetrators of a crime against the people. Perhaps Enlightenment philosophers had wanted to liberate us from fear and superstition by proposing that the general exercise of reason was both the right and the capacity of all human beings, but their secularism had failed to provide structures of meaning for ordinary people. For Left intellectuals, reason itself had been hopelessly deformed as technoscientific rationality. Increasingly complex forms of difference, rather than communicative or persuasive forms of solidarity, would become the foundation of a new political imaginary. During the 1980s and 1990s, antielitism was the banner under which the academic populist insurgency gathered its strength. For the most radical of these thinkers, divesting themselves of a misplaced investment in reason was the most challenging task of all.

In the historical struggle between reason and belief that intensified three hundred years ago, this was an unexpected turn of events. Enlightenment philosophers had dared to see themselves as a vanguard in the struggle against both church and king, but their contemporary avatars had allegedly morphed into soulless "professional" experts who were now declared by Right and Left as the laggards of both history and politics. Academic populists saw the truth of this situation: they were the ones who could point to the fact that intellectuals were left shamefully holding up the rear in a new struggle for freedom from the oppressive demands of thinking itself. The Enlightenment had launched progressive thought as a social and political project that "was aimed at liberating men [sic] from fear and establishing their sovereignty," but the actual political achievements of the republics seemed to fall far short of the Utopia of self-rule and self-determination promised by popular democracy. Not only had "What Is Enlightenment?," Kant's promotion of emancipation from tutelage, lost its appeal, but the benefits of rational, political citizenship had been tarnished in the eyes of the most sophisticated cultural critics. American liberal democracy was merely a disguise for imperial and economic ambitions: in more Foucauldian terms, participatory citizenship and the public sphere reproduced both surveillance and discipline. For the New Left, the Vietnam War and the Nixon administration revealed the dark side of American liberalism: for a new generation of academics, participation in dissent and the political process was complicity in disguise.[9] From a theoretically sophisticated, antielitist point of view, Kantian "maturity" or the very notion of political majority seemed biased against the "immature" and the minor: those who were marginalized by dominant ideologies could not even figure as legitimate sources of dissent. Political rationality was too restrictive as a category to accommodate the new politics of the popular, the different, the queer. In any case, the developmental trajectory proposed by Kantian philosophy sketched its history with that most hated of representational tools: the linear narrative. Meanwhile, a generation of scholars found relief in Foucault's analysis of power because it confirmed that liberalism was merely another form of "governmentality."

By the late 1980s and early 1990s, enthusiastic Anglo-American readers of "French Theory" and proponents of cultural studies could agree that the era of "grand narratives" was over.[10] American critics of Enlightenment reason dismissed the work of midcentury intellectuals who were seen as sponsoring the consensus liberalism of proprietary individualism and political rationality. Widespread discontent with academic specialization spurred deeper engagement with other cultures, other ways of knowing. Counterculture-driven distrust of the uses and abuses of expertise resonated with general feelings of populist discontent with the increasing powers of the state. If in the 1890s the People's Party demanded economic justice for producers, the populists of the 1980s demanded freedom from cultural condescension. In the neopopulist revival, secularism and reason became cast as twin tyrants that had to be overthrown in the name of freeing the people from that most overweening of potentates: cultural elitism.

In the wake of countercultural discontent, academic populism emerged as a strong arm of cultural studies: this remarkably charismatic academic reform movement in the 1980s and 1990s shaped academic debates as well as the positions defended by the Left during the culture wars. Although it may have appeared that Dinesh D'Souza disagreed with Fredric Jameson and William Bennett with Henry Louis Gates, Jr., they could all agree that culture had become a privileged site of political struggle. Victory or defeat on the cultural battleground could translate into any number of portentous social consequences—Western civilization could be saved or lost. Oppressed peoples could be freed—or not. In *Nixonland*, Rick Perlstein argued that Richard Nixon's dark vision of politics gave shape to the logic of American cultural apocalypse.[11] For Perlstein, Nixon was haunted by the idea that American values were on the verge of extinction. In his struggle to save his country, there was no law he would not break, no tactic he could not stomach, no area of dispute he would not enter. He showed us how to wage a culture war: up the ante until your adversaries are cornered and have to fold. Left and Right alike participated in the escalation of the culture wars, when education and curriculum were turned into matters of baleful portent. Western civilization had to be rescued from barbarians; Western civilization had to be undone from within. Once the battle lines were drawn, serious discussion of education and its goals and histories had to be eclipsed, if not suppressed. Most significantly, the academic Left was so distracted by its own attacks on liberalism that it failed to grasp what the long-range consequences of antielitism as a cultural program would be.

For the most extreme academic populist, any criticism of popular culture and popular taste was associated with elitism, universalism, normative masculinity, consensus politics, liberalism, and Marxism. While the Left denounced critique and negativity as the true usurpers of the sovereignty of the people's will, conservatives construed public goods such as public universities oxymoronically as socialist luxuries that had parasitically attached themselves to the aggrieved "American taxpayer." In 2001 historian and journalist Thomas Frank argued in *One Market under God* that "market populism" was the most dynamic business ideology of the past decade: in its attempts to secure more freedom for markets rather than people, it marshaled a motley crew of enemies who possessed all the sins of greedy plutocrats from a century ago.[12] Market populism was an exotic hybrid of laissez-faire business ideology and populist outrage that purposefully appropriated the emancipatory promises of 1960s political movements in order to give "power [back] to the people." For Frank, populist agitation for economic and cultural self-sufficiency was skillfully woven into the rhetoric of free market ideology, creating the intellectual and moral ground for market populism's demands and attitudes. The most satisfying target of new populist rage turned out not to be the banks or trusts; by the late twentieth century, it was the government itself that had emerged as predatory and corrupt. In the populist imagination of the recent past, the government has replaced the plutocrat as a parasite on the body of the innocent "producers."

Frank showed that the New Economy boom of the 1990s animated a passionate antielitism of free markets. Government interference in the form of either taxation or regulation was seen as hindering the progress of the rugged individual as nonconformist and entrepreneur. In fact, during the 1990s, business and management ideology touted the market as a miraculous "global plebiscite": Walter Wriston condemned any government or union interference with market forces as obstructing the actualization of the people's will itself; George Gilder denounced skepticism about the free market as the cause of economic downturn.[13] Wriston and Gilder were Reagan era economic visionaries. Wriston was a banker and former chairman of Citicorp. From 1982 to 1989 he served as the chairman of Reagan's Economic Policy Advisory Board. George Gilder was an early defender of techno-Utopianism and author of *Wealth and Poverty*, a book that promoted with a missionary passion technological progress, free markets, and small government. Wriston and Gilder shared the conviction that a free market and technology could realize a better world. They also could lay claim to Promethean ambitions to break the backbone of New Deal and Great Society reforms of the American economy. The two men legitimized and defended Ronald Reagan's economic policies with intellectual ballast and effective business practice.

In Gilder's world, the power of positive thinking had taken on a whole new dimension, while Freud's concept of the "omnipotence of thoughts" was taken as a "how-to" injunction to work on creating "one's own reality."[14] Cultural historian of new media Fred Turner showed that, by the early 1990s, Gilder played a critical role in marrying supply-side economics from the Reagan era with the technolibertarianism of the New Economy.[15] Gilder believed that markets mirrored natural phenomena and should be left alone to develop "organically." In a wide-ranging interview with Kevin Kelly for *Wired* magazine in 1993, Gilder used social Darwinist metaphors to argue that government should leave the Internet and the New Economy to develop without interference or regulation so that the fittest might prevail.[16] For Gilder, markets were spontaneous and naturally antihierarchical systems; in 1993 Gilder and Kelly concurred that the Internet was free market Utopia made digital flesh. In the 1990s, corporations made claims on authenticity and creativity by appealing to populist style. Moreover, flexibility and networked horizontality were principles by which profit making and creativity could be reconciled. Wooed by intellectuals, economists, and the greatest corporations of the late twentieth century, ordinary people were alleged to possess unique powers of critical and cultural discernment.

For David Harvey, embedded liberalism, based on Keynesian economic principles, described the post–New Deal compromise worked out among corporate power, government, and workers. Neoliberal economic policies destroyed this compromise by continually attacking as cumbersome the unwieldy state bureaucracies that supported "embedded liberalism." Conflating the demand for individual freedom and expressivity with market freedom and its need for "expression," a savvy capitalist class helped by economists and think-tankers was able to back up its grab for power with the antistatist demands of the popular protest movements of 1968. According to Harvey, "neoliberalization required both politically and economically the construction of a neoliberal market-based populist culture of differentiated consumerism and individual libertarianism."[17] Conservative culture warriors found that the fertile ground of popular and mass culture should not be ceded to the tenured radicals. Instead of defending Plato and Rousseau, a new generation of right-wing pundits rushed to embrace NASCAR, pork rinds, and barbecue.

Claiming a novel form of solidarity with the people through their embrace of popular tastes, academic populists also rushed to proclaim their hatred of experts, bureaucrats, and elitists. They asked themselves how they could make their work relevant and more whole. They chafed at narrow, artificial forms of specialization. Academic populists gave voice to a general sense that we had become trapped by the steel cage of professionalization and professionalism: how, then, were we to break out of these institutional confines? Theory, interdisciplinarity, popular culture, cultural studies: a vast array of new methods and objects emerged to challenge the idea of proper academic research. Pragmatism was an early articulation of the dilemma of the American academic, torn between a mugwump contempt for both democracy and business and a devotion to the sanctity of a newly forged sense of scientifically oriented specialization. Pragmatism had offered a way out of these two equally confining alternatives and, because of its impetus to ground thinking outside the narrow concerns of academic philosophy, it emerged as a powerful intellectual force during the Progressive Era. "Experience" became John Dewey's watchword, a bridge term between the practice of philosophy and an engagement with industrial democracy. If Dewey originally insisted that the experiences and problems of ordinary people had to be accounted for in meditations of philosophy, then cultural studies, as a newly configured pragmatism, took "ordinary" to mean something specific to "culture" itself. American pragmatism was founded on Dewey's injunction that philosophy had to address the ordinary problems of ordinary people. The key word "ordinary" may have had a scandalous inflection in the cultural work of Raymond Williams: it was quickly embraced as a legitimizing force for a new kind of critique.[18] Routinized antielitism became ensconced in American academic life during the 1980s and 1990s. Furthermore, academic populism was uniformly hostile to ideals of liberal education as well as aesthetic and intellectual autonomy, once defended by midcentury thinkers like Richard Hofstadter and Theodor Adorno. Anglo-American cultural studies scholars of the 1980s almost universally dismissed Adorno's theory of culture industry as an idiosyncratic system of cultural critique that was both elitist and simplistic.[19] In fact, for Lawrence Grossberg, denouncing elitism became one of the most important forms of political struggle tout court. In an attempt to open up the "political horizon" of postmodernism, Grossberg urged us to reject those who refuse to see the positive effects of the postmodern on everyday life and ordinary people. For Grossberg, noxious forms of elitism abounded: there was the elitism of the vanguard, the elitism of producerism, the elitism of frontiers, deconstructive elitism, textual elitism, and, of course, aesthetic elitism, all waiting to be rooted out and denounced by what can only be described as an "ultrapopulism."

For progressive scholars who yearned for relevance and immediacy, academic populism and cultural studies promised to sweep away all that was obsolete and moribund about humanities and social sciences education. The anticanonical, antiliterary animus of cultural studies had a much easier time than expected reshaping already fluid ideas about the American curriculum. Gerald Graff and others have shown that in the United States, humanistic disciplines never partook of the explicit nationalism that marked literary criticism in Great Britain and on the European continent. By the twentieth century, American professors were preoccupied with academic freedom, standardization, and normalization of the research university and its curriculum. As Graff has pointed out, a fundamentally pragmatic and professionalizing attitude about research universities would have long-range, cascading consequences for the development of a distinctively American notion of the social function of meritocracy and higher education. For instance, it was only with the rise of standardization in college entrance examinations that secondary school reading lists for English literature were formed. The consolidation of the study of literature as the discipline of "English" occurred as a result of concerted institutional efforts to establish uniform standards in secondary school education.[20]

Richard Hofstadter was a troubling figure for the academic populist. As a historian of educational reforms and American anti-intellectualism, he was a harsh critic of the mythologization of ordinary people. His denunciation of American anti-intellectualism would make him an enemy of academic populists. Hofstadter saw something essentially American about the various forms of anti-intellectualism that shaped both reactionary and progressive politics. For Hofstadter, American admiration for the self-educated man and his mastery of erudite and practical knowledge was accompanied by a deep suspicion of book learning. In the 1960s Richard Hofstadter's account of American anti-intellectualism became the focal point of a massive reassessment of the political and historical significance of American populism. In *Anti-intellectualism in American Life*, he launched a harsh critique of the agrarian myths upon which populist politics were founded.[21] He wanted historians to reevaluate the agrarian myth in light of McCarthyism and Cold War anti-Communism.

The Progressive education movement that Deweyan philosophy inaugurated, organized, and legitimized never hid its world-transforming ambitions. In many senses, Hofstadter was arguing against it in the name of a more restrained but rigorous set of standards in education that could only be generated by the critical and historical demands of intellectual work itself. Like Theodor Adorno's notions of aesthetic autonomy, Hofstadter's conception of intellectual autonomy remained remarkably negative. If midcentury intellectuals such as Clement Greenberg and Meyer Shapiro, along with Hofstadter and Adorno, were unsparingly critical of populism in politics and culture, the late 1980s and 1990s saw young critics on the Left turn decisively against their predecessors. What Angela McRobbie called "'68 educated radical professionals" launched wave after wave of criticism against their "high modernist" and "elitist" elders.[22] But it was with the rise to power of Ronald Reagan and Margaret Thatcher that a turning point in academia was reached. On the Left there appeared a marked historical shift away from criticism of popular culture and consumption toward a sympathetic reappraisal of consumption's awesome powers. Andrew Ross's *No Respect* offered an implicit indictment of Hofstadter's theory of American anti-intellectualism. Ross found that American popular culture was filled with examples of popular subservience before intellectuals and their expertise: if Ross sensed a rebellion brewing against the eggheads, he felt that the eggheads could only blame themselves for their sense of entitlement and condescension. In his history of American intellectual life, the 1950s and 1960s were a period when intellectuals enjoyed unprecedented prestige and power. They became apologists for the powerful, while their aesthetic elitism alienated ordinary people. From a cultural studies perspective, Hofstadter's negative assessment of American populism would of course appear as the height of intellectual arrogance and elitism.

From outside of cultural studies circles, Christopher Lasch condemned Hofstadter for his intemperate dismissal of populism.[23] Lasch was Hofstadter's student and one of the most prominent cultural historians of his generation. If he criticized Hofstadter, he also defended the Old Left values against the countercultural revolt within the academic world. A dissenter on all fronts, Lasch refuted Hofstadter's charge that a sustained sentimentalization of farm life eventually yielded the "paranoid style" in American politics. Lasch praised the populist refusal of progress as one of the most important and powerful dissenting political movements in the United States. He embraced a return to agrarian values and civic vigor against the consumerism of the 1960s and 1970s. In his defense of populist politics, he excoriated the neoliberal confidence in technocracy and limitless economic growth as the most distinctive characteristic of post-McGovern Democratic politicians. According to Lasch, "the rise of neoliberalism in the mid-seventies made it easier than ever for the right to appropriate the rhetoric and symbolism of populism."[24] For both Lasch and Hofstadter, however, Progressive politics and liberal institutions relied too much on expertise and institutional solutions for social problems. They viewed the popular and neopopulist backlash against liberalism with much more trepidation than Ross: Lasch's defense of populism took place in the name of an anti-Enlightenment, antiprogressive, civic militancy. At his most radical, he rejected the growth and progress models of economy and culture, urging his readers to embrace a properly republican sense of duty and sacrifice, all in the context of a darkly realistic sense of the limitations of representational politics. In fact, Lasch abhorred the easy hedonism and smug self-involvement of the countercultural New Left. For him, only the producerist ethic of populism was capable of reviving a positive Puritanism, grounded in stoical self-sufficiency and coupled with passionate civic-mindedness. Only through active cultivation of this attitude could Americans overcome the facile sensuality and perpetual dissatisfaction of consumerist culture: "The progressive conception of history implied a society of supremely sophisticated consumers; the populist conception a whole world of heroes."[25]

Lasch dismissed Hofstadter and Adorno's concerns about the racist and often anti-Semitic cast of militant and heroic provincialism. He participated in the backlash against midcentury liberal cultural critique even as he denounced the rise of theory and its proponents. The 1990s saw many positive, historical reappraisals of populism, including historian Michael Kazin's analysis of the power of populist rhetoric.[26] Kazin took an ambivalently affirmative view of the populist movement and focused on its rhetorical power to inspire collective action in the name of political change. Kazin's analysis of populist rhetoric offered a theoretical and historical redemption of the religious and spiritual aspirations of populist politics and its egalitarian and ethical aspirations. The son of New York intellectual Alfred Kazin, Michael Kazin proposed a self-critical, theoretical reevaluation of the kinds of populist politics that were particularly difficult for urban, cosmopolitan, secular Jewish intellectuals of his father's generation to understand, much less affirm.

Mark Fenster's book *Conspiracy Theories: Secrecy and Power in American Culture* offered a cultural studies critique of Richard Hofstadter's historiography and the cultural position of "postwar intellectual elites."[27] In 1999 Fenster's goal was to rescue conspiracy theory from Hofstadter's 1965 work, *The Paranoid Style in American Politics*.[28] For Fenster, Hofstadter's dismissal of conspiracy theory thinking as a legitimate form of dissent within the polis participated in the liberal pathologization of marginal voices and identities. Focusing on a close reading of a passage from *The Paranoid Style*, Fenster showed that Hofstadter had compared paranoia with ugliness and distortion in painting, thereby using aesthetics to describe the political difference between liberalism and populism. Liberalism was beautiful, conspiracy theory thinking was ugly.[29] In the 2008 expanded and updated reissue of Fenster's book, his criticism of Hofstadter's work was blunted. It seemed that after September 11, 2001, Fenster was less enthusiastic about conspiracy thinking given the rise of extremist politics both at home and abroad. He ceded no ground, however, on his description of Cold War intellectual elites: they were still described as anxiety-ridden, patriarchal defenders of 1950s "normativity." In the cultural studies version of the American 1950s, Fenster decided that Hofstadter was a little "paranoid about paranoia." Drawing upon Andrew Ross's and Antonio Gramsci's work on hegemony, Fenster pointed to the postwar alliance between the intellectuals and the state. He concurred with C. Wright Mills that Cold War intellectuals readily embraced their roles as functionaries and servants of the power bloc: "In this sense, consensus historians, as part of an entire class of dominant intellectuals, played a central role in the legitimation [*sic*] process of Cold War policy and ideology."[30] According to Fenster's and Ross's versions of the 1950s, intellectuals such as Hofstadter were so complicit with statecraft and played such a central role in American politics that they were blind to the political expressiveness and critical legitimacy of popular culture and populist conspiracy theories. Fenster's critique represented the standard cultural studies historicization of the role of intellectuals during the Cold War: intellectuals allegedly pandered to power and were committed to producing a flattering and fundamentally fraudulent image of American liberalism.

Fenster's and Ross's intellectual activities were no longer in danger of being complicit with organized forms of power. Their cultural politics were aligned with radical, nonnormative, transgressive, ordinary, populist, and denigrated forms of dissent. Fenster's methodology, if not Ross's, was inspired by the work of French historian Michel Foucault's critique of normalizing and disciplinary apparatuses deployed by "power" to reproduce itself. "Problematization," "subversion," "complication," and "disruption" were favorite watchwords used in defiance of political and economic legibility. In Fenster's 2008 conclusion, he used verbs like "to complicate" and "to disrupt" as positive descriptors of contemporary academic methodology. Hofstadter's analysis of conspiracy theory was simplistic and normative: the absence of the critical and complicating matrix of "race, gender, and class" made Hofstadter's work appear fundamentally flawed to the cultural studies scholar. Although Fenster shared Hofstadter's concern with status politics and resentment, he was unable to accept Hofstadter's liberal turn of mind. David S. Brown, in his recent biography of Richard Hofstadter, attributes Hofstadter's skepticism about agrarian life to his deep attachment to the cosmopolitanism and intellectual stimulation of New York City, especially of the Upper West Side neighborhood around Columbia University in which he lived and worked.[31] Hofstadter's work also shows evidence of being influenced by *The Authoritarian Personality*, a postwar investigation of totalitarianism and its relationship to prejudice and anti-Semitism.[32] Populist suspicion of middlemen and financiers struck Hofstadter as unpleasant reminders of Nazi propaganda against the Jews. Populist rage may have fueled a thirst for authentic economic and political justice, but Hofstadter saw it as a potentially malleable force that could be easily volatilized into a toxic cocktail of racist resentment and reaction. A rough and righteous populist rage may have expanded the base of representative democracy, but Hofstadter never accepted democratic aspirations at face value. He would be dismayed but not surprised at discovering the contemporary conspiracy theories about the U.S. government and a New World Order or a president's allegedly doctored birth certificate elaborated by more recent grassroots insurgencies.

Charles Postel's *The Populist Vision* represented a historian's critique of Hofstadter's critique of populist anti-intellectualism.[33] In this reappraisal of American populism based on new archival research, Postel forcefully argued that the historical Populists of the 1890s were modernizers. Postel's arguments are derived from archival evidence he found in nineteenth-century Populist papers as well as the correspondence of Populist activists and ordinary rural Americans who were drawn into Populist politics. Postel found that Populists saw the gap between urban and rural life as one of the great problems of late nineteenth-century America. For Populist thinkers like Charles Macune, the postal service was one of the great modern innovations that served the cause of rural modernization by connecting isolated farmers with cities and with each other. They were not hidebound traditionalists, nor were they agrarian sentimentalists. Postel's book addressed the question of race and gender by presenting the People's Party agenda as one in which rural women found a way of expressing their own public and political aspirations. Women played a prominent role in the movement because Populist politics addressed the concerns of rural society as a whole. Postel showed that Populists demanded improvements in rural communication, culture, and education. Populists believed in education and self-education: the Farmers' Alliance sent lecturers all over rural America to teach those who tilled the earth about the importance of rural organization. Unfortunately, Populist views of race and their affirmation of white supremacy and segregation were justified by their embrace of the pseudoscience of racial hierarchy, especially in the South. In fact, for Postel, their faith in science resembled the scientific optimism of both Gilded Age and Progressive Era elites.

Not all young scholars have been critical of Hofstadter's legacy. Thomas Frank certainly owes a great deal to Hofstadter's historical work. In *The Conquest of Cool* Frank showed that 1950s corporate leaders yearned for countercultural revolt as much as their hippie and bohemian counterparts: in advertising, corporate America's connection to countercultural aspirations became visible in the effective mass marketing of "cool."[34] Frank's against-the-grain reading of the connection between the 1950s and the 1960s drew upon Hofstadter's consensus theories. In *What's the Matter with Kansas?* Frank suggested that right-wing cultural and religious populism had appropriated the rhetorical strategies of its erstwhile adversaries by demonizing cultural elitism and intellectual elitists as the most shameful enemies of the outraged people.[35] Frank and his collaborators had used their gadfly publication the *Baffler* to satirize the cultural politics of highly contorted cultural studies and postmodern theories of difference. In a way, their work represented a return to a certain midcentury skepticism and a commitment to the value of reasoned dissent and participation in public policy debates. Frank married a postpunk sensibility with a midcentury critique to cast a jaundiced eye on the boomer theorists of the Left. In so doing, Frank kept his focus on the ways in which cultural populism had been repurposed by the Right. In his return to the 1950s critique of mass culture as political manipulation, Frank pointed out that an antielitist emphasis on cultural grievances and cultural marginality had the strategic political effect of suppressing an economic critique of finance capital. Frank showed that the Right was able to use race and religion to make a reactionary and emotional appeal to the lost values of the American pastoral. The rational and economic interests of his middle-class, middle-American Kansans were eclipsed in favor of cultural battles over values and meaning. Meanwhile, in academia, Frank was called a neoconservative, and leftist scholars expressed outrage whenever someone like Frank dared to impugn the robust independence of mind and intellectual self-sufficiency of ordinary people. During the past decade, right-wing pundits from Ann Coulter to Bill O'Reilly, from William Kristol to David Brooks have deftly used the antielitist rhetoric forged by the Left to its own advantage. This "repurposing" of antielitism was certainly a sign of its power as cultural critique.

Unfortunately, the demise of cultural hierarchy masked and marked the rise of economic polarization: a class war was being fought alongside the culture wars, but the redistribution of wealth was not of central concern in Jameson's interventions. Antielitist cultural critique attacked normative, dominant, and central agencies of oppression, taking out of the equation anything that smacked of totalizing accounts of exploitation or expropriation. As conservative political analyst and historian Kevin Phillips showed in his analysis of the 1980s Reagan era tax reforms, the 1970s marked the end of the economic gains in purchasing power and economic strength hard earned by the American working and middle classes.[36] In 1989 Barbara Ehrenreich had already tried to draw attention to economic polarization in her sweeping analysis of middle-class anxiety and economic insecurity: "According to the U.S. Census the income gap between the richest and the poorest families was wider in the mid-eighties than at any time since the bureau began keeping statistics in 1946."[37] A new concentration of economic power followed Reagan's tax reforms and the deregulation of banking while undermining social welfare assistance to the poor. The concerted attacks on unionized labor destabilized the lives of the poor and working classes: a new oligarchy was emerging that would indeed care much less about high culture and its achievements. Yet Jameson emphasized, in his attempts to define postmodernism, that its emergence as the "logic of late capitalism" in the 1970s and 1980s oversaw a period that saw the welcome demise of a cultural aristocracy. Even business journals such as *Barron's* and *Business Week* appeared to be more critical of tax reforms and the rise of information society than America's most famous Marxist theorist. In fact, business journalists more than left-wing academics remarked that these conditions were creating a new class of "left-behind workers" as well as a "fragile middle class" whose incomes, while rising, could not keep pace with the increase in after-tax incomes for the very wealthiest.[38] In fact, during the periods of economic growth under Reagan and Clinton, working families saw their debt burden grow in proportion to earned income. In his study of American wealth, Phillips showed that, according to one analysis of the Congressional Budget Office, the United States saw a dramatic polarization of incomes as a result of the 1980s tax reforms. Changes in the tax code allowed the top 1 percent of after-tax salaries to grow at the rate of 115 percent (adjusted for inflation) between 1977 and 1990. "By contrast, the inflation-adjusted, after-tax income flowing to the middle 60 percent of households in 1999 was slightly below the same figure for 1977." The bottom fifth of households in the United States saw a decline of 9 percent in after-tax income. And yet, during the same period, one could find in cultural studies journals and anthologies an optimistic mood about the transgressive and liberatory potential of the enigmatic people, these "consumer-sphinxes" who were inventing new forms of empowerment behind the back of the liberal elites. I think it is critical to juxtapose the academic success of a new politics of culture with the political and economic successes of Reagan's tax codes, which strengthened a new financial elite by undoing the New Deal's fiscal policies.[39] For Richard Sennett in *The Culture of the New Capitalism*, "inequality has become the Achilles' heel of the modern economy."[40] Inequality was the thorn in the side of American democracy by the 1980s and 1990s: it appeared in the language of academic and conservative populism in displaced and symptomatic ways but most often as antielitist outrage that tried desperately to avoid any association with vulgar Marxism. Former president of Harvard and former treasury secretary Lawrence Summers may have believed that he was addressing social inequality head on when he boasted about offering full scholarships to Harvard for deserving low-income students, but the normally hardheaded economist was ignoring the facts. Expanded access to higher education has not solved the problems of economic and social injustice. Sociologist Richard Arum and Josipa Roksa's groundbreaking study of higher education and learning outcomes demonstrates that outside of the Ivy League and elite private institutions, disparities in academic achievement across the lines of class and race are actually reinforced and not diminished after four years of college. Class and cultural privilege is already deeply entrenched by the time students are in secondary school, and talk of education as America's "great equalizer" seems to pander to an administrative fantasy while diverting attention and resources from the conditions that have undermined economic and social security for the majority of Americans outside of financial and professional elites.[41]

In the chapters that follow, I would like to show that popular resentment and discontent have been all too justified, but not because the people are essentially indifferent to political rationality. Quite the contrary. Ordinary people have been deprived of spaces for participation in wide-ranging political discussions that aim at a complete picture of the contemporary situation. Ordinary people are all too capable of reason but feel themselves powerless and deprived of the right to exercise that reason in public. Reason did entail the expression of an objective and critical grasp of people's situation, but the counterculture and the Left abandoned reason as the grounds for a general critique of the social totality. Under the banner of antiuniversalism, academic populism gained ground in American academia. In addition to Andrew Ross's *No Respect*, the 1992 volume *Cultural Studies*, edited by Paula Treichler, Cary Nelson, and Lawrence Grossberg (the proceedings of a cultural studies conference at University of Illinois at Urbana-Champaign in 1990), was a field-defining anthology. In both these books, strong arguments were made for the pursuit of an aggressive campaign for populist theory and politics in cultural studies.

Populist cultural critique expressed itself in myriad academic channels—and it was fueled by its conviction that high culture's fall from grace would bring about a necessary and revitalizing cultural revolution. Few in academia were willing to concede the problems with the leftist turn toward cultural populism. Along with Wendy Kaminer, Todd Gitlin, Neil Postman, and, more recently, Susan Jacoby criticized the celebration of unreason by their academic counterparts, but there was little sustained debate about their critique and even fewer responses to their criticisms. I keep their interventions in mind as I consider the intellectual history of academic populism and the ways in which it forged, along with the very forces it sought to repudiate, a distinctively modern concept of education.[42]

The book is organized in a modular way: while each chapter builds on previous arguments, each chapter also has a minimally autonomous character and can stand alone and be read separately.

Chapter 1, "The Problem with the Meritocracy," lays out a brief history of standardized testing as the most critical social technology of the meritocracy. I outline the principles of technocratic selection and argue that it is the basis of administered elitism. I give a brief account of how standardized testing emerged as the most compelling administrative instrument by which educational opportunity would be rationally distributed in postwar America. In this context, I deal with the 1980s and 1990s antitesting movement, which produced muckraking critiques of the testing industry by journalists such as David Owen, Nicholas Lemann, and Peter Sacks. I situate their critiques of standardized testing in the context of the Frankfurt School and midcentury critiques of progressivism. The testing industry became an integral part of the "administered life" that existed side by side with an ever more entertaining and prolific culture industry. In claiming to distribute educational resources more efficiently, the testing industry justified the ubiquitous principle of competition, which made the most persistent forms of inequality seem manageable and even ethically acceptable.

In chapter 2, "Ordinary Americans, Average Students," I look at how standardized testing and ranking produced the concept of the average student. I examine the ways in which the needs of this statistical fiction are constructed and flattered as well as how standardized testing has transformed the concept of education as a social technology. Furthermore, this chapter argues for a theoretical understanding of the average student in the context of C. Wright Mills's white-collar worker and Freud's aggrieved Everyman.

In chapter 3, "The Curious Cult of Religious Practicality," I look at the rise of the advice industry as a critical part of the culture industry. Specifically, I examine the ways in which Hofstadter's analysis of self-help and inspirational literature addresses a highly constructed ordinary American. I try to elaborate a relationship between self-help literature and utilitarian notions of education. In doing so, I hope to show that Hofstadter expands upon many of Adorno's ideas about the authoritarian personality and the relationship between fascism and popular culture. The first half of the chapter offers a close reading of Hofstadter's conception of spiritual technologies in relationship to Adorno's own theories of the authoritarian personality. The second half of the chapter situates Adorno's 1953 essay, "The Stars Down to Earth," in the historical context of his own relationship to American sociological research and Adorno's personal and professional prospects at that uncertain moment. Furthermore, I consider Adorno's close textual analysis of the *Los Angeles Times* horoscope in the context of the 1952 presidential election results and the defeat of Adlai Stevenson.

In chapter 4, "Against All Experts: No Experience Necessary," I look at the mythologization of 1960s student radicalism and try to locate countercultural attacks on the university and the rejection of elites and expertise as a critical moment in the formation of leftist cultural politics of the following decades. I take up Philip Roth's *American Pastoral* and its novelistic treatment of liberal and countercultural visions of Utopia and reconciliation, which, I argue, must be considered as an eloquent and troubling example of the conservative view of the culture wars launched by the militant antiwar politics of the 1960s. While Roth is repelled by the counterculture's rejection of the American consensus and liberal values, academic radicals celebrate the unraveling of the "postwar settlement." The American pastoral to which Seymour Levov, Roth's hapless protagonist, is committed appears both tragic and pathetic. I make an argument for recognizing cultural studies as the institutionalization of countercultural values within the context of the university.

Chapter 5, "The New Age of Cultural Studies: Crisis in the PMC," considers the founding rhetorical moves of an academic discipline that uncannily reflected both the aspirations of the eclectic and alternative spiritual movement identified as the "New Age" and the crisis in the "professional-managerial class." I look at the ways in which the attacks on "objective" reason emanating from the privileging of personal experience implied a breakdown of transactional and minimal communicability of reasoned argument contained by a highly unstable public sphere. The "Science Wars" and the Sokal affair emerge in a vexed environment where the struggle for leftist-progressive legitimacy confronts science and the formation of professional legitimacy within a counterculture-driven critique of objectivity and rationality.

Finally, in the conclusion, I look at the escalation of the culture wars between 1989 and 1990, at the moment when cultural studies itself was consolidating its own populist powers of persuasion within the American academy. In a brilliant tactical move, Jesse Helms took on the National Endowment of the Arts as an elitist government institution using taxpayers' money to fund obscene work that would repel the "ordinary American." In his attacks on the federal arts agency, the ordinary American emerges full force as a powerful actor, alleged to possess an unshakeable integrity of both political and aesthetic judgment. The ordinary American was the major protagonist in both progressive and reactionary dramas of antielitist cultural critique. I argue that in a struggle to deal with growing economic and social polarization, politicians and academics alike identified cultural resentment as a powerful fuel for political mobilization. The rise of the American meritocracy is one of the factors responsible for fanning the flames of antielitist resentment, which continues to underwrite the most extreme forms of political expression today.

chapter one

the problem with the meritocracy

Richard Hofstadter and Theodor Adorno were both deeply concerned about the relationship between anti-intellectualism and the cultural politics of the twentieth century. They were both interested in the emergence of an antiliberal bent of mind in the modern era. They were, at the same time, both opposed to the instrumentalization of thinking and the administration of human experiences. They were both implicitly critical of routinization and professionalization and harbored deep suspicions about the Progressive Era's reformist zeal. Their defense of critical and liberal values made them especially unpopular "elitists" during the rise of academic populism in the 1990s. In reevaluating the significance of their work, Hofstadter's critique of American anti-intellectualism should be integrated with Adorno's conception of the culture industry to render a more vivid portrait of the ways in which administration and scientific management shaped the emerging education and testing industries of the mid-twentieth century.

For Hofstadter, a starkly utilitarian and American vision of knowledge reveals itself in periodic hostile attacks on the educational system, which is then subject to the efforts of wide-ranging and often radical reformism.[1] Hofstadter's work isolated a singularly American configuration of ideas regarding education: suspicion or resentment of intellectual endeavors was accompanied by a "faith in popular education" as a means of resolving social contradictions and meeting social needs. He saw the politicization of education in its embrace of what he saw as populist-Progressive as indulging in a particularly American brand of reactionary anti-intellectualism that plagued the American body politic. In *Anti-intellectualism in American Life*, Hofstadter remarked that despite their suspicion of book learning, Americans were remarkably confident that education could improve society and that massive reorganizations of curricula in the name of relevance and utilitarianism would make both teachers and students better individuals in the most amplified, expressive sense of that term; that is, they would be more aware of who they are and where they come from. They would acquire the sensitivity and consciousness to be tolerant of difference and to recognize in others a magnificent diversity. It was assumed that students of Progressive education would learn to be better citizens and better critics, and they would acquire a kind of hard-won sensitivity that they would want to transmit to their benighted peers. Just as they would not tolerate injustice or violence, so it was imagined that they would organically become curious about and respectful of the arts. All interest was alleged to originate in the students themselves: the school was a place that merely responded to the spontaneous set of passions that each student brought to bear on the materials offered. Instead of joining the chorus singing the praises of this antiauthoritarian reorientation of the teaching process, Hofstadter pointed out that educational reforms seemed to lead to an embedded, institutionalized anti-intellectualism. Progressive policies inevitably and wrongheadedly subordinated education to "life."

Based on the preceding critique of Progressive education and its goals, Hofstadter would argue that the Progressive Era reforms actually produced many of the problems within American schools and universities. He concluded that the tenets of progressive education supported the introduction of an anti-intellectual, pragmatic business ethos into the administration of mass education. Like his colleague Daniel Bell, Hofstadter sought to defend the values of liberal education and critical negativity in his historical study of anti-intellectualism. Both Hofstadter and Adorno saw critical thinking and intellectual life as increasingly besieged, but Hofstadter did not blame the excesses or simplification of mass culture for the poverty of twentieth-century intellectual life; instead, he fingered hubristic educational reformers and administrators for betraying the values of education itself.

It is not easy to grasp the broad outlines of a history of educational reform and administration in the United States. When the first shocks of an economic and social crisis reach American schools, educators and administrators respond by promoting urgently needed innovations, reconfigurations, and cutbacks in order to increase efficiency. In the twenty-first century, educational reforms, imposed by the force of social and economic pressures, result in cuts in resources but are justified by demands for accountability. These perpetual calls for reform in the name of efficiency and accountability in fact disguise the ways in which these two tenets had already taken hold in the mind of administrators who adopted them as the watchwords by which the American educational system was reimagined as a business, subordinated to the needs of business. In hopes of shedding light on this history, this chapter offers a broad and no doubt incomplete overview of the tenor and aims of educational and institutional reform over the past century, with particular attention to the origins and rise of standardized testing as the critical social technology of the meritocracy and its system of administered elitism. The ultimate goal of this chapter is to demonstrate how the testing industry has shaped a concept of the ordinary or the average student that would come to dominate critiques of hierarchy and elitism during the 1980s (discussed in more detail in chapter 2).

In 1892 the National Council of Education was formed to address the pressing crisis in American education: urbanization, industrialization, and immigration were reshaping the nation, and the school system was hard-pressed to catch up with the quickly changing nation. The council proposed the universal ideals of humanist education as a national core curriculum in secondary education in an attempt to remedy the uneven and unsatisfactory quality of high school education. Convened by presidents of prestigious universities, the Committee of Ten, as it came to be known, was led by Charles W. Eliot, president of Harvard University. It consisted of mostly Ivy League professors who wanted to modernize and standardize an academic curriculum deemed suitable for all high school students regardless of class background or intellectual capacities: the committee insisted that, under this system, "there would be no distinction between those preparing for college and those preparing for 'life.'"[2] At Harvard, Eliot was an institutional reformer who introduced the elective system and the written examination, the latter of which replaced the stifling oral recitation during which students were obliged to demonstrate that they had committed large portions of the textbook to memory.[3] Under Eliot's presidency, Harvard was reshaped as a research university, with the requisite bureaucratic structures of professional credentialism that would come to distinguish the modernization of these former seminaries. At the same time, however, Gerald Graff points out that it was also at Harvard that the most distinguished gentlemen generalists found their institutional homes.[4] These gentlemen scholars would spurn the pedagogical innovations and forms of professionalism that would usher in the new age of technocratic rule in higher education. Although Eliot seemed like a radical innovator and callow modernizer to his peers, to the next generation he belonged to the world of traditional education they hoped to lay low.

The Committee of Ten revealed its commitment to Eliot's notion of mental discipline, based upon the idea that students, regardless of class or ethnicity, could benefit from being thoroughly schooled in a general curriculum. Despite Eliot's insistence on educational modernization and reform, the actual methods of imparting such mental discipline were retrograde indeed and still grounded in large part on the rote memorization and recitation that Eliot had sought to change in the oral exam process at Harvard. Mental discipline valued physical control of the self as well as psychological stamina to withstand boredom, while memorization of the classics developed out of literary study as a core intellectual pursuit. In the years that followed the Committee of Ten's report, the committee was attacked by all proponents of progressive education, and most of its findings were eventually repudiated. Educational reformer and pioneer American psychologist G. Stanley Hall criticized the Committee of Ten as being woefully out of touch with the science of child development. It was also condemned by pediatrician and educational reformer Joseph Mayer Rice as being "unscientific."[5]

From the point of view of enlightened middle-class reformers like Hall and Rice, "social efficiency" and science promised the creation of an enlightened form of social cohesion—produced and transmitted through schools—that could answer the popular demands for massive social change and political upheaval with a cool, balanced program designed by the new experts.[6] In Henry Kliebard's history of American educational reforms, there was no clear victor in the struggle for the American curriculum. During the nascent years of the Progressive Era, schools became battlegrounds on which the struggle for cultural and political hegemony took place. Political winds shifted so rapidly, however, that yesterday's reformers were transmogrified into today's reactionaries. Educational reform movements encouraged the fantasy that school reform itself could be an effective means of achieving both social change and social control. But the pioneering thinkers of educational reform at the turn of the last century were not a scientific vanguard as much as they were following an industrial (and business-oriented), instrumentalist ethos in their theories of development and pedagogy. So charismatic was the doctrine of efficiency that educational theory came to be dominated by ideas completely foreign to what John Dewey tried to identify as the self-sustaining and self-defining goals of education itself. Educational antitraditionalism had and would continue to have, throughout the twentieth century, unforeseen consequences.

Dewey criticized academic education because he thought that universalism and formalism in philosophy and pedagogy had produced a deadening and unscientific method of education that was ill-suited to the needs of a burgeoning and bustling industrial democracy, massive immigration, and an ethnically diverse working class. Traditional education was designed for oligarchy: it taught the sons and daughters of the elite to participate in luxurious display but did nothing to initiate them into the "right use of products of industry." Democratic education would be designed to teach students to participate in all areas of life as active and engaged thinkers, but, even more important, it would not think itself beneath teaching students how to make a living. Dewey envisioned students acquiring "the ability to make [their] way economically in the world and to manage economic resources usefully."[7] His advocacy of vocationalism was coupled with a rejection of externally imposed "aims" for education and their application in shaping the ambitions and aspirations of its students. Democratic education hoped to attend to each and every person's capacities as an individual and to place him in an environment where he could achieve self-realization through the cultivation of respect for the peculiarity and particularity of those individual capacities.

For Dewey, it was clear that this kind of education would produce capable, critical subjects for robust participation in American political life: progressive education would not only seek to "correct unfair privilege and deprivation," it would also make it apparent to its students that social efficiency, a term that appears strange and inimical to our twenty-first-century sensibilities, should aim at cultivating a "capacity to share in a give and take of experience."[8] In progressive thinking, education became deeply invested as an "efficient" means for solving social problems, resolving social contradictions, and bringing about an end to inequality or even transforming the sensibilities that would tolerate inequality. In fact, Dewey seemed to suggest that children, guided by the correct methods of supportive noninterference, would learn to participate in "necessary collective efforts" and that laissez-faire individualism would meet its end in the pragmatically oriented, socially enlightened classroom. If this seems to overburden the Progressively minded teacher with an impossible task, it did not dampen later curriculum reformers' enthusiasms for certain kinds of scientific solutions in the application of Dewey's most powerful ideas.

For Hofstadter, Horace Mann idealized the public school as guarantor of American democracy and prosperity. For Mann, universal education "would be the 'great equalizer' of human conditions, the 'balance wheel of the social machinery,' and the 'creator of wealth undreamed of.'"[9] Mann's optimism was founded on his faith in the Enlightenment notion of the perfectibility of human beings and human institutions: his ideal of the American school "would not be a school for the common people . . . but rather . . . a school common to all people."[10] However, by the end of the nineteenth century, the problems presented by mass immigration, industrialization, and urbanization would pose daunting and unforeseen challenges to Mann's common school.

Joseph Mayer Rice's 1892–93 articles on the American public school system (later published in book form as *The Public School System of the United States*) revealed that the actualization of Mann's ideals of compulsory public education was rather dire.[11] Rice discovered in his far-flung investigations that primary schools in the United States were for the most part tyrannically and fitfully ruled sites of absurd authoritarianism. Most classroom exercises reproduced the drudgery of work life: the curriculum appealed almost exclusively "to mechanical memory" rather than "the reasoning faculty."[12] The most authoritarian of the schools seemed to follow Dewey's facetious description of traditional philosophy's view of history and creativity: "If there ever was creation, it all took place at a remote period. Since then, the world has only recited lessons."[13] Rice also minced no words in condemning the public school system as a backwater of corruption and machine politics. In the places where he found the tenets of progressive education upheld (Minneapolis and Indianapolis as well as La Porte, Wisconsin), teachers and experts in pedagogy in "normal" or education schools did not labor under the yoke of political appointees. In cities like New York and Philadelphia, politicians and hacks hired barely qualified teachers and rewarded their cronies with plum positions in administration. In turn, the schoolroom itself saw these barely educated, overtaxed teachers impose rote learning, cramming, and cruel disciplinary measures on their wards.

Rice called on parents and local communities to rise up against the school boards and call in experts who, professional educators themselves, would be given free rein to run schools without interference from the unqualified opinions of political and business appointees. Education experts would hire and supervise teachers in the science of child development. At one point, Rice described a meticulously worked out schedule by which he determined how the superintendent of New York City's public schools would be able to "meet all his four thousand teachers once a month."[14] Rice shared one assumption with Horace Mann: improving schools would improve the nation, but for Rice, this improvement could only be achieved if we accepted the principles of science into the administration of education.

Rice called for the enfranchisement of the educational expert to combat the political hack who had hitherto dominated public education and its distribution of resources: scientific expertise in educational theory would liberate the common people's children from the twin tyrants of "mechanical education" and political machines. In this way, Rice introduced the concept of expert administration into the debate about the American school. What C. Wright Mills called the managerial demiurge appeared in progressive educational reform as the enlightening power of science and expertise. This was to have far-reaching consequences in determining the direction of school reform. Rice's science, however, was founded on a great wellspring of sentimentality about children that allowed him an almost limitless optimism regarding the possibilities opened up by the new education's methods. In Hofstadter's words, the scientifically trained normal school graduate would be able to observe her pupil "in order to learn [his] innermost thoughts so that she may be able to render her guidance intelligible to him. As she learns to understand him, she begins to sympathize with him, and in return she secures his love; once his love is secured, he will follow her to the end of the earth, and the examinations will take care of themselves." Hofstadter recoiled at such an overblown vision of education as two parts telepathy and one part sympathy.

Dewey's pragmatic antiuniversalism, however, seemed to be a radical and progress-making break with the methods of rote memorization that had become a hallmark of humanist education. Given its pedagogical apparatus, it is easy to see how critics of traditional education would identify "humanist" and liberal education with a rigid "authoritarianism." Reformers like Mann and Rice idealized the school as the key to the promotion or prevention of authentic social change while also insisting on the authority of the expert whose knowledge was based on scientific method and its findings. In this context, the struggle over the best way to educate American students became increasingly politicized. Dewey's theories were mobilized as one front in a struggle for social efficiency even though he himself rejected the notion that education should serve as merely "preparation" for work. Pragmatist antitraditionalism set down the basic principles for mass education in an industrial democracy at the same time that it promoted a highly compromised form of Deweyan adjustment to the contemporary realities of inequality.

In 1911 the National Education Association, an emerging professional organization of educators, appointed the Committee on Economy of Time in Education and charged it "with the systematic removal of waste from the school curriculum."[15] The committee concluded that in order to teach students more efficiently, "educational measurement" would have to take the upper hand in setting curricular content. Lawrence Cremin describes this critical juncture of American educational history as particularly marked by a strong faith in scientistic, or pseudoscientific, solutions to all sorts of problems: "If science promised nothing, it promised efficiency; this ultimately was the plum the educational scientist dangled before the taxpaying public."[16] In the committee's imagination, waste was everywhere and had to be eliminated. The one critical resource that was being needlessly squandered was education itself. This was the discovery of the Commission on the Reorganization of Secondary Education, which reported its findings in 1918 in an influential report called *The Cardinal Principles of Secondary Education.*[17]

Hofstadter was scathing in his critique of *The Cardinal Principles*. He could bare-ly contain his dismay that educational administrators had declared "health" and "worthy home membership" as legitimate goals of secondary education. Its proponents and supporters praised the way in which *The Cardinal Principles* emphasized democracy as one of the conditions of modern education. Only democracy and democratic education, the report implied, most effectively promoted and encouraged the development of the individual's personality in coordination with the pursuit of public goals: "The purpose of democracy is to organize society so that each member may develop his personality primar-ily through activities designed for the well-being of his fellow members and of society as a whole."[18] According to *The Cardinal Principles*, secondary education should promote "common ideas, common ideals, and common modes of thought, feeling and action, whereby America, through a rich, unified common life, may render her truest service to a world seeking for democracy among men and nations."[19] In Hofstadter's view, the common life was hardly adequate to describe a systematic understanding of history and the objective conditions for progress in scientific and humanistic research. Adorno would have identified in such educational goals the false "personalization" of modern education: the system pretended to adjust itself according to each student's ability in order to engage in the ideological promotion and reification of subjective reason and experience over objective critique and dialectical analysis.

In Judith Sealander's account of American attitudes about children and edu-cation, *The Cardinal Principles* represented the fruit of a historically innovative alli-ance between the federal government, university professors, and urban school administrators. This coalition or "triumvirate" was able to turn the spotlight onto critical issues in education while promoting the consensus that education was the key to "national improvement."[20] The reforms offered by *The Cardinal Principles* were inspired by the general application of Carl Campbell Brigham's and Robert Yerkes's Alpha and Beta tests for intelligence, discussed in detail later in this chapter in relation to the SAT. With the introduction of mass intel-ligence testing for the army recruits of World War I, scientists and educators had come upon an astonishing fact: the great majority of test-takers were unable to benefit from a traditional academic curriculum. They simply did not have the in-tellectual capacity or aptitude. Reformers proposed that the curriculum be ad-justed to suit the needs and capacities of students; student needs were dictated by the demands of the social status quo, and student capacities were measured by intelligence testing. Reformers felt that curricular content should always be determined by the identification of the "common social needs" of American students, namely, what "the majority of normal children" had to master in their everyday lives. Efficient use of education resources had to take into account the average skills and capacities of "normal children," who needed to acquire skills for life and work. In making efficiency the watchword of mass education, the authors of *The Cardinal Principles* casually and surreptitiously discarded academic content or liberal education as the driving force behind the shaping of secondary school curriculum. Rather, the average or normal student was created as an innovation on and a by-product of the standardized intelligence test. The construction of the average student's needs and limitations determined the criteria of efficiency and waste management that fired the imaginations of administrators and reformers alike.

In 1917 the U.S. government signed into law the Smith Hughes Act, which provided federal support to expand the secondary school curriculum to include crafts and technical training. Widespread public concern about the "crisis in the schools" and wartime preparedness had led to federal intervention after intervention, with the channeling of public funds into the establishment of agricultural, trade, and industrial subjects along with home economics as part of the secondary school curriculum.[21] These federal interventions opened up the academic curriculum to the needs of industry and business. Labor unions were ambivalent about this development, since they were worried that vocational education in public schools was going to take over the apprenticeship model and weaken their membership, but business associations welcomed these developments. By introducing technical training into the curriculum, administrators seemed to be affirming the dignity of labor in the educational system. Lawrence Cremin asserted bluntly, however, that in a time of massive industrialization, "the onrush of technological advances" consigned the crafts-oriented vocational education supported by the Smith Hughes Act almost immediately to obsolescence and relegated the workers who took on teaching jobs in this area to marginality with regard to "mainstream industrial innovation."[22]

Vocationalism cast into relief the difficulty of institutionalizing "practicality" in education: for Cremin as well as for Hofstadter, vocational education actually affirmed the popular idea that a few lessons in the school of hard knocks were infinitely more educational and profitable than by-the-book knowledge imparted in school. For them, schools could not and should not be charged with keeping pace with business demands. But efficiency became an irresistible slogan of educational policy makers. After all, efficiency expert and management innovator Frederick Winslow Taylor's principles of scientific management had touted efficiency as the most desirable goal of any form of modern administration.[23] In 1944, to supplement or expand upon the pragmatic mission of secondary education, the Educational Policies Commission of the National Education Association published "Education for *All* American Youth." Where *The Cardinal Principles* may not have been clear enough about the goal of its educational agenda, this report was more explicit. According to Diane Ravitch, professor of education and policy expert turned defender of liberal education, "this report . . . portrayed the public school as the fulcrum of social planning, designed to meet all the needs of all children and youth, as well as the needs of their communities. The report treated the once-central academic curriculum as an antique inheritance of dubious value, to be set quietly aside in favor of the 'imperative educational needs of youth,' such as gaining job skills, learning about family life, etc."[24] Ravitch criticized the regimes of testing and progressive education in her analysis of race and African American education. She noted that during the era of school reforms, African American intellectuals such as W. E. B. Du Bois as well as African American parents objected to the introduction of vocational education in the schools: they found that the tracking system created de facto educational segregation, and they were more committed to the traditional curriculum than white parents.[25]

The public school became the contested site of social control—from a Foucauldian point of view, education served discipline. But it was with the increasing reliance on the scientific authority of the education expert as well as the promotion of social efficiency and vocationalism as educational aims in the first half of the twentieth century that reformers found a way to justify the transformation of educational institutions into instruments for the "rational" distribution of "opportunity." In 1958 Michael Young, a British Labour politician and sociologist, had coined the term "meritocracy" as a grotesque neologism for his satirical novel, *The Rise of the Meritocracy*.[26] Young flatly asserted that feudalism is bad because its means of social promotion, nepotism, is simply an inefficient way of maximizing the value that can be extracted from human intelligence. Rather, this critical national resource could be much better managed for international competition and national security through a perfectly administered system of intelligence testing. In the novel's Great Britain of 2033, all children are sorted through a national testing board into schools and jobs appropriate to their IQs. The appearance of a rationally distributed educational opportunity is maintained even as the "myth" of both formal and substantive equality of all citizens has been destroyed. According to Young's fictional narrator, "the gradual shift from inheritance to merit as the ground of social selection was making (and finally made) nonsense of all their loose talk of the equality of man."[27] In Young's novel, violent, populist revolt against the meritocratic system would bring it down in the year 2033. At the end of the novel, his smug, well-educated narrator is surrounded by signs of massive civil unrest that he chooses stubbornly to ignore. Young was writing satire, after all.

In sum, Young predicted that meritocracy as the rationalized rule of an elite would eventually lead to violent, populist revolt. His skewering of the postwar Labour Party's promotion of bright working-class lads and lasses into the ranks of government and business elites looked balefully toward a future in which a volatile and leaderless underclass would revolt against an increasingly complacent and entitled elite. In reality, in both the U.S. and the U.K., enlightened administrators were proposing meritocratic solutions to the problems of social injustice by promising that the most gifted and talented members of any underprivileged group could emerge as fully invested members of the highest ranks of society after being pressed through the sorting mechanism of higher education. In Young's novel, the populist revolt of a misused underclass is directly attributed to the rise of the meritocracy. Under such rule, the system of education had become a sinister pipeline of promotion for gifted and talented working-class children and underrepresented minorities: the school drew them up out of their impoverished neighborhoods and benighted communities, moving them swiftly along the path toward academic and professional achievement, until they no longer identified with their communities or class of origin. Young described familiar figures of a global educated elite who were sophisticated, restless, ambitious, and jet-setting, although he refused to idealize the very political discontent that he predicted. Young's critique of "irrational" popular revolt betrayed an Old Left belief in revolution and reason that the new generation of counterculture-infused cultural studies activists and scholars would find so infuriating.

Young lived long enough to greet with dismay the acceptance of "meritocracy" in the educational and political discourse as a laudatory moniker. In 2001 he wrote in the *Guardian*: "I have been sadly disappointed by my 1958 book, *The Rise of the Meritocracy*. I coined a word which has gone into general circulation, especially in the United States, and most recently found a prominent place in the speeches of Mr. Blair. . . . A social revolution has been accomplished by harnessing schools and universities to the task of sieving people according to education's narrow band of values."[28] Young meant for the neologism to communicate a philological and political monstrosity—and to contain within its awkward mixture of Latin and Greek roots an obviously repellent form of social and economic organization. Furthermore, even if we were to accept that a group of especially meritorious people could be identified by tests, how could we, citizens of a democracy, agree that this group, presumably a tiny minority of high scorers, could legitimately supplant rule by the people, the "demos," as the sovereign force of democracy? Young thought the rule of the allegedly meritorious would appear sufficiently awful to all his readers and that his linguistic invention would inspire outrage and revulsion. He never imagined that the term itself would come to mean the unquestionably desirable administration of increasingly efficient and desirable forms of selection within the educational system.

In the *Guardian*, Young described the new meritocratic elite as feeling more entitled to their wealth and privileges since they believe that they have been scientifically selected to their positions. This new class, or the "business and financial elite," feels no compunction about arrogating to themselves the most outrageous rewards in salaries, bonuses, and fees. Social polarization and economic inequality accompany the triumph of this class.[29] Young pointed to two prominent members of the Labour cabinet of 1944, Ernest Bevin and Herbert Morrison, both of whom lacked diplomas and could only lay claim to work experience, the former in unions and the latter in local government, as their sole credential for service in national government. Yet they distinguished themselves as foreign secretary and deputy prime minister, respectively. Civil servants and political leaders who were genuinely self-educated or at least who had received their education in the workforce were a disappearing breed. William Lamb, an American Farmers' Alliance leader, lecturer, and organizer, received twenty-five days of formal schooling in his entire life. Abraham Lincoln was the last entirely self-taught American president. The point is not to lionize such men but to point out that their rise to power has been made impossible by the meritocracy, which organizes a reward system that has privileged credentialism and potential over work and organizing experience.[30] American schools did not always serve the function of sorting and selection. As historian Paula Fass has pointed out, nineteenth-century American schools were simply not designed to select a class of elites.[31] Education may have reproduced cultural and political prerogatives and privileges, but it certainly did not produce the ideal of rational selection. Self-educated leaders like Lincoln did not hold schooling in contempt because they had none; in fact, Lincoln's own deprivation deepened his respect for erudition.

Thorstein Veblen identified this problematic relationship between power and merit in his economic and social theory of domination and emulation.[32] In response to the prevailing ideology of social Darwinism, Veblen's economic anthropology demonstrated that the qualities of a dominant class were meritorious insofar as they commemorated the violent exploits of hunters and warriors in predatory societies. The admiration that these qualities attracted came at a direct cost to the denigrated category of everyday labor, feminized as drudgery. During historical periods when violence was no longer necessary, the exploit remained valorized as more deserving of merit than other forms of work and experience. Veblen used "meritoriousness" in a highly contingent and relative manner: he never allowed his readers to believe that it could be defined or determined by immutable or even measurable capacities. For Veblen, modern society was entirely anachronistic, since it was still operating by the brutalizing division of labor that had prevailed in predatory societies. He believed that the devaluation of one kind of labor in favor of the exploit served to justify the domination of one class over all others, allowing for the perpetuation of gross inequalities in the distribution of industrial wealth.

While eugenic thinking and the social Darwinist philosophy upon which it was based gained an enthusiastic following among American scientists and statisticians in the 1920s, by the Great Depression generalized economic suffering had forced the experts to abandon their position that the poor deserved—biologically—to remain in the underclass. Decades later, Stephen Jay Gould felt that the return to biodeterminism and its misuse of evolutionary theory to justify the persistence of social inequities were related to the revival of right-wing politics in the wake of the 1960s. For Gould, scientific racism was spurred on by the election of Richard Nixon and the fears of social disorder following a decade of civil unrest. Richard Herrnstein's article "The Bell Curve," published in the *Atlantic Monthly* in 1971, labored to legitimize theories of racially determined and inheritable intelligence in order to justify the logic of unrestrained competition as a social, philosophical, and biological ideal.[33] In fact, Herrnstein's arguments blithely echoed Young's satire of meritocratic rhetoric. Aristocracy, for Herrnstein, was incapable of rewarding the biologically superior members of a society. That was why there were revolutions and revolts. For him, the present system of social triage had produced inevitable natural stratifications. Ironically, this came about because "society" had removed "artificial barriers" between classes, allowing biological ones to replace them. The wealthier and more privileged members of 1971 America were simply more capable than the poor and the miserable. It would be best for us as a society to renounce our philosophical ideals of egalitarianism and to give competition a free hand in determining who gets to the top and who is abandoned at the bottom of social and economic hierarchies.[34] Gould pointed out that Herrnstein's science justified his politics: Herrnstein was politically opposed to government intervention in the face of entrenched social and economic inequalities. Supporting Gould's critique of the social thought behind the measurement of intelligence was the fundamentally liberal assumption that it was in the public interest for the government to act to improve the plight of the poor and the underprivileged.

From a more conservative perspective, Christopher Lasch criticized meritocracy and bureaucracy as the building blocks of a narcissistically driven counterculture elitism. He concluded with an affirmation of the values of "moral discipline" and "decency," which were ostensibly opposed to the values of the meritocracy, as "a parody of democracy."[35] In his view, an increasingly cosmopolitan class of meritocratic liberals found themselves increasingly detached not only from the core of ravaged and deindustrialized cities but from "public services" in general.[36] This new elite was especially deficient in civic virtue, since its members saw no advantages in investing in the practices of local citizenship or local institutions. As Lasch pointed out, even the optimistic Robert Reich, secretary of labor under President Bill Clinton, was critical of the "secession of the symbolic analysts," whose ways of being and working in the world, following the flows of capital across national borders, represented a "striking instance of the revolt of the elites against time and place."[37]

Lasch was unrelenting in his critique of contemporary elites: from his 1978 *Culture of Narcissism* to 1994's *Revolt of the Elites*, he continued to expand upon his condemnation of new forms of privilege and the moral and political turpitude to which they gave birth. In Lasch's sustained analysis, bureaucracy, counterintuitively, had taken up with an essentially elitist counterculture in order to erect the stages upon which the new narcissists were allowed to display their empty charms. Lasch argued for a return to yeoman-like independence and a renewed sense of self-sufficiency, crafts oriented in its respect for labor processes rather than the semiotic and consumerist manipulations of styles and signs. For Lasch, "growth" and "awareness" would lead to nothing more than the self-indulgent navel-gazing of the "Me" generation. Lasch argued that all bureaucratic organizations "devote more energy to the maintenance of hierarchical relations than to industrial efficiency. . . . Domination and subordination within management take on as much importance as the subordination of labor to management as a whole."[38] Government and corporate capitalism conspired to produce personalities at once narcissistic and dependent. For Lasch, "professional self-aggrandizement" was identified as another phase of the "process from competitive to monopoly capitalism." Therefore, "the struggle against bureaucracy requires a struggle against capitalism itself."[39]

Lasch excoriated the culture of self-aggrandizing consumerism, superficiality, and social survivalism: he urged Americans to forge deeper relationships with history and local communities. In doing so, he betrayed his own susceptibility to the temptations of the agrarian myth, so harshly dismissed by his mentor Richard Hofstadter. About the new elite and its corruption Lasch wrote: "It has created new forms of illiteracy even in the act of setting up a system of universal education. It has undermined the family while attempting to rescue the family. It has torn away the veil of chivalry that once tempered the exploitation of women and has brought men and women face to face as antagonists."[40] Lasch recommended a return to "moral discipline"—an amalgam of restraint, craftsmanship, wisdom, and material self-sufficiency. As a whole, his analysis and critique were limited by his incapacity to see the "culture of narcissism" as a symptom of anything more than a lack of moral and psychological strength before the seductions of consumerism and monopoly capitalism. Lasch seemed certain that a return to the small-town, small-farm forms of preindustrial production would guarantee psychological and political forms of autonomy necessary to a functional democracy.

In a sense, David Brooks continued Lasch's critique in his breezy analysis of "bobos," a hybridized social category he identified when he saw yet another species of the American elite emerge before his very eyes: these new elites boasted bohemian tastes that were supported by bourgeois wallets. Brooks offered a more accessible and popularized version of Lasch's harsh critique of the privileges of a countercultural elite. Like Lasch, he saw meritocracy as connected with the formation of a new American elite whose view of the world was increasingly estranged from the problems of ordinary Americans.[41] Both writers shared what Barbara Ehrenreich identified as the American middle-class fear of being overtaken by modern hedonism and of consumer culture's nullification of the principle of deferred gratification.

By the 1990s large numbers of Ivy League graduates had applied to and were hired by prestigious financial firms, from Salomon Brothers to Goldman Sachs to Morgan Stanley. An Ivy League bachelor's degree was one of the required credentials for entry into the dizzying world of high finance. An Ivy grad could radically increase his or her earning potential with the right kind of MBA program or a JD from a prestigious law school. The Ivy paths to wealth had become well-trodden itineraries, with investment banks and hedge funds ready to recruit the best and brightest graduates from elite schools. There was another kind of meritocratic student who had entered the class of cultural and professional elites: Nicholas Lemann calls them "the Mandarins."[42] The Mandarins, as the name reveals, were just as privileged as their Ivy-educated business counterparts. They believed that their expertise could serve socially progressive ends. They went into government service and occupied less profitable but equally prestigious positions. More often than not, however, beneficiaries of the meritocracy, as Michael Young predicted, were not shy about reaping the full material rewards of high scores. In fact, a swathe of highly privileged high scorers could be said to represent the ethos of financial work, with its emphasis on risky, short-term solutions to complex but abstract and decontextualized problems. High scorers performed well in high-stakes, high-pressure situations where astronomical profits could be gained by quick, decisive thinking.

The American meritocracy and its adjuncts had by all accounts produced a new postwar elite and an entire industry meant to select and manage their smooth integration into the proper institutions of higher education.[43] In the 1980s and 1990s a trio of highly gifted investigative journalists, David Owen, Peter Sacks, and Nicholas Lemann, delved into the American meritocracy and investigated the little-understood history of its major institution: the privately held, not-for-profit organization known as Educational Testing Service (ETS). As a critical player in the modern testing industry, ETS guarantees the efficient implementation of meritocratic measures. It has been producing and distributing not only the SATs, the MCATs, the LSATs, and the GREs but also a whole battery of other examinations for professional credentialization. Founded in 1947, ETS played a critical role in the transformation of American higher education after World War II: as universities and student populations exploded, the efficient management of educational resources and opportunities became increasingly important. ETS provided the standardized test as a critical instrument in evaluating and assessing diverse new populations of students for whom higher education had become a possibility but not a right or an entitlement. Furthermore, the equitable distribution of these resources would demonstrate the fundamentally democratic ethos of postwar American society itself. In the words of David Owen, "historically and in spirit, ETS is a product of the American Century (circa 1945–1973)."[44]

Even as the sale of standardized tests to public schools doubled between 1960 and 1989, a small movement against testing gained strength, spurred on finally by Allan Nairn and Ralph Nader's legal struggle against ETS. Nairn, an investigative journalist, and Nader's demands for more transparency in the testing industry led eventually to the passage of the 1980 truth-in-testing law in New York State. The law required ETS to release test questions and graded answer sheets to students who requested their results.[45] In fact, ETS felt the heat from its critics and responded by abandoning the term "aptitude" in the Scholastic Aptitude Test. No mention of aptitude can be found in company literature after the 1980s, even though there continue to be references made to "assessment." In 1993 the SAT was separated into two parts, the SAT I Reasoning Test, or SAT I, and the SAT II in Subjects. By 1999 even "assessment" proved too controversial, so ETS retained the SAT name but insisted that as an acronym it no longer stood for anything else. An ETS test-maker is quoted in David Owen's *None of the Above: The Truth behind the SAT's* as saying, "SAT is not an initialism; it does not stand for anything."[46] Evidently, ETS was perfectly in tune with the linguistic turn and the arbitrariness of signs.

SAT as an acronym had become emptied of meaning and referentiality, but it remained a rite of passage for almost all four-year and elite college aspirants. SAT itself was transformed into a pure "brand" name, detached from any semantic ground, and with this truncation the tests tried to divorce themselves from early twentieth-century attempts to measure minds. Despite the waves of criticism and suspicion around these tests, ETS and its multiple-choice tests have indelibly marked the academic itinerary for generations of American high school students. Daniel Bell noted in the 1960s that ETS's Advanced Placement tests were beginning to dominate the determination of high school curricula in math, science, and English. High school students who did well on Advanced Placement examinations could get college credit for high school coursework.[47] ETS had not only cornered the college entrance exams, it had also won a monopoly on college preparatory courses for the gifted high school student.

Journalists like David Owen, Peter Sacks, and Nicholas Lemann tried to communicate to a concerned public the destructive impact of the testing industry on the American body politic. In *Standardized Minds: The High Price of America's Testing Culture and What We Can Do to Change It*, Peter Sacks identified the 1983 publication of the report *A Nation at Risk*, prepared by a commission appointed by T. H. Bell, Ronald Reagan's secretary of education, as marking an intensification of the political struggle for determining the direction of American education. *A Nation at Risk* became the "New Testament" of accountability reformers of the 1980s. It painted such a stark picture of American education that no reform appeared drastic enough to address the danger we faced. We needed a full-scale revolution:

> Our Nation is at risk. Our once unchallenged preeminence in commerce, industry, science, and technological innovation is being overtaken by competitors throughout the world. This report is concerned with only one of the many causes and dimensions of the problem, but it is the one that undergirds American prosperity, security, and

civility. We report to the American people that while we can take justifiable pride in what our schools and colleges have historically accomplished and contributed to the United States and the well-being of its people, the educational foundations of our society are presently being eroded by a rising tide of mediocrity that threatens our very future as a Nation and a people. What was unimaginable a generation ago has begun to occur—others are matching and surpassing our educational attainments.[48]

The report offered a terrifying prognosis: educational failures, not fiscal policies and global politics, were actually responsible for the economic torpor and slow growth of the 1970s. Reformers promised nothing less than national transformation and rejuvenation, if only lazy teachers were held to greater levels of accountability. In response to the perceived crisis in education, a federal system whereby failing schools would be penalized and high-testing schools rewarded was established under the aegis of pursuing "excellence." The standardized test, whether in the form of the ACT, the STAR test, the SATs, or the GREs, presented a set of tools to counteract the danger posed by the decline in educational quality. Accountability became associated with the containment of risk, and the tools of assessment appeared as social technologies that had to be refined in order to bring to an end the dangerous mediocrity of American schools. In an age when deindustrialization and globalization were accelerating, students as future workers had to be trained to be more "competitive." As educational funding became linked to test results and the massive administrative overhaul of the schools, public expectations were stoked to create the idea that our schools could restart the economic engines of the nation: revamped schools could lead to economic growth and expansion, global competitiveness, and the end of double-digit inflation. George H. W. Bush, the self-proclaimed "education" president, and Bill Clinton both accepted the findings and remedies presented by A Nation at Risk while fanning American anxieties about losing economic ground because of a failing educational system.

Owen's None of the Above, Sacks's Standardized Minds, and Nicholas Lemann's The Big Test: The Secret History of the American Meritocracy offered sobering accounts of the failures of standardized testing to produce better schools and a more equitable distribution of educational opportunity.[49] All three journalists gave devastating critiques of the overweening belief that all we needed as a nation was a more "scientific" test of scholastic aptitude to prevent the kinds of stratification that John Dewey thought would be fatal to a democracy. It was Owen who demonstrated most cogently how flawed the actual tests are, specifically, the ad hoc method ETS uses to produce its questions and scores and how defensive the company is about being accountable to the public it serves. Sacks deplored the misuse of an "educational crisis" for political mobilization in conservative campaigns to undermine the authority and autonomy of teachers and their ability to set their own curricular goals. Standardized test results, for Sacks, are deeply skewed by family background, wealth, and education while remaining poor predictors of future performance. What Sacks offers in place of standardized measurement is vaguely Deweyan: work experience, civic engagement, interest in the world outside of school.[50] Lemann focuses on a generation of American testing experts whose racist and eugenicist idea of social order exerted a powerful influence on their image of the public good. Lemann's historical account of standardized testing is more fleshed out, and while he shares Sacks's recommendation that affirmative action would be a moot point if standardized testing in admissions were abolished in favor of a different form of evaluation, his conclusions are more radical. According to Lemann's analysis, if universities really want to be instruments of social change, they should institute open admissions and free tuition, policies that have proven far more effective at promoting social mobility and economic opportunity than either high-stakes testing or affirmative action. All three journalists took pains to situate the SATs squarely within the American history of intelligence measurement and mass testing, showing how the testing industry participated in forging a hegemonic vision of the world.

Hofstadter believed that standardized testing and progressive education worked together to undermine liberal and academic education in American schools. He also thought the progressive ethos paved the way for the introduction of mass testing in secondary schools. In his view, Dewey's critique of academic education went too far, undermining support for academic content and an understanding of objective methodologies of finding and arguing for historical truths. Hofstadter felt that education should serve intellectual rather than social ends: like Adorno, his elitism was linked to a ruthless commitment to the creative capacities of negativity in critical thinking. For Dewey, education would attend to differences in individual capacities on a mass scale. He did not anticipate that universal standardized testing would become the means by which "differences" in student capacity could be accurately assessed. Testing was meant to create a new form of selection and meritocracy that would break the back of the inherited privilege of an East Coast WASP elite. As standardized test results emerged as the proper measure of merit by forward-looking university administrators, achieving rule by the meritorious became one of the most important goals of educational institutions in twentieth-century America.[51] Even harsh critics of the SATs and the College Board such as Peter Sacks believed in the meritocracy: they just want a better, more holistic form of evaluation.

Hofstadter's targeting of progressive thought no doubt had to do with its special form of cryptoreligiosity—in short, it idealized building community feeling over encouraging intellectual effort. In promoting a kind of communion between teacher and students, progressive education gradually eviscerated academic content from the school curriculum. In this way, progressive curricula contained the seed of an anti-intellectualism that would find fertile ground in the twentieth-century political imagination. In fact, Joseph Mayer Rice did not believe in curricular content at all: he believed that proper management by properly trained supervisors would liberate children and teachers alike from tyranny.[52] For other critics of progressive education such as Samuel Bowles and Herbert Gintis, scientific management of schools was merged with business methods. The fatal application of "business methods" reproduced in schools society's pyramidal structures of authority and privilege. Bowles and Gintis, writing in the 1970s, thought that school reform was meaningless without a revolution in social forms—or the very destruction of capitalism itself. Eighty years of progressive educational policy, according to them, had produced only unhappy results. The demands for administrative accountability reduced the teachers to "the status of a simple worker, with little control over curriculum, activities or discipline," while students became "objects of administration" with "'busy-work' and standardized tests coming to prevail over play and self development."[53] Two decades after Bowles and Gintis's critique of American schools, Peter Sacks observed with outrage that teachers in financially beleaguered school systems, reeling from the need to raise test scores, do just what the testing industry recommends that they *not* do—teach to the test. Even standardized test producers concede that drilling students to take tests produces only ephemeral learning results, but in economically beleaguered school systems serving the poorest American students, test preparation has taken the place of teaching.[54] For Sacks, shifting accountability to the administration was part of the problem in our schools, not the solution.[55]

Charles W. Eliot made his mark on the American educational scene when he responded to the pressures of a rapidly changing country with institutional reforms. Another Harvard president, James Bryant Conant, discussed below, would become the administrative author of the American meritocracy. In the early twentieth century, however, it was Columbia University that would find itself most directly challenged by the pressures of urbanization and immigration. By the end of the nineteenth century, American universities and educators found themselves challenged by the demands of industrialization and the pressing need to address new immigrant populations. Because of its location in New York City, Columbia was at the forefront of these problems. In the early twentieth century, Columbia College changed its admission standards to admit a more diverse student body. It was the first Ivy League university to allow a New York Regents Credential to fulfill part of its admissions requirement.[56] This early attempt at diversification did indeed change the demographic of the student body. By 1916 Columbia College's third dean, Herbert E. Hawkes, complained about the new kind of Columbia student who commuted to class and thought of his education as merely another step toward a better life. These commuters were the sons of New York's Lower East Side immigrants, many of them Jewish. These second-generation immigrant students were enormously energetic and ambitious: Hawkes and Nicholas Murray Butler, then Columbia's president, looked on with dismay as their numbers threatened to transform the culture of these administrators' beloved university. These new students brought something of the Lower East Side to the Upper West Side, and this was not a welcome consequence of the change in admissions policies. Lionel Trilling pointed out that it was the abolishment in 1916 of the Latin requirement that opened Columbia College's admissions to the brightest young men of limited means who were educated in the New York City public school system, where Latin was never made part of the curriculum.

For the most part, Hawkes was right: the new students viewed their education as a means of climbing the socioeconomic ladder.[57] James Crouse and Dale Trusheim, academic critics of the SATs, remarked that the intelligence test was meant to discourage immigrant students and reduce the number of Jewish applicants without imposing an explicit quota on their admission. So convinced were educators by social Darwinism that they believed that immigrant students were simply not going to be able to make the grade. Their alleged biological inferiority would be revealed by the test, and immigrant children would be legitimately disallowed entrance into New York City's premier private university.[58] John Wechsler writes, "Within the vortex of the late nineteenth–early twentieth-century world, two related processes—immigration and education—emerge as especially dynamic social forces. For just as mass immigration was a symbol for—even the embodiment of cultural disruption—education became its dialectic opposite, an instrument of order, direction, of social consolidation."[59] The dual ideals of efficiency and social control emerged as dominant principles of value in American educational institutions.

Nicholas Murray Butler was not simply a reactionary or an authoritarian. His view of college admissions and the identity of Columbia was complicated. He was tired of his institution being used as a site for the reproduction of what Nicholas Lemann called the "Episcopacy," the Episcopalian aristocracy that had long dominated American politics and culture.[60] Butler worked with Charles Eliot of Harvard to form the College Board, a board of examiners "to administer uniform college entrance examinations."[61] The attempt to standardize college admissions sought to address the chaos and nepotism that characterized American higher education: many colleges admitted students solely on the basis of recommendation or certification by preparatory school. Those colleges that gave admissions examinations put students who lived far away at a distinct disadvantage.[62] Butler did believe, then, in rewarding the merit of exceptional students who were not born into privileged families residing on the eastern seaboard. He just did not believe that the energetic and ambitious sons of Lower East Side immigrants possessed enough merit for Columbia to accept them in great numbers.

The management of university admissions would undergo a striking change after World War II. James Bryant Conant, president of Harvard from 1933 to 1953, can lay claim to shaping the exceptionally powerful version of American meritocracy that arose after the war. Conant was a full blue-blooded member of the American WASP elite. He wanted to shake things up in the bastions of inherited privilege. In his eyes, the new sciences of testing and development would be capable of realizing the Jeffersonian traditions in American schools because they combined objectivity and progressive pragmatism. In order to meet Dewey's exhortation for educators to respond to "industrialism" and the demands made by industrialization upon the workforce, Conant focused on assessment and selection. The American meritocracy could be adequately described as a unique invention of the Episcopacy, whose most capable and service-minded members—Eliot, Butler, and Conant—presided over the midcentury reforms of American education, government, and culture.

By the 1940s Conant wanted "to depose the existing, undemocratic American elite and replace it with a new one made of brainy, elaborately trained public-spirited people drawn from every section and every background."[63] I would argue that his ambitions were more complex. First, he wanted to draw upon the resources of the new science of testing to create a system of education that would counter the dual threats of new social organizations, Communism and Fascism, which are both based in large part on class antagonism. Second, Conant wanted to avoid Columbia College's errors and backtracking in admitting only the right kinds of high scorers. Deeply concerned about the proper form of education for a tumultuous and democratic country and writing in the shadow of a world war, Conant laid out his case for decisive educational reforms and "drastic action" in an article the *Atlantic Monthly* called "Education for a Classless Society." Conant's Jeffersonian ambition was to select "youths of genius" from among the poor as a means of opening up careers to all talented and worthy Americans. Although he agreed with his contemporaries Theodor Adorno and Max Horkheimer that the idolatry of reason was a form of superstition, Conant maintained that the setbacks of the Enlightenment project were only temporary. The expansion of freedoms and the defeat of tyranny would take place through the development of the new discipline of the social sciences (in this too he seemed to concur with views that were promoted by Theodor Adorno). This new science would develop new tools to produce a truly democratic, socially fluid nation that would act as a model for the entire world. Newly forged institutional tools would then allow for the peaceful abolishment of class difference in the name of social mobility. Conant envisioned the transformation of the public secondary school system into an instrument by which the Jeffersonian dream could be successfully realized. Non-academic students who demonstrated "manual dexterity" or were gifted in arts and crafts would also be identified and provided with the proper education to guide them toward the correct career opportunities. In the ostensibly anodyne statement "Abilities must be assessed, talents must be developed, ambitions guided," we find the origins of the kind of thinking that would turn schools into sorting mechanisms and testing itself into a global, multi-billion-dollar industry charged with identifying the brilliant and helping the average student. Conant chose to ignore the extent to which "manual dexterity" was increasingly obsolete for Taylorized systems of manufacturing even as he promoted high-stakes testing tools that would reward the sorts of mental gymnastics that his intellectual hero, John Dewey, deplored.[64] Conant was not a man of idle words: in 1943 he created the University Committee on the Objectives of General Education in a Free Society; its members were drawn from the Faculty in Arts and Sciences and Education. The committee's deliberations were published in 1945 as a book called *General Education in a Free Society*, known as the Harvard Redbook.[65] In the introduction to the committee's report, Conant defended his abandonment of "liberal education" for "general education" in the name of the committee and the title of the book. In his own words, "we are concerned with a general education—a liberal education—not for the relatively few, but for a multitude."[66] The populist inflection was unmistakable.

Conant's multitude was going to present itself in full force by the end of World War II. He was determined to meet the challenge of a reconfigured American university by producing a nationally accepted standardized test that would undo the inheritance of privilege and entry into elite institutions of higher learning. In Conant's search for a like-minded young man who might help him develop the best tools for testing the new multitudes of college aspirants, he did not have to look far. Henry Chauncey, an enthusiast of intelligence testing, was a young assistant dean at Harvard. Conant invited him to develop tests that would produce a more rationalized form of selection in the process of college admissions and gave him the mandate to select outstanding public school students from the Midwest for a new scholarship program at Harvard. Descended of Puritan entrepreneurs and ministers, Chauncey brought to the mass application of testing a missionary zeal. Although his own family was poor compared to his peers at Harvard and Groton, he benefited from the informal scholarship system that kept the WASP elite in the right schools. He would go on to be the first director of the Educational Testing Service and is a mythical figure in that organization. Conant gave Chauncey the means to realize their shared dream of finding a test that could be given to the masses in order to select the most outstanding students.

In fact, Chauncey discovered rather than invented the multiple-choice tests that would become the basis for the SATs: they were developed by Carl Campbell Brigham, a professor of psychology at Princeton who wrote *A Study of American Intelligence*, an analysis of the army mental tests he helped administer to World War I recruits.[67] The army mental tests in turn owed a great debt to Lewis Terman's modifications of Alfred Binet's intelligence tests, which were developed to identify learning deficiencies in Paris schoolchildren. Binet had hoped to develop a test that would find deviations from the norm. His tests were made up of mental puzzles corresponding to specific ages: if 65 percent of children of one particular age, say, seven, could correctly answer one of his puzzles, that question became a seven-year-old question. The IQ produced factored in both the biological age and the "tested" age of a student. In 1910 Lewis Terman discovered the tests and enthusiastically adapted them into a revised version that came to be called the Stanford-Binet IQ Test that is still used today. Terman had only tested a few hundred Californians when the opportunity for mass application came up: the federal government was in desperate need of a means of sorting officer material out of its 1.7 million recruits. Before this time, Terman's test had already inspired heated critique from Walter Lippmann, who in 1922 had published a series of seven articles in the *New Republic* on the subject.

Lippmann focused on the development of the tests and their assumptions that human intelligence from the ages of four to sixteen could be calculated by measuring individual test results against an average mental capacity. For Lippmann, "the intelligence test does not weigh or measure intelligence by any objective standard. It simply arranges a group of people in a series from best to worst by balancing their capacity to do certain arbitrarily selected puzzles, against the capacity of all the others."[68] Binet's tests were meant to identify learning deficiencies and difficulties; they were not meant to produce intelligence rankings or assess potential achievement. But the content-free nature of his mental puzzles was deeply appealing to American psychologists and social scientists. They thought they had found a neutral instrument that could be used objectively to assess test-takers from diverse backgrounds.

In *A Study of American Intelligence*, Brigham elaborated on what he and his mentor, Robert M. Yerkes, firmly believed: that intelligence was both measurable and quantifiable. In addition, they wished to use the science of the Stanford-Binet IQ test to prove that intelligence was not only measurable, it was inherited. Moreover, Brigham believed intelligence to be the determining factor in predicting the future achievements of test-takers. The Alpha tests were given to literate recruits; the Beta tests, which had fewer language-oriented problems, were given to illiterate ones. Like Alfred Binet's mental tests, both were filled with brain twisters and puzzles, remarkably similar to today's SATs. Test-takers were presented with a series of questions and a list of different possible answers, from which test-takers had to choose the correct one. While Binet felt that his tests should be given on a one-to-one basis for a full assessment and diagnosis of a child's needs, Yerkes and Brigham tested army recruits by the tens of thousands. Brigham shared with Chauncey a quasi-religious belief in the science of testing and his own expertise, but Brigham also believed in a racial hierarchy of intelligence. As part of his critique of the army mental tests' cultural bias, Stephen Jay Gould cites the following multiple-choice question as an astonishing example of what the test-makers thought was a measure of innate capacities: "Crisco is a: patent medicine, disinfectant, toothpaste, food product."[69] Because Yerkes insisted that his tests measured "native intellectual ability," the results of World War I mass testing and its interpretation confirmed for many American scientists their ingrained suspicions that northern Europeans were biologically superior to southern and eastern Europeans. Brigham and Yerkes would eventually conclude that "Negroes" were mentally deficient to such a degree that their very existence on American shores had become a eugenic problem for white European settlers. In his analysis of the results of

44

the army tests, Brigham concluded that the marked decline in American intelligence was so dire that restrictions on immigration and naturalization would not be sufficient to improve the level of national intelligence. He saw no reason why "legal steps should not be taken which would insure a continuously progressive upward evolution. . . . The really important steps are those looking toward the prevention of the continued propagation of defective strains in the present population."[70] Brigham was proposing the political and legal imposition of policies meant to winnow out the intellectually and cognitively unfit.

Brigham's ideas about race and eugenics never prevented him from being assigned by the College Board to develop university assessment tests. Later, under the auspices of ETS, Chauncey collaborated with Brigham and the College Board to disseminate the tests and to convince large sections of the population that the SATs were socially valuable instruments for the building of a better, more open world. It may seem unfair to juxtapose Brigham's sinister insinuations with Henry Chauncey's and James Bryant Conant's progressive attempts to rationalize selection for America's top universities. However, if we ignore the ignominious origins of the SATs, we cannot hope to understand the range of consequences of what David Owen called "the cult of mental measurement."[71] Conant was in essence a bureaucratic author who did not need to sign his name to his far-reaching innovations, either his renaming of liberal education as general education or his critical role in empowering Henry Chauncey to found ETS, one of the most powerful postwar, unregulated, nongovernmental educational institutions in this country. University admissions policies underwent massive transformation in the name of Conant's and Chauncey's progressive reforms. As enlightened members of the Episcopacy, they felt entitled and empowered to improve the nation according to their values. Conant and Chauncey did not share Brigham's virulent racism; they merely believed that the science of testing and the redistribution of educational opportunity would produce generations of grateful graduates of elite universities.

Chauncey guided ETS through a period of almost unimaginable growth: "Only 81,200 SAT's were taken during 1951–1952. Ten years later the number had increased to 802,500."[72] He was an energetic corporate leader who was able to shape ETS's mission decade by decade, from the late 1940s, when he emphasized expansion of educational opportunity, to the late 1950s, when a backlash against progressive education and Cold War anxieties allowed him to frame testing's goals firmly within the interest of national security. Crouse and Trusheim put an interesting twist in the story of the relationship between progressive education and standardized testing. For them, "Chauncey put ETS squarely against the jargon, slogans and anti-intellectualism when he expressed concern for 'talent waste' and a more effective utilization of human resources."[73] ETS was able to convince a large swathe of policy makers, administrators, and the public that its tests would identify the unhappy underachiever whose fantastic standardized test scores would inspire him (or occasionally her, but this was the 1950s, and Chauncey was concerned about identifying engineers) to apply to an elite school and be trained to serve his (or her) country. ETS would help prevent human resource "waste" while promoting educational efficiency.

Low scorers, on the other hand, would have their expectations "cooled down" and be advised by teachers and guidance counselors not to waste everyone's time by enrolling in challenging college prep classes and/or applying to elite schools. As if in direct response to the discontents of C. Wright Mills's white-collar worker, Chauncey suggested that early identification of low scorers could prevent worker malaise. Everyone would find their place in the educational system and the workforce. Rational distribution of resources would be guaranteed by America's "secret weapon," testing and guidance.[74] The American system of selection would achieve not only greater "social mobility," James Bryant Conant's dream, but also greater national security and international competitiveness. In the United States, talents and gifts would not be squandered. They would be copiously rewarded.

No matter how humble their family backgrounds, students identified as gifted and talented would be awarded entry into the nation's top universities. After their course of study, they would choose to enter government and public service in order to pay back the social system that had allowed them to gain access to the inner sanctum that had once been reserved for America's ruling classes. This sort of top-down reform anticipated the rewards of scientific philanthropy while discreetly covering up the uglier aspects of its intellectual and cultural inheritance. For Lemann, "the notion that they are participating (and succeeding) in a great, broad, fair, open national competition is at the heart of their idea of themselves, and indeed you do have to be very intelligent and able to get the most prestigious of billets distributed by the meritocratic machinery."[75]

Standardized testing emerged as a pillar of the American meritocracy as curriculum was continually adjusted to meet the alleged needs and interests of modern students. Elementary education was no doubt improved under progressive reforms, but what happened in secondary and higher education was more complicated. "Relevance" and "life" were configured and institutionalized by progressive reformers who unwittingly provided a powerful set of justifications for making the world of school nothing more than a series of prepara-

46

tory exercises for the worlds of work and consumerism. Praising the cultivation of liberal arts at the expense of "specialization" may still be acceptable at commencement ceremonies, but as the twentieth century drew to a close, the mind would not so much practice "awareness of contingency" as it would be engaged in perpetual "reorientation" and "adjustment."

According to David Owen, the College Board and ETS were unwilling to recognize Brigham's bigotry: they preferred to dismiss "Brigham's virulent racism as a sort of irrelevant eccentricity."[76] In its official histories, ETS emphasized the fact that Brigham eventually renounced his defense of the science of "comparative racial studies." He acknowledged that his tests did not measure innate intelligence but a kind of literacy in the cultural vernacular that put immigrant and rural test-takers at a distinct disadvantage.[77]

The acceptance of standardized testing in American schools has been the result of a long historical process: it has taken a hundred years to make the school into an instrument of mass social triage and teachers into its unwilling accomplices. The meritocracy, as it has developed in the United States, justified the unequal distribution of wealth and privilege by promoting the measurement of a narrow and pseudoscientific concept of intelligence. Standardized testing wanted to produce a value-free measurement of individual capacities, but its own investments in early twentieth-century anxieties about social unrest and grotesque economic inequality shaped the horizon of political and social reform. The science of standardized testing had to be confident about its ability to predict the future achievement of even the most diverse pool of test-takers. For this reason, standardized testing as a social technology rooted itself in early twentieth-century eugenic thinking and attempted to produce a stable and unilinear conception of pure capacity that had no relationship to mastery of academic content.[78]

In raising serious questions about standardized testing and social selection, Lemann identified the formation of a new and entrenched elite in the postwar United States. In his investigation of the origins of the Educational Testing Service, Lemann cast doubt upon the overweening belief that a more "scientific" test of scholastic aptitude would naturally lead to a more egalitarian and democratic society. The SATs did present a more efficient and rationalized means of triage, and the widespread acceptance of SAT scores for college admissions did crack open the monopolization of Ivy League education by eastern seaboard WASPs with inherited wealth while also becoming a tool for recruiting the best and the brightest across the races, the classes, and the nation for entry into prestigious high-paying jobs in business, finance, and law. Nevertheless, in

part because the Ivy League has found its selective process of admissions justified by testing, the institutionalization of aptitude tests as the de facto university entrance examinations has not brought about the radical democratization
of higher education, if this was indeed Conant's intention. Henry Chauncey
and the Educational Testing Service claimed to depose "character," a mystifying quality that was part sociability, part sportsmanship, part group loyalty that
had been held in higher esteem than anything like intelligence or curiosity by
the American aristocracy. To replace the aristocratic prerogative of character,
Chauncey and the testing industry came upon "scholastic aptitude" as a scientifically quantifiable quality that would organize social distinction by order of
merit rather than family or privilege. The perfect SAT scores of the incoming
freshman class provided a "scientific" rationalization for a new form of elitism.
Harvard, Yale, and Princeton undergrads no longer hailed exclusively from Puritan blue-blooded families and Yankee preparatory schools. They were admitted to these exclusive colleges because they were simply found to have greater
scholastic aptitude and academic potential than the rest of their peers. Free
public universities were simply dismissed as part of the "embedded liberalism"
and deficit spending of yesterday. Nevertheless, the testing industry emerged
from the scientific activity that produced theories of racialized biological determinism. Its innovations represented a uniquely American contribution to the
application of intelligence-testing principles to mass education. Meritocracy,
which was supposed to expand educational opportunity, instead served to rationalize and to widen the gap between elite and public universities as well as
urban and rural incomes. Testing justified the continued and intractable nature
of economic and social inequality: what it offered was scientific measurement
of different degrees of merit. It may have appeared that giving gifted and underprivileged students entry into elite universities furthered the cause of social
justice, but it merely obscured the demise of an ideal of free public universities
and open admissions policies. In Lemann's words, the ETS-shaped meritocracy
allowed American universities to be turned into "a national personnel department" that was able to charge increasingly prohibitive fees for its educational
and social networking services.[79]

Indeed, the function of universities in the meritocratic order should inspire
much more popular suspicion and debate. The meritocracy was established by
a small group of men, and it became the accepted means of distributing educational opportunity in a democratic society. Its most important features and
institutions have not been subject to public debate or government legislation:
ETS was founded in a series of patronage deals made among the administra-

tors and professors at Harvard, Yale, and Princeton. Considering this history, it is perfectly understandable that "people worry and squabble" obsessively over universities and that these debates within the academy and the public sphere have often been colored by resentment of education, resulting in the persistent demand for more efficiency in the educational process. In their study *The Meritocracy Myth*, Stephen J. McNamee and Robert K. Miller, Jr., have shown that expansion of educational opportunity through meritocratic instruments of selection has not led to greater social mobility for underprivileged and minority populations: "Increases in educational attainment are completely compatible with stable levels of social inequality and class reproduction."[80]

In 1966 Daniel Bell was commissioned by Columbia University to undertake a study of general education at the university. He was given the same mandate as the Harvard Committee of 1945: to explore the future of the liberal arts in the expanded functions of the university. Whereas the Harvard Redbook directly addressed itself to the task of educating the multitudes, Bell showed a deeper sympathy for allegedly elitist forms of humanistic inquiry and liberal thinking. He praised the value of liberal education and the humanities as the ground of general education itself: he put himself in the position of a universal subject, grounded in Western traditions and forms of cultural achievement that both progressive reformers and the countercultural Left would find wasteful and compromised. After the Vietnam War, Bell's idealized view of liberal education came to represent a decidedly "conservative" perspective on general education:

> Liberal education, for me, is more than the cultivation of the humanities, although it certainly is that. It is an emphasis on the grounds of knowledge. . . . When a subject is presented as received doctrine or fact, it becomes an aspect of specialization and technique. When it is introduced with an awareness of its contingency and of the conceptual frame that guides its organization, the student can then proceed with the necessary self-consciousness that keeps his mind open to possibility and to reorientation. All knowledge, thus, is liberal (that is, it enlarges and liberates the mind) when it is committed to continuing inquiry.[81]

According to Bell, liberal education entailed a kind of endless, free-ranging, nonspecialized curiosity that would contribute to a general sense of self-awareness. The liberal sensibility was agnostic and skeptical: it took nothing for granted as essentially necessary or essentially valuable or essentially good. It rejected specialization in favor of "continuing inquiry." Americans have tended to believe, even at the height of economic prosperity, that the cultivation of such critical and aesthetic sensibilities is an unaffordable luxury and that transmitted knowledge should be easily converted into an instrument for social, personal, and economic improvement.

According to John Dewey, liberal education was "linked to the notions of leisure, purely contemplative knowledge and a spiritual activity not involving the active use of bodily organs."[82] Dewey undertook a critique of the relationship between privilege and liberal education and concluded that all teaching, thinking, and learning must be situated in the complexity of "shared concerns" and concrete situations. This situatedness is what makes education in a democracy distinct: learning should not take place in a vacuum but should address and be firmly grounded in "the community of interests." Education can serve to prevent "stratification into separate classes." According to Dewey, we must "see to it that intellectual opportunities are available to all on equable and easy terms."[83]

Liberal education was meant to educate a genteel elite: in an industrial democracy, intellectual life should be made to rhyme with new forms of association and rhythms of experience. If the modern world needed new ways of teaching, learning, and knowing, modern intellectuals needed to immerse themselves in the shared concerns of ordinary people. Dewey's complex position was often reduced to the doctrine of "learning by doing," and the application of his theories produced results and methods he would be hard put to recognize. Even as education itself became a technical area of specialization, hyperbolic claims for its ability to train, normalize, discipline, and integrate students into the workforce continued apace. It seemed that average students and ordinary people felt more estranged from intellectual life, even as progressive principles of education achieved greater institutional legitimacy. Adorno and Hofstadter would see this particular situation as symptomatic of the administered life. Efficiency would begin to usurp all other standards of educational assessment, and as the twentieth century waned, it would become harder and harder to argue forcefully and publicly against the administrative imagination. Liberal education seemed increasingly to be wasted on the majority of American students who, in the imagination of countless commissions and committees, did not need to master academic material spanning centuries or millennia of human culture and history. They certainly did not need to master the practices of an updated aesthetic education, set out in Bell's version of the liberal arts as the cultivation of detached self-reflection and "endless inquiry." Average students needed to be prepared for work and "active home membership." They needed to be taught how to maintain their "health" and be informed consumers, and, for some reason, they needed to be taught these things in school.

chapter two

ordinary americans, average students

Hofstadter's analysis of American ambivalence about education is essentially an interpretation of a modern American fantasy about the relationship between the classroom and the workplace. Since education was supposed to prepare students for both work and life, administrators and reformers imagined that it could be a tool to mitigate social inequality and social tension. When schools fail to train docile workers and to move people up the economic ladder, to educate students and produce a docile workforce, the institutionally embedded anti-intellectual tendencies within the educational system itself explode. Administrative solutions are sought to discipline and reward teachers, rein in the power of corrupt unions, and help passive victims of an allegedly nefarious system—the foundering students themselves. When politicians act forcefully in this arena, they appear to be responding to popular demands for "excellence," accountability, and efficiency. In the previous chapter, meritocracy and the standardized testing industry emerged as two of the most important political and technocratic innovations of the American century; in this chapter, we will see how the emergence of the free public high school represented another extraordinary and vexed achievement in the history of American education. The progressive ideal that schools should be deeply linked to and immersed in the problems of industrial democracy made possible by midcentury the institutional focus in public secondary schools on socialization, vocational training, and civic education, holding in reserve critical self-reflection and liberal education for a small minority of high scorers. I would like to suggest that the sorting function that high schools played in creating a division of education is related to a distinctly modern American animus against liberal education, but the ideal of free public secondary education that prepared students for citizenship took hold as a specifically American educational aim. American academies of the early nineteenth century imitated the European model of an explicitly elitist and aristocratic system of education. It was only gradually that an American theory of democracy made itself felt in the promotion of a common secondary school. Despite his dim view of the American high school's academic profile, Richard Hofstadter pointed out that a free community-based secondary school is a positive achievement in the history of education, one that in the postwar world, western "European nations have found worthy of emulation."[1]

According to Judith Sealander, "less than 7 percent of all seventeen-year-olds in the country were high school graduates in 1900. By 1940, almost half were."[2] Throughout the nineteenth century, Americans had been content to fund their schools on a voluntary basis: elite academies could charge prohibitive tuition, while country schools were supported by donations of food, supplies, and money from the rural communities they served. As the population became increasingly urban and foreign born, urban elites realized that expanded public education was critical to building a common culture and common identity. National anxiety about educating these new Americans spurred state legislation that mandated property tax–supported secondary schooling. With this legislation, a massive sea change took place in the way in which Americans of the future were to be educated. The family as a site of social and cultural transmission was deemed inadequate, especially in urban areas where large percentages of the working-class population were made up of recently arrived immigrants. Fueled by fears of public education for African Americans, the South showed the greatest resistance to these compulsory schooling laws. Southern states were able to set up segregated high schools and required the least number of days in school during the academic year. As we will see, the mass secondary school was a distinctly urban phenomenon, supported primarily by early twentieth-century urban elites.

Into this mass secondary school streamed a stunning diversity of students, many of whom were from working-class families who had relied on their children's incomes for support. These new students were subject to the new compulsory education laws and were in attendance under conditions of coercion. Many of the educational reform movements that sprung up in the interwar period were attempts to engage just this kind of the reluctant student. In our times, it is easy to criticize vocational education and its management of expectations because it is grounded in producing a docile working class. Vocational education's stated intention, however, was to engage the unwilling secondary school student by forging a more durable link between what he or she learned in school and his or her work life beyond the classroom. The students of voc-ed had given up college aspirations, but high school would provide the skill sets by which these low and average scorers could receive the proper education. Reformers held fast to James Bryant Conant's belief that low scorers were often miraculously gifted with a compensatory manual dexterity. From the perspective of the cultural and economic elite, students as future workers needed to be managed and adjusted to what Harry Braverman described as work in its "capitalist form," that is, work characterized by increasing fragmentation of tasks, "swiftly changing technology," and "antagonistic social relations."[3] According to Braverman, "manual dexterity," "intelligence," and "accident proneness" were among the areas of aptitude that industrial psychology of the 1910s and 1920s sought to identify for a variety of American corporations. Although the tests proved poor predictors of actual work performance, they left a distinct mark on the future of managerial methods and objectives. The tests were abandoned during the labor crises of the 1930s, but industrial psychologists continued to believe that they could find new instruments of calibration and measurement that would serve to promote worker/management harmony.[4] Meanwhile, Lewis Terman of World War I army intelligence test fame pushed intelligence testing on American schools. Sealander notes that in 1925 "almost 90 percent of urban school districts used some form of intelligence testing and urban systems employed staffs of full time psychologists." Even as the United States surpassed other nations in proportion of the population attending high school, its students became the most IQ tested in the world. Testing and education for the masses had become intimately and inextricably intertwined ways of managing social progress and resolving the nagging problem of inequality.[5]

Manual dexterity needed cultivation and refinement as well. Confronted with their average to low standardized test scores, ordinary students would naturally want to excel at manual labor, and, given voc-ed electives such as woodworking, automotive mechanics, home economics, and metalworking, they would embrace such classes and assume their places reasonably, if not contentedly, in the American workforce. High schools therefore played a critical role in the division of labor across the student body. The skills required by manual and vocational labor were discretely separated from those necessary for intellectual work and academic mastery. The institutional imagination of the meritocracy subtly but inexorably configured the separation of two distinctive sets of human skills and aptitudes, one "manual" and one intellectual, each with its own place in the industrial and economic order. Conant's fantasies about low scores and manual dexterity notwithstanding, it is quite obvious that secondary education with a vocational twist was a way of dealing with economic and social inequality. It did this, on the one hand, by providing free high schools as the institutionalization of the American ideal of social mobility. Simultaneously, it offered a way to manage the expectations of poor and economically marginal students who found themselves in a high school holding pattern, unable to go straight to work because of the new laws against child labor but alienated from academic subjects at the same time.

The compulsory and coercive aspect of high school thus becomes more obvious. Even though American industry needed manual laborers, labor unions and social reformers agreed to work together to keep young people out of factories: the first group was worried about competition and unemployment, the second about the moral question of exploiting young people. Vocational education, as compared with academic training in foreign languages, arts, math, literature, and science, seemed to provide a more responsible way of bridging the gap between the working-class student and his or her life after school. In light, however, of the evolution of Taylorism and management science's relationship to craft skill and manual labor in the twentieth century, it would be simply disingenuous to maintain such a rosy vision of the powers of "manual dexterity." The drive for efficiency had led to the degradation of the conditions of labor and the fragmentation of the work process, leaving manual dexterity for most American workers increasingly beside the point. Vocational education notwithstanding, "compulsory education law allied with applied psychology condemned millions of American teenagers to several years of meaningless schooling."[6]

By the 1940s, innovative practices and educational reform had made elementary school classrooms more cheerful and child-friendly places. Desks were no longer bolted to the floor, and students were no longer seated in strict alphabetical order. The walls were not covered with abstruse and difficult material but rather were decorated with the drawings and writings of the children themselves. At this time, few teachers or administrators would question the need to address the "whole child" or even the imperative to shape curriculum to children's "interests." In the preprogressive education world, discipline, authority, and indifference to the "personality" had produced a stable distance between the interests of the teacher and the interests of the students. According to 1950s sociologist David Riesman in *The Lonely Crowd*, in this tradition-oriented school "the teacher is supposed to see that the children learn a curriculum, not that they enjoy it."[7] In assessing educational authoritarianism, Riesman was ambivalent about the relative autonomy it fostered in its inner-directed teachers and students. Its exclusionary, talent-crushing potential wreaked a kind of damage he did not choose to focus on. Riesman was worried about forms of other-directed conformity that, according to him, were being fostered by new objectives in education. By the early 1950s, for Riesman, as for Hofstadter, Progressive theories of education had fostered an innovatively invasive form of social control. For example, the old school basically left play alone, allowing children

53

to work out among themselves the harsher pleasures of rough and unsupervised blacktop justice. In the new school, "play, which in the earlier epoch is often an extracurricular and private hobby, shared at most with a small group, now becomes part of the school enterprise itself, serving a 'realistic' purpose."[8] Cooperation and collaboration often centered on "contentless" projects that had evolved out of Dewey's idea of learning by doing.[9]

From Riesman's point of view, the language of Progressive education had become the language of educational administration itself: enlightened teachers and parents were to act as rationalizers or managers of children's talents and emotions. The rhetoric of Progressive education not only had become routinized but had emerged as a badge of professionalization and middle-class sophistication. Progressive education claimed to produce greater freedom for students and teachers while being grounded in the scientific facts of child development. To Progressive education's midcentury critics, it allowed for the takeover of schools and their new, expanded functions by a new breed of administrators less interested in academics than in promoting more managerial control over what went on not only in secondary school classrooms but in teacher training programs across the country. From Arthur Bestor's 1953 perspective, "American intellectual life is threatened because the first twelve years of formal schooling in the United States are falling more and more completely under the policy-making control of a new breed of educator who has no real place in—who does not respect and who is not respected by—the world of scientists, scholars, and professional men."[10]

In 1947 the Department of Education held a conference on vocational education at which Charles Prosser made a statement that would eventually pass as a resolution on "life" education. In 1912 Charles Prosser was working for the business lobby group the National Association of Manufacturers as its full-time secretary. In 1914 he was appointed to the Commission on National Aid to Vocational Education. The commission was charged with the goal of measuring the need for vocational education. Not surprisingly, it determined that needs were "great and crying."[11] The commission's findings led to the passage in 1917 of the Smith Hughes Act, which channeled federal funds into school systems to promote and design vocational education courses. The state of national security was at stake since industrial education was seen as augmenting the nation's "preparedness for war." The piece of legislation allowed for the introduction of electives and a whole course of study that generations of American public high school students accepted as an inevitable part of their educational "choices": carpentry and auto mechanics, home economics and typing. Prosser wanted to use American schools to build "a working class to meet the needs of a burgeoning industrial economy." He was decidedly not interested "in contributing to a middle-class mythology of individuals getting ahead."[12]

In 1948 Prosser reemerged as a major player in educational policy when his statement at the vocational education conference appeared, slightly revised as a government paper issued by the Office of Education in 1948, *Life-Adjustment Education for Every Youth*. Prosser felt that vocational education had been neglected by federal agencies; it had become the underfunded stepchild of public education and needed a reconfigured, modern look. According to Prosser's 1947–48 analysis, 20 percent of students were bound for college and 20 percent for the "desirable skilled trades."[13] The remaining 60 percent would perform unskilled work. By putting into place a more "relevant" secondary school curriculum entirely oriented toward "life-adjustment," he hoped to help the neglected majority of American students. Their "sad tales of the social and economic maladjustment of millions of America's citizens is evidence of the failure on the part of the general high school itself."[14] Prosser looked at standardized test results and saw that students from underprivileged or newly arrived immigrant families "scored lower on intelligence and achievement tests, and lacked interest in school work."[15] These students deserved a specially designed curriculum made just for their needs, their lives, and the limited horizon of their working-class futures. It was simply inefficient and wasteful to teach students what they could not use later in life.

In one way, Dewey's arguments, amplified for secondary school education, would seem to support Prosser's vocationalism. But Dewey had opposed "making the schools an adjunct to manufacture and commerce." According to him, education that focused narrowly on vocational training would become "an instrument of perpetuating unchanged the existing industrial order of society."[16] Prosser would not have disagreed about the aims of vocational education: for him, this description would have been a positive assessment of what he hoped schools could do for society. He believed that working-class unrest and discontent could be pacified through proper education, since vocational education would produce properly trained and adjusted workers. This kind of preoccupation with training students can be seen in the child labor laws that were supposed to prevent the exploitation of children as workers but that also functioned to prevent poor and working-class youth from participating in contributing to the family income.

In 1933 the pressing problem of youth unemployment had made itself felt with stark urgency: an estimated three hundred thousand teenagers were living as tramps, homeless, hungry, and unemployed.[17] More stayed home, unemployed and no better nourished by unemployed and harried parents. The Civilian Conservation Corps (CCC), a New Deal program, almost derailed Prosser's educational agenda. According to Sealander, this emergency work program was one of Franklin Delano Roosevelt's favorites, and he won the support of labor when he appointed labor leader and machinist Robert Fechner as its head. Fechner had been vice president of the International Order of Machinists and was a high school dropout himself. By the time the CCC was closed down, it had employed over three million American boys to "replant the country's forests, improve its soil and refurbish its parks."[18] In the history of the CCC, over three million young men ages seventeen to twenty-eight were fed and clothed in camps. They received a cash allowance of $25 to $30 a month, which was sent home to needy families. The outbreak of World War II allowed CCC members easy entry into the military; its success as a public works program for disadvantaged youth was in some part eclipsed by the smooth mobilization of CCC workers as army GIs.

In the 1920s Prosser was already a tireless advocate for vocational education. In 1925 he coauthored *Vocational Education in a Democracy*.[19] Not content with the passage of two federal laws supporting vocational education, he saw educational relevance as a cause that needed continual renewal. The economic catastrophe of the 1930s put a damper on the realization of his agenda, but Prosser never wavered in his insistence that the average American student was a victim of an unjust and inadequate educational system. He called for changes in secondary education that would allow for greater efficiency in the education of the average student and presented himself as an advocate for this particular student's interests. Professor of English and critic of management theory Evan Watkins effectively argued that Prosser's theories of education owed more to Frederick Winslow Taylor's ideal of managerial efficiency than Dewey's philosophy of education. Taylor wanted to find and train the best and most motivated workers, like the hardworking and compliant Schmidt made famous by the tract on scientific management. Schmidt was either manipulated or motivated, depending on one's point of view, into moving pig iron more efficiently than his coworkers. Prosser "foresaw vocational education as capable of *producing the kind of workers appropriate to specific slots in an industrial economy*."[20] In 1898, Taylor was hired by Bethlehem Steel to increase the amount of pig iron moved by the average worker. According to Taylor, it was management's scientific obligation to increase the amount of work a worker could do in a determined amount of time. A promise of increase in wages for each individual worker did not hurt his cause either, but Taylor's goal was to increase the amount of profit that Bethlehem Steel could enjoy through maximized efficiency. Taylor did not think highly of his guinea pig Schmidt, but he selected him because of his physical capacity and psychological malleability. Taylor alluded, in fact, to Schmidt's stupidity as being one factor in the management team's selection of this hardworking, slow-witted laborer: "The selection of the man, then, does not involve finding some extraordinary individual, but merely picking out from among very ordinary men the few who are especially suited to this kind of work."[21]

Prosser's educational Taylorism could not have been possible without the appearance of a new figure in the discourse of education reform: the average student, whose education had to be made both scientific and efficient. A statistical fiction took on flesh and blood, and many claims were made on the average student's behalf by education reformers, the most notable of which was that his or her needs had gone woefully unmet in traditional secondary schools. For Prosser, academic education was simply useless to the great majority of secondary school students who were going to grow up to work on the assembly lines in the nation's factories. Prosser played a critical role in Richard Hofstadter's history of American anti-intellectualism: he was also precisely the kind of educator with an anti-intellectual animus as described by Arthur Bestor. Prosser was a fervent crusader for vocational education: his heartland values were embodied by his suspicion of universal academic training. For Prosser, it was better "to teach them [80 percent of American students], for example, not physiology, but how to keep physically fit."[22] In fact, Prosser simply did not believe that all Americans were born equal: it was the task of the public school to "adjust" rather than educate the majority of American children "to the bitter fact that they are good for nothing but undesirable, unskilled occupations, and that intellectual effort is far beyond their feeble grasp."[23] Since practical knowledge was precisely not synthetic, an average student's capacities were best characterized as a series of separate, measurable aptitudes. Ordinary students should not be taught how to generalize. Prosser argued that because 80 percent of the secondary school population was ill suited to academic education, the needs of the average student had to be restricted to "practical training in being family members, consumers and citizens." Prosser's condescension was as boundless as his zeal for reform; to him, ordinary students were not only incapable of the simplest forms of common sense but also "less emotionally mature—nervous, [and] felt less secure."[24] They came from economically deprived families and also simply did less well on tests. Life-adjustment education claimed that it could offer a reassuring and familiar educational environment for these sorts of cognitively and psychologically challenged students.

Like vocational education, life-adjustment education presupposed the acceptance of statistically determined hierarchies and translated the statistical enthusiasm and social determinisms of the late nineteenth century into a rational educational program. It added something interesting to the formula of hierarchical thinking: it celebrated the average student as the neglected and overlooked victim of education itself. Life-adjustment education derived from the needs of the average student, however, a system of education for "all American youth." This implicit denigration of the liberal arts and the undermining of content in education produced the resentment of "book learning" as the exclusive purview of a select and arrogant minority. Before we delve more deeply into Prosser's theories of life-adjustment, we should pause to consider how deeply educational administrators felt about the need to confront the new student population entering secondary and higher education at the end of World War II.

If the humanities (and the concept of liberal education upon which it was founded) was destined to be only one discipline among many, the defenders of general or humanist education struggled to find a coherent argument for common ground, or at least for universal experience. General education advocates might have argued for the importance of a unified cognitive field based upon a strong conception of history that would offer a conceptual background for struggles and conflicts against which works of art, culture, and philosophy could be studied. They took, however, an entirely different tack, one that sought to ground universal experience not in history but in the uplifting experience of a private confrontation with aesthetic "greatness." As Gerald Graff described them, the battles in literature departments between scholars and critics took a new turn during the postwar period. Once again, James Bryant Conant played a critical role in spearheading postwar educational reforms. As noted in the previous chapter, Conant, president of Harvard, formed the Committee on the Objectives of General Education in a Free Society to investigate general education in the United States after the war. Conant and forward-thinking university administrators saw a need to formulate the principles of a new general education that would be able to address increasingly diverse and diversely educated undergraduates who were admitted to universities under the GI bill after the war. He appointed famed rhetorician and literary critic I. A. Richards to the committee. Richards was one of the most prominent proponents of literary criticism in that era, and he made his influence felt. New Criticism, with which Richards was identified, asserted that literary texts were highly self-contained aesthetic forms whose deeper meanings were tangled up in self-referentiality rather than historical and social conditions. Since the 1930s, New Critics had been engaged in a struggle against literary history in the halls of American academia, and they saw their star rising after the war. Therefore, with Richards's participation, the 1945 report on general education, also called the Harvard Redbook, supported the idea of a "unified cultural tradition that was felt to be latent in the great literary texts beneath or above the merely fragmentary and incoherent flux of history and historical knowledge."[25] Greatness in literature was monumental, lasting, transmissible, temporally transcendent, and ahistorical. History appeared marginal to general education. Instead of founding general education on history, the Harvard Redbook committee took a sweeping look at Western civilization and saw that a universalism founded on literary explanation might offer an immediate and accessible mass experience of the common ground. In this study, historical knowledge was eclipsed in favor of New Criticism–inflected close reading.

We cannot understand the fate of general education in the United States without appreciating the role that the professionalization of academia played in homogenizing and improving the overall quality of humanist education while at the same time resituating it as only one field of study among many. Professionalization secured an implicit demotion of the prestige of the humanities within the university itself. Whereas the preprofessional concept of liberal education was aristocratic, cryptoreligious, profoundly elitist, and decidedly antivocational, the new university, with its general education requirements, its professional schools, research specializations, and distinct departments, was both secular and technocratic. Underlying the driest of philological practices, however, was the assumption that a total picture of a language, a culture, and a history would emerge for the devoted student of language. In Graff's description of early nineteenth-century liberal education, he reminds us that there was a presumptive communal and collective experience of literature and the classics accessible to all, even in the most difficult courses on Latin or Greek grammar. The universal experience of beauty or ethics could be imparted during recitation of classical texts, and this universality was supposed to be reproduced through the reading aloud of literary texts. The building of character would take place during these exercises and drills.

In order to overturn such archaic models of pedagogy, educational reformers had to argue against a whole set of presumptions about the legitimacy of universal categories as such. The aesthetic and literary experience of "great literature" was judged to be too "foreign" and "irrelevant" to the lives and needs of an increasingly diverse and average student body. Even the Harvard Redbook criticized the aims and methods of traditional liberal arts education by calling them aloof and inaccessible to the majority of American students. Henceforth, academic content could not be coy; it would have to be unabashedly promiscuous in order to meet students halfway. At the same time that it held the greatness of literature to be aloof from the ravaging forces of history, the Redbook was unabashed in its support of the Deweyan heritage. But its presumptions actually represented something closer to Prosser's ideas of aptitudes, appropriateness, and relevance in education. The Redbook was explicit about using general education to forge a unified sense of national identity: whereas Dewey hoped to make work whole again by forging a kind of education that married intellectual inquiry with physical labor, the authors of the Redbook hoped to heal the divides in the social body through close reading of literary works that would engage the lives and experiences of the new student of both mass and elite education.

Meanwhile, in secondary schools, average students who had no hope of ever going to Harvard had to learn to accept the judgment of experts, that is, the statisticians, test-makers, and test-givers who claimed to be able to measure their faculties and aptitudes. The needs of average students were to be provided for through life-adjustment. Like voc-ed students, average students of life-adjustment did not need to think about the bigger picture, achieve a historical perspective, or struggle fruitlessly with anything like analytic or systematic thinking. For Hofstadter, Prosser's theories of education presented an unlikely merging of populism with business values. He pursued a zealous course of vocational and then life-adjustment advocacy in educational policy that was colored by a sense of confidence in his methods and outrage at the holdouts in intellectual life who disagreed with him. Prosser would at first blush appear to prove Hofstadter's point that populism was shaped by a suspicion of all things related to the "life of the mind." Prosser's philosophy of education, however, represented business interests more than it ever represented the interests of the people. Prosser was unable to destroy liberal education completely: it was deemed wasteful for the majority of students and appropriate only for a gifted minority. How those students were identified and how the rest were to manage would be greatly dependent on the application of mass intelligence and aptitude testing.

Prosser's brand of business-friendly anti-intellectualism arose in the ashes of Populist revolt and was shaped more by the managerial ethos than by the agrarian insurgents. He could ignore the arguments that were being made

against biological determinism and testing, offering his social Darwinist predecessors new tools for institutionalizing economic hierarchies as cognitive
limitation. The average and below average students were consigned to a life
of highly regulated and coordinated leisure and "adjustment" to work, even
as their individual needs were both catered to and measured. This "mental
measurement movement provided the technology necessary for the kind of assessment and prediction that a curriculum based on social efficiency doctrine
required."[26] Prosser was able to build on a Progressive Era reformism married
to Taylorist ideas of managerial efficiency to argue that the secondary school
curriculum had to be entirely remade for the average American student—nothing of it should be left intact. According to the tenets of life-adjustment, intellectual development and cumulative knowledge were not useful goals in a mass
education program. Hofstadter emphasizes the repetition in life-adjustment
manuals that "intellectual training is of no use in solving the 'real life problems' of ordinary youth." In its own words, life-adjustment education emphasized "life values" over the "acquisition of knowledge," inspiring Hofstadter to
remark upon the casual but critical dissolution of the link between the latter
and the former.[27]

If humanist education seemed wasteful and obsolete, it appeared so because
it was deemed inadequate and irrelevant in preparing average students for their
lives outside of school.[28] It did seem doubtful that education in literature, foreign languages, and math beyond basic calculations was useful to the average
student in finding profitable work and raising a family. While the association
of academic subjects with irrelevance was not what Dewey had intended in his
formulation of Progressive education's basic tenets, the pragmatic concept of
"life" as a set of dynamic experiences, problems, and demands that should be
brought to bear upon the traditional classroom underwrote the gradual de-
emphasis of curricular content for the "general" or "average" student body.
Dewey was trying to formulate a notion of extra-academic knowledge and experience that had to be accounted for in the educational setting. Prosser produced
a "scientific" justification for two tracks in secondary education, an academic
one for the higher IQ students and a more utilitarian one for slower learners.
The techniques and tools at his disposal provided for a way of making differences in student abilities manageable. As Harry Braverman puts it, during the
intensive period of industrialization at the turn of the last century, "capitalists
were groping toward a theory and practice of management. . . . As capitalism
creates a society in which no one is presumed to consult anything but self-interest, and as the employment contract between parties sharing nothing but the

inability to avoid each other becomes prevalent, management becomes a more perfected and subtle instrument."[29] The new, efficiently managed form of modern education claimed that it was geared to the individual needs and abilities of each student, especially average students who had to be taught how to deal with "life." In the minds of administrators and educational theorists, the misuse of academic content became associated with waste and inefficiency. Self-interest, as conceived of by Dewey, was always collectively formed, and the Progressive classroom would be a place where self and group would find a proper relationship. But self-interest for Taylor and Prosser was entirely individualistic. Since Dewey thought that life outside of school was influenced and shaped by industrial democracy in ways that schools did not acknowledge, his call for educational reform aimed at producing an educational method that was inherently flexible and responsive to a diverse and shifting set of student needs. Collective existence and social change would be the most important if impossible aims of Deweyan pedagogy.

Standardized testing and the science of measurement worked together to shape curricular innovations that would make the high school curriculum appear at midcentury to be at once more individualized and more stratified. Support for free American public high schools galvanized around both moral and vocational imperatives that were clothed in the language of civics and citizenship. Vocational and, later, life-adjustment education became the policies that most aggressively and confidently claimed to be able to fulfill a complicated mission. In 1918 Mississippi became the last state to pass a mandatory education law requiring students to remain in school until the age of sixteen. Along with these laws came a whole apparatus of control such as attendance and truancy officers who would keep track of reluctant high schoolers. In Sealander's words, "The public high school, funded by local property taxes, had arrived."[30] Her account of compulsory secondary education confirms Hofstadter's critique of popular, institutionalized anti-intellectualism in American schools: she emphasizes that the Progressive Era was very clear that the public high school would teach civic education and cultural assimilation more than academic content.

The high school became a mass institution where most of the students were not only "unselected but also unwilling." Whereas the free high school had once seemed to be a "priceless opportunity for those who chose to take it, the high school now held a large captive audience that its administrators felt obliged to satisfy."[31] Hofstadter is devastating in his description of what happened next: in this sort of institution, the average, academically ungifted student became exalted as a kind of American "culture hero." He or she had particular interests that had to be met, and the secondary school was mandated with doing its utmost to meet them. How did the low-to-average-scoring high school student become such an important figure not just for educational administrators but for an entire cultural imagination? How did the reluctant student, clothed in the charismatic and rebellious silence of James Dean, create a counterpoint to the cheerful B student as the all-American kid? And how does this description of the exaltation of the average student as ordinary American in training fit in or not with Watkins's and Braverman's idea of educational control of working-class discontentment?

To answer the first question, we have to seek help from English professor Louis Menand's epic intellectual history of pragmatism, published in 2001, the first half of which concerns the evolution of nineteenth-century statistics in shaping philosophical and epistemological positions. I cannot recapitulate Menand's deft summaries of statistical thinking, but a few thorny concepts useful to this project emerge from his account of statistics and their relationship to probability. According to Menand, Belgian mathematician Adolphe Quetelet's discoveries in statistics in the 1820s and 1830s not only seemed to be able to provide scientific proof for social determinism but also produced a new general category: *l'homme moyen*, or the average man, a critical figure in constructing a mathematical schema for a national identity. The average man was not only a precursor of the average student but also a modern incarnation of the Everyman. Deviance and pathology are always measured against a statistical norm, and this average as norm, or Everyman, is also related to the formation of early nineteenth-century national identities: *"L'homme moyen* is in a nation what the center of gravity is in a planet."[32] He was related to a national character that could be identified and measured.

For the nineteenth-century scientific mind, to measure something was to both know and understand it. What could be more important to know and understand than national identity? The bell-shaped curve emerged as the graphic visualization of norms of measurement: the top of the curve is the statistical mean, and the elegantly gentle rise and fall of the bell represent the ascending and descending numbers surrounding the magical, mathematical rendering of normalcy. Quetelet's most famous case study produced a statistical mean for the chest measurements of Scottish men. As Menand points out, "The term 'statistics' is etymologically linked to 'state': statisticians were sometimes called 'statists,' and before the adoption of the German term *Statistik*, their work was referred to, in English, as 'political arithmetic.'"[33] Statistics were the stuff and substance of new regimes of measurement that promised new powers for the nation-state in being able to identify its contours. In fact, the "average student" was a creation or by-product of the IQ, which is derived from a comparison between a child's cognitive abilities and the average ability of his or her age group. We arrive at the IQ of a child based upon the difference between his or her abilities and the age group average multiplied by 100. There is no IQ without a theory of the age-based average ability.

The average American emerged as an elusive object of study for social scientists, pollsters, advertisers, and market researchers. Sarah Igo's recent analysis of how statistics and market surveys helped the science of marketing catch up with the Taylorist science of management offers a fascinating background for the problems considered here.[34] After Robert S. and Helen Merrell Lynd's study of "Middletown" was published in 1929, Americans interrogated themselves publicly and privately about their relationship to averageness as much as they debated the virtues of this study of "averageness."[35] Averageness turned out to have an aura of complexity and substance, becoming an object of heated discussion among experts and in popular culture. According to Igo, "surveyors were . . . abetted by print and broadcasting networks that saw a profitable market in reports about 'average' Americans." In Igo's study of the relationship between the rise of social science and the evolution of the media, she underscores the "merger between new facts and new outlets" and suggests that "ordinary people now had access to . . . data once reserved for a few."[36] The data and information produced and consumed concerned the isolation and identification of averageness against which readers could measure themselves.

The surveys and questionnaires used by the Lynds to compile their portrait of "Everytown, U.S.A.," could be easily repurposed by market researchers to locate, identify, and isolate the national average, which in this case represented "the widest possible market for their homogeneous goods."[37] Prosserian theories of education provided the theoretical justification for the transformation of schools into sites of intensive management of attitudes not only toward work but toward leisure and consumption as well. The transformation of education into management process could be well coordinated with the regime and administration of testing and statistical self-representation. Lawrence Cremin's study of the transformation of the American school in the 1940s and 1950s offered a scathing critique of vocational education and Prosser's theories. As Evan Watkins has pointed out, the explicitly class-based construction of vocational education eventually faded into obsolescence as a feature of secondary school education in the 1980s and 1990s. It was replaced by "career education," which

"heated up" expectations rather than "cooled them down." A classless, postindustrial workplace was one of the Utopian conditions of the New Economy.
The people who worked in such places were not just workers, they were "smart
workers." They were not just students, they were lifelong learners. Smart workers and lifelong learners were allegedly taking part in career education, tech
prep, and School to Work (a federally funded secondary school program focusing on work training and helping students prepare and find jobs after gradua-
tion) while participating in the Reagan/Thatcher era critique of class identities
and class processes.[38] Standards education would be touted by reformers of the
1980s and 1990s as the magical key to training workers for the New Economy and
the reality of global competition. Students were imagined as smart workers-
to-be, with education for "smart" work replacing voc-ed as the rallying cry of
reformers. The new postindustrial order demanded worker flexibility more
than worker acquiescence. In fact, in 1998 the American Vocational Association
changed its name to the Association for Career and Technical Training in order
to distance itself from the negative and limiting connotations of voc-ed.

The liberal-vocational education opposition had broken apart. Self-cultivation was simply not the strict set of exercises to be performed while reading
the classics. It had been absorbed and dispersed into the language promoting
critical thinking, workplace flexibility, and problem solving. Daniel Bell's 1960s
ideal of the endless inquiry and self-inquiry in the liberal arts no longer seemed
irrelevant or foreign to business life; instead, it seemed redundant when enlightened management and human resources discourse promoted something
called "lifelong learning" and "flexibility." The values of self-cultivation, personal growth, and satisfaction in work, accompanied by the promise of con-
tinuous lifelong learning, were no longer explicitly restricted to the privileged
few. However, the curricular and administrative reforms that reorganized the
inherently undemocratic academic education of the nineteenth century had
made way for a version of secondary education that concentrated enormous
powers in the management of educational and class formation processes.

Administration would eventually decide on the proper application of scientific methods of management and pedagogy. Reformers were involved in a
heated romance with the average student of the 1930s and 1940s: the child of
this unlikely couple was "a class process" that Watkins theorized as one of the
most important goals of educational management theory. Class process, in
short, was simply the production of class identification and identity: the New
Economy's class process was founded on antihierarchical nondifferentiation
between workers and management. Vocational education, on the other hand,

very explicitly aimed at producing workers who were supposed to accept their subordinate role as manual laborers under scientific management.

Moreover, newspapers and magazines reproduced different versions of the social scientists' questionnaires to produce answers for their readers' questions about where they stood in relationship to the norm. By the 1930s the true American turned out to be the average American: the average American had some relationship with Dewey's common man as an important philosophical fiction, but he was more squarely situated in the field of statistics and social science surveys.

By the time Theodor Adorno and Max Horkheimer arrived in the United States, where they would spend their years of exile, the general popular resentment against culture, arts, and intellectual activity struck the German Jewish intellectuals as politically reactionary. Adorno and Horkheimer arrived at the height of the Progressive Era reform movement, between 1938 and 1949.[39] Outside a small elite, humanities as the core of academic education with its grounding in Latin and Greek (as they had experienced it in the German *Gymnasium*, or preparatory academy) never occupied a large part of the American educational imaginary and found itself, as we saw in chapter 1, on very shaky ground by the 1930s. If Horkheimer and Adorno denounced what they saw as the American faith in "subjective" over "objective" reason, they were attacking in part what they saw as the institutionalization of pragmatism as part of the reform movement within American education. Horkheimer was outraged at pragmatism's subsumption of means to ends: he took Dewey's concept of "use" for an endorsement of simple self-interest. But Horkheimer did not grasp Dewey's historical radicalism within speculative philosophy, and he misread Dewey's critique of the scholasticism of philosophy departments.

Even though the American critique of the liberal arts education as the leisure activity of thoughtless privilege may have had Progressive origins, Veblen's and Dewey's critique of contemplative detachment from productive labor appeared to the exiles as one more facet of the protofascism of an American version of authoritarian personality. This is one of the great conundrums of Hofstadter's theory of American anti-intellectualism that we still grapple with today. Even in Henry James's novels of American and European manners, we see a suspicion of overrefinement as a product of financial parasitism. In James's ambivalent accounts of American philistinism, the most corrupt characters are the ones who are at the farthest remove from productive labor and the creation of wealth. Adorno and Horkheimer would find that American popular culture and American philosophy earnestly sought to bring culture "down to earth." In the United

States, Adorno and Horkheimer encountered the simultaneous existence of a permissive, hedonistic, but standardized bohemianism with required listening and reading lists that included jazz innovators like Thelonious Monk and Charlie Parker along with European modernists from James Joyce to Marcel Proust to Franz Kafka with a large dose of Sigmund Freud. At the same time, the airwaves carried the inflammatory message and evangelical rage of Father Coughlin and Martin Luther Thomas. In movie theaters, the films of Frank Capra promoted rustic innocence and naïveté against political machines, class prejudice, and aesthetic pretension.

In Adorno's mind, this nefarious conflation of the physically defenseless intellectual with moral corruption and parasitism became one of the building blocks not only of the authoritarian personality but also of anti-Semitism.[40] Strikingly, Adorno, late in his career in 1966, revised his opinion and described the work of John Dewey as a "humane" version of pragmatism in *Negative Dialectics*.[41] In this work Adorno indicated that a metacritique of philosophy can be reconciled with pragmatist attempts to redeem philosophical questions through its sustained engagement with the problems of ordinary people. The Frankfurt School exiles arrived in the United States skeptical of the rhetoric of world-changing policies and technocratic innovation. What they found was an industrial democracy in love with technological and scientific solutions to its own social problems. All of the most innovative elements of measurement and the new social sciences formed the intellectual basis for Progressive reforms. Statistics and reformism oriented the answers that were provided to questions like, What should be taught in schools that would speak to and engage the ordinary person—or, as Dewey called him, "the common man"? Was it possible or even desirable to compare the common man or ordinary person to the average student? How was the average student a product of statistics and the norms of age-based means?

Adorno's own protest against the philosophy behind "adjustment" has been analyzed by Detlev Claussen, one of Adorno's biographers and a former student, as a resistance against his own position of dependency on Progressive and New Deal institutions such as the Rockefeller Foundation–funded Princeton Radio Project. A pioneer of social research and media in Europe, Paul Lazarsfeld had secured funding in the mid-1930s from a number of different donors, including the Rockefeller Foundation, to do research on radio listening practices. Paul Lazarsfeld, an exiled Austrian sociologist, was uniquely talented at bridging the gap between granting agencies and intellectuals. The Princeton Radio Project was supported by government and private foundation funding to explore the social and political potential of the new medium. Lazarsfeld was Adorno's first formal employer, and there was much friction between the two of them. As Claussen points out, this was Adorno's first position in a "proper organization," where he found himself working as both professional and employee. Later on, some of the most poignant and infuriating moments of his writing would have to do with his denunciation of the professionalization of American academia. Adorno insisted that intellectual life could be and was deformed by the naked need for survival. Despite this, "the American decade socialized him as a scholar, even though he continued to defend his autonomy as an individual."[42]

Horkheimer, Adorno, and Hofstadter criticized two aspects of a "flexible" subject-centered philosophy of education: first, the science of measurement in identifying the capacities of the student, which represents a narrow and limiting positivism; and second, the dangerous vagueness of its definition of life. It should be noted that Adorno and Horkheimer wrote The Dialectic of Enlightenment as an anguished response to American pragmatism and its implicitly flawed view of the world as a series of problems that needed to be solved.[43] Dewey, in fact, felt that renewing philosophy meant addressing the problems of ordinary people. In the post–IQ test world, Adorno and Horkheimer saw that this attitude could reduce all of thinking to an aptitude for finding solutions to puzzles. Their insistence on objective reason, independent of self-interest, as the grounds of intellectual solidarity was directly opposed to what they saw as pragmatism's callow concessions to individual survival. Their own struggles to "fit in" and adjust to American society were embodied by their struggle with what they saw as a philosophy of fitting in that governed everyday life in their country of exile.[44] Horkheimer and Adorno saw encrypted in the products of the culture industry a message that survival was inextricably linked to an individual's ability to adjust to new realities at all costs.

The advocates of life-adjustment education had no commitment to Dewey's understanding of the complexity of the contemporary world and our collective need to respond to it. The average student was thought to have many good qualities and a few intractable limitations: one of the latter was not being at all interested in academics or any field of study that did not seem immediately relevant or useful to his or her life. In short, the average student lived by subjective reason alone, and the school would have to reach into that realm in order to be able to educate him or her. This newly configured form of "subjective reason" reflected a set of values made up of self-interest, "personal experience," and self-preservation. Subjective reason thus configured would provide new forms of justification for education as an endless series of adjustments to the vicissitudes of "life," construed as merely a euphemism for "the demands of industry and business."

Measuring and adjusting education to fit the capacities of individuals displaced universalist principles from a shared and transmissible common culture to statistics as the only grounds upon which students could compare themselves to one another. The banalization and routinization of Dewey's reform-minded pragmatism provided a fig leaf for new forms of institutionalized antiacademic sentiment and promoted social triage and peer conformism in secondary schools. What Dewey hoped for was much different: he claimed that educating the whole child would allow teachers and children to abandon the spectatorial or "contemplative" approach to life and work. The Progressive classroom would engage and engross the whole child. Dewey hoped to dignify everyday life and labor in the classroom. For him, practical education dramatized the importance of social efficiency because it provided the most compelling arguments for the institutionalization of social equality and social justice. Progressive education would guarantee the assimilation of children of all classes into a harmonious and orderly classroom that replicated and presaged a better world. According to Dewey, since it is quite obvious that "the natural or native impulses of the young do not agree with the life-customs of the group into which they are born," education must serve as a means of "socialization as participation." Participation was a critical concept for Dewey's notion of democracy and describes a state of active engagement. Traditional methods of socialization and control had hitherto been "indirect, or emotional and intellectual, not direct or personal. Moreover, it is intrinsic to the disposition of the person, not external and coercive. To achieve this internal control through identity of interest and understanding is the business of education."[45] Control for Dewey has two vectors: forces outside of the student do try to control him or her, but education leads also to positive forms of self-mastery and self-control. Authoritarian forms of control produced indifference and passivity rather than active, personal interest in both objects of study and the welfare of others. Dewey's system of the establishment of common interests, fitting into the social scene, and noncoercive integration of the individual into the "life customs of the group" forms the basis of the simultaneous exaltation and rational reconstruction of the personal or internalized reason of the individual. The common good is demolished as too abstract a ground upon which to found the disciplining of the young; instead, personal interest replaces common good as a final "good." To make it in the personal interest of the student to achieve "internal control" is an important innovation in the institutionalization of social con-

trol. "Fitting into" the social and collective enterprise was for Dewey inseparable from "growth." But later, personal growth was so powerful and compelling an ideal that, as Eli Zaretsky has pointed out, "personal life" emerged in the
mid-twentieth century as one of the most compelling and charismatic categories of modernity.[46] Dewey insisted that all hierarchies of value in the curriculum had to be connected to the interest of children. He assumed that children
were naturally inclined to democracy rather than tyranny, cooperation rather
than competition, social exchange rather than isolation. To preserve the child's
spontaneity and creativity, a teacher would have to practice quiet encouragement and active observation, creating in the classroom the world as it should
be. Hofstadter identified this as a "utopianism of method." Hofstadter, writing
in midcentury, is animated by a kind of radical, Enlightenment skepticism. Traditional education imposed its demands from the outside and failed to produce
a real sense of active engagement in the world: "Like Freud, Dewey saw the process by which a society inculcates the young with its principles, inhibitions and
habits as a kind of imposition. . . . For Dewey, the world as a source of misery for
the child is largely remediable through the educational process."[47]

Hofstadter had accepted Freud's lesson that instinctual gratification and
"civilization" were tragically at odds but, more importantly, that the instincts
themselves demanded some kind of control and limitation. Spontaneity and
curiosity arose out of their respective psychoanalytic correlates, aggression and
sexuality: the emancipation of instinctual life would not necessarily result in
a pretty tableau of happily cooperative children. Rather than set up a series of
authoritarian prohibitions to produce a sense of the need for participation,
Dewey suggested that young students should be presented with situations
where they "have to refer their way of acting to what others are doing and make
it fit in. This directs their action to a common result, and gives an understanding common to the participants."[48] For Hofstadter, Dewey's new philosophy of
education helped to encourage the institutionalized denigration of the life of
the mind—in secondary school. What he saw was the institutional outcome
of Deweyan ideas in high school reform. The democratic ideal of a common
school for all was betrayed for the needs of producing, pacifying, and dominat-
ing low scorers. High schools became places where the majority of students
would be prepared for a life of work and the minority for higher education. Hofstadter would concur with Adorno that such practical education would produce
indifference and contempt in that great mass of average students: the object of
student resentment, however, would not be the tests that had relegated them

to the lower tier but the life of the mind and the academic education of which they were being deprived.

To Hofstadter, a Progressive reconfiguration of education goals would sound like a blueprint justifying the 1950s bogeyman of conformity, but Dewey emphasized the voluntarist, participatory aspect of "fitting in" as a mode of active participation in a common project. In Dewey's school, the desire to be social and to join the collective would come spontaneously to the student. Rather than remaining aloof from collective endeavor as the individualist subject of laissez-faire capitalism and competition, Dewey's student would take from her classroom experience the properly democratic and collectivist attitude toward experience and social engagement. The sense of collective enterprise would extend to include the working and laboring class's struggles for social justice. The student would emerge from school as a progressively oriented citizen who was well equipped to guide the just development of industrial democracy. This internalized sense of the necessity of "fitting in" replaces the traditional external, coercive authoritarianism. Hofstadter suggests that "self-deceit" was necessary in both student and teacher for "new education" to work. The student-centered classroom produced a false sense of solidarity between student and teacher that disguised a persistent power differential: "personalized" soft coercion would engender resentment instead of traditional and authoritarian education's "fear of failure."[49]

Dewey's notion of participation was formed on the idea that every student is an artist and that aesthetic experience forms the core of democratic culture.[50] Along with Walter Benjamin, Dewey saw the democratization of aesthetic experience as one of the most critical features of modernity. In Dewey's school, all citizens and students were potential artists. Artists were the kinds of people who were able to have and to exchange meaningful experiences: if every student was an artist, then each one would be able to deduce the fundamental ways in which "aesthetic experiences are tied to everyday experiences through this [the educational] structure of rational instrumentality."[51] Schools were the places where "the artist within" could be animated. Art education was a powerful instrumentality that could activate all sorts of innate capacities in children. If in the mid-twentieth century Hofstadter recoiled from this democratization and diffusion of aesthetic experience and talent, he did so from the point of view of an absolutely different conception of democracy, one that was already in formation in the 1920s and 1930s among "democratic realists." In David S. Brown's recent biography of Hofstadter, he argues that Hofstadter saw Progressivism as a cryptoreligious worship of rustic innocence embodied in both yeoman and child. Hofstadter blamed Dewey's naive optimism for devaluing intellectual and academic content in the school curriculum. Furthermore, Dewey's theories had offered theoretical justification for administrative zealots of practical education. "The more humdrum the task the educationists have to undertake, the nobler and more exalted their music grows. When they see a chance to introduce a new course in family living or home economics, they begin to tune the fiddles of their idealism."[52] Hofstadter was concerned about the McCarthyite, anti-intellectual populism that had unleashed its fury upon writers, intellectuals, and academics during the early 1950s. Brown argues that *Anti-intellectualism in American Life* is a partisan defense of the speculative life of the mind, the values of the metropolis, and the autonomy of intellectuals like himself. To reduce this work to a biographical curiosity would be wrong. Brown does, however, emphasize that Hofstadter was participating in a massive re-evaluation of the Progressive tradition and of its provincial, nativist defense of thinly veiled forms of Christian community that, while ostensibly loving, were suffocating and oppressive in their refusal to value intellectual speculation. The values that Hofstadter represented were secular and liberal, firmly rooted in the cosmopolitan life of the city.

The depth of the difference between Dewey's and Hofstadter's conceptions of the value of innocence and the problem of experience is exemplified in their relationship to the relationship between life and the life of the mind. Dewey's growth model stakes the power of education on its ability to awaken in all of us an inclination to learn from life itself and "to make the conditions of life such that all will learn in the process of living." This is the finest "product of schooling."[53] Hofstadter would insist that the life of the mind may have its own territories, ruling over a space and time that is in fact divorced or at least detached from the interests of everyday life. In this idea, he could have found an advocate in Dewey's own advocacy of academic disinterestedness: Hofstadter would find that "life" and its "processes," with their demands for practicality and applicability, could easily censure and circumscribe thinking. These were not Dewey's intentions necessarily, but, nevertheless, they emerged in the American mid-century as the most prominent features of a reaction against intellectuals and their ways of working.

For Hofstadter, a truly tolerant democratic culture would not despise the life of the mind nor have contempt for aesthetic experiences that were not immediately translatable into popular taste or understanding. Hofstadter defended an urban cosmopolitanism, as both his critics and supporters noted of *Anti-*

intellectualism in American Life. He was drawing upon a set of autobiographical experiences in establishing his point of view on the value of robust skepticism, intellectual freedom, and aesthetic autonomy. According to Brown, Hofstadter's critique of Dewey focused on the ways in which "new education" would fail immigrant students like himself: "Rather than equip a rising immigrant class with coursework designed to promote personal autonomy through the mastery of critical thinking skills, Dewey stressed public education as a means to acculturate the new citizens into the mainstream of American life."[54]

The Freudianism in Hofstadter's work is evident here, for Hofstadter is not shy about attributing to anti-intellectualism all the contradictory qualities of a symptom of modern American institutions. In his critique of Dewey, he seems to echo Freud's critique of Christianity, which is a religion that suppresses distinction. For Freud, ordinary people are swindled in the deal they make with religious institutions to suspend their capacity for reason for the promise of redemption in another world. Peter Gay described Freud in positive terms as an "intellectual populist" who does not indulge in the relativism of "subtle reasoners." Freud often adopted the standpoint of the common man: and it was in this sense that he insisted that "there is only one truth."[55] Freud's impatience with piety belied his interest in religion. Religion was the most accessible, popular, and common form of delusion that provided some modicum of relief and solace from the unbearable suffering and uncertainty of life. But this ordinary consolation was a panacea, and one that extracted a high price and great sacrifice in return for its occasional solace and consolation. If religion claims to offer us relief from everyday life's humiliations and dangerous pleasures, Freud insists on their slippery inescapability. From harrowing obsessions to half-forgotten dreams, smoldering resentments, and crippling obsessions, from blind rages to slips of the tongue, Freud took on the detritus of psychic life and cognitive experience and built his theories on them. For Gay, Freud's Enlightenment militancy about the consolations of religion and the illusions of superstition prevented him from reserving any amount of truth value for metaphysics or theology, while he always took fantasies and delusions very seriously.

Religion offers the ordinary person some relief from suffering and sin by offering a single path to collective salvation. Freud himself underscored certain universal truths about the unconscious that would make him an enemy to postmodernists. His insistence upon the universality of truth was linked to his affective identification with the "Everyman," who had emerged as the skeptical interlocutor of theory itself. Instead of performing acts of heroic resistance, bold transgressions, and subtle subversions, Freud's ordinary person suffered from lapses of memory, told jokes at the expense of others, made stupid mistakes, lost treasured keepsakes, dreamed incomprehensible dreams, and harbored conscious and unconscious fantasies, superstitious feelings, muted resentments, and so on. If everyday life had become more rich and dense under Freud's scrutiny, it was because at every moment, everyone is betrayed by instincts more or less badly tamed. Rather than flattering ordinary people into submission, Freud quizzically considered the ordinary person's plight, first as an external observer but then increasingly as an ordinary person himself. In Peter Gay's account, "[Freud] is the point in the discourse where the scientist and the common man come together."[56] Unlike the Victorian and Progressive Era elite, who recommended asceticism and moral uplift as the solution for alleviating mass immiseration, Freud considered that addiction, regression, and resentment are perfectly justified reactions to the stringent demands of modern life: "Life as we find it, is too hard for us."[57] Freud joined his voice in the first-person plural to this experience of life's difficulty. For psychoanalysis to function in the clinic, the analyst has to have experienced the first person on the couch as the radical nonspecialist, the nonexpert, the nontheorist: the analyst has merged with and emerged as the ordinary subject of the unconscious. Modernization and modernity (terms Freud himself never used), accompanied by the semblance of progress wrought by scientific and technological achievements, have not brought about a higher degree of happiness for the ordinary person, and modern unhappiness is all the more bitter because it confronts the gap between promise and reality. In fact, demands for self-control and self-surveillance intensified with little reason or reward: witness, for example, the late nineteenth-century American bourgeoisie's imposition of stringent regimes of self-control within "modern" spaces of public recreation like the theater and parks. These regimes in turn produced aggression against *Kultur*, or civilization, promoted by the consolidators of cultural authority. For Freud, such displaced aggression is dangerous for both the individual and the society in which he or she lives.

Freud's sympathy for the average person and his intellectual populism resembled that of C. Wright Mills. In the mid-twentieth century, Mills was writing a sociology of the working life of the average American salaried employee or worker. In describing the decline of craftsmanship in twentieth-century America, Mills pointed out that handicraft, having been trivialized as a "hobby," "is confined to minuscule groups of privileged professionals and intellectuals." Mills saw the de-skilling of work accompanied by rising levels of mass education as producing a workforce condemned to underemployment: "As school attendance increases and more jobs are routinized, the number of people who must work below their capacities will increase."[58] Mills would point out that the de-skilling of white-collar work followed the devaluation of work skills and experience imposed by scientific management on the assembly line earlier in the twentieth century: "Even on managerial and professional levels, the growth of rational bureaucracies has made work more like factory production. The managerial demiurge is constantly furthering all these trends: mechanization, more minute division of labor, the use of less skilled and less expensive workers."[59]

In fact, Freud felt that the constraints of civilization actually forced great numbers of people to live below their intellectual capacities. The discontent produced by such massive subjugation for both Mills and Freud is simply inevitable. Freud was interested in everyday life, not miracles or exceptional circumstances: he expressed an indifference to extraordinary human beings, from mystics to geniuses, from yogis to artists. He was interested in the everyday life of the average person and found that to be the terrain richest in meaning. In Freud's later work, the twentieth-century Everyman, or *Jedermann*, played a central role as a fictional interlocutor whose arguments against psychoanalysis are anticipated and parried: this character, most distinctively evoked in *Future of an Illusion* and *Civilization and Its Discontents*, is anonymous, a follower rather than a leader, on the conservative side of things, but skeptical. Freud was concerned with the untalented, ordinary person, the one who is in fact born with "a specially unfavorable instinctual constitution," or someone whose desire for pleasure and instinctual satisfaction is stronger than her capacity for sublimation. What happens to this person in her attempts to extract some degree of happiness from the world? For Freud, she has few options: flight into neurotic illness, addiction, or the desperate rebellion of psychosis. For Mills, following Kracauer, the dissatisfaction of the disaggregated mass of employees makes them susceptible not to organization and collective actions but rather to an inarticulate authoritarianism, a hardened, cynical attitude, and inchoate and volatile resentments. Freud's symptomatic paths of escape bring substitute satisfactions that are extremely isolating and atomizing. Another available option is one that has a distinct advantage over the others, for it brings Everyman into contact with others who seek similar forms of solace: religion. For Freud, religion "imposes equally on everyone its own path to the acquisition of happiness." The social aspect of religious experience is a critical part of its appeal. Freud deflates or at least marginalizes the gifted spiritual virtuosi, those yogi masters, mystics, or hermits who decide to seek happiness by isolating themselves from human society in their attempts to "kill the instincts."[60] He is not interested in extreme spiritual practices because, unlike religion, they are not accessible to ordinary people.

For Freud, religion relies upon a "technique [that] consists in depressing the value of life and distorting the picture of the world in a delusional manner—which presupposes an intimidation of the intelligence."[61] Infantile helplessness and the desire for an all-powerful protector are universal experiences for which religious illusions offer temporarily consoling delusions of satisfaction. The analyst finds the grounds of religion extremely unstable for the building of an authentically ethical character. In fact, religion offers a form of collective regression that prefigures and gives a structure to the mass regression offered by an unconscious, but it simultaneously requires unconditional surrender of our capacity for reason. Freud concludes that all religions demand unconditional submission, which would mean the renunciation of that capacity for skepticism and thought before God's "inscrutable decrees." For Mills's white-collar employee, the renunciation of reason takes place not before God but before "the centralization of decision and the formal rationality that bureaucracy entails. . . . [R]ationality itself has thus been expropriated from work and any total view and understanding of its process. No longer free to plan his work, much less to modify the plan to which he is subordinated, the individual is to a great extent managed and manipulated by his work."[62] Mills, like Freud, finds the worker and Everyman the victim of a series of bad deals. By the 1980s the Everyman would no longer be understood as a victim: for academic populists, the Everyman would be deemed beyond manipulation, just as the allegedly universal capacity for reason itself would be relegated to a fantasy of the Enlightenment. Andrew Ross and John Fiske criticized both Mills and Adorno for representing average Americans as robots: the fault lay not in industrial organization or culture industry but in the condescension of midcentury sociologists! Freud found that the individual's most profound sacrifice had to do with an abstract capacity, a mode of cognition, a capacity for reason that is not formal but objective. Postmodern thinkers would find that objective reason itself should be renounced on the grounds of an entirely new set of cultural conditions that eventually led to a cultural theory of politics that Freud and Mills would find baffling.

In C. Wright Mills's mind, mass leisure involved the fateful separation of work and pleasure. If Mills's sociology offered division of work and leisure as absolute, Adorno and Horkheimer offered a slightly different interpretation of the situation. They would continue to emphasize that the culture industry coordinated work and leisure, making the latter adapt to the demands of the former. When Freud urged us to confront the Christian injunctions, he assumed, like the Enlightenment *philosophes*, that a native capacity for reason, unfettered by the force of habit or intimidation, would naturally bridle at specious arguments, absurdities, and unreasonable demands. Freud celebrated the folkloric and popular feeling for constitutive aggression and the irreplaceable pleasures of sexual love in his analysis of jokes and their relation to the unconscious. In Freud's writings, then, there appears an ordinary and "naive" person who is the very touchstone of reason and skepticism and who is also the subject of repressed experiences of unsettling pleasure. Freud's own radical skepticism is demonstrated in his reasoned refusal of the Christian ideal to "love one's neighbor as oneself." He called his bewilderment before such an injunction "naive"; let us call it irreligious or respectfully impious. Its very absurdity, however, is that the injunction exerts its demand for belief and the unconditional surrender of the believer's intellectual faculties. In *Future of an Illusion*, Freud's guarded optimism about the ordinary person's capacity for reason is even more evident. In his debate with his fictive sparring partner, who reminds him that religion and religious ideals may be necessary to maintain moral order, Freud responded by insisting that this is much too cynical a view of human beings. His adversary accepts the intellect's powerlessness before instinctual life all too willingly. Freud proposed that a moral system founded on reason rather than "religious delusion" would be more stable, more durable, and less apt to inspire resentment because it would be based upon principles that could be modified, questioned, criticized, and reformed. For Freud, "The voice of the intellect is a soft one, but it does not rest until it has gained a hearing. Finally, after countless rebuffs, it succeeds." He then proposed that this is one of the few causes for optimism: "The primacy of the intellect lies, it is true, in a distant, distant figure, but probably not in an *infinitely* distant one."[63] Religion sets its expectations for a better world on God and his infinite wisdom. But within the limits of reason, the dreams of a better world to come in which the intellect might be the new sovereign is not to be given up, even in the face of a string of setbacks and crushing defeats. Freud wants us to place our hopes on the soft but undeniable voice of reason: "There is no appeal to a court higher than that of reason."[64] The persistence of reason is one of its unique features: even in the face of coercion and illusion, it retains its integrity. The voice of reason, once audible, is not easily silenced. Repressing our capacity for reason is a risky project because its denial produces the ordinary and everyday resentment about civilization's and religion's absurd demands and unfulfilled promises. In following the spirit of Freud's reasoned skepticism, Hofstadter insists upon the intellectual necessity of defending autonomy in intellectual affairs. His defense of intellectual life and intelligence may appear as grandiosely confident liberal elitism, but he defied the kinds of cultural intimidation he saw in American politics. In Freud's later works, the revolt against the irrationality of religion takes place in the mind of the ordinary person, not the philosopher or "professional thinker."

Adorno and Horkheimer shared Hofstadter's sense of commitment to intellectual, if not academic, freedom as the freedom to be reasonable. In the 1980s this secularizing and "modernist" position was discredited as outdated universalism, Cartesian rationalism, and yet another Western metanarrative of development. But the grounds of objective and critical reason as well as the shared capacity for self-determination and skepticism were undermined in the attempt to theorize a new decentered selfhood.[65] The hardening of processes like personalization was both seductive and inadequate in managing student and worker discontent: pseudopersonalization produces a residue of suspicion or resentment. The language of therapeutic "empowerment" of the individual has routinized what was once an authentically novel and innovative way of looking at the classroom. Despite differences in student ability and an inherent inequality in intellectual capacities, universal, humanist education should be available to each and every student in order that all citizens can have a share in the legacy of intellectual life. In some sense, Hofstadter's predictions about the doomed attempts of the curriculum to reach student interest have borne strange fruit—contemporary students feel empowered to judge "good" and "bad" teaching as well as "interesting" and "uninteresting" material even as they have quietly, and seemingly without protest, acquiesced to a pitiless regime of standardized testing.

At first glance, we might want to jump to the conclusion that it has been the corporatization of university education and research that is responsible for the radical undermining of liberal education through the application of purely utilitarian goals in higher education. But something else has been at work in the last three decades: in the postindustrial age, Dewey's language of growth and "addressing the whole self" as well as Daniel Bell's idea of self-reflection have been absorbed into the discourse of both management and popular culture. In this reconfigured concept of flexible, infinitely retrainable selves, cumulative knowledge and experience would be increasingly devalued in favor of explosive, future-oriented potentiality. A highly limited, descriptive, case-study approach to problem solving would make historically decontextualized close readings of both literary theory and cultural studies appear more user-friendly for new generations of American students.

Hofstadter pointed to another critical weakness in applying the methods of progressive education to secondary schools: child-centered education failed to recognize its own limitations. It may have been a fantastic method of teaching younger children, but what of secondary school education and its intellectual or academic foundations and conceptions? As the postwar educational reform movement focused on secondary education, it contributed to the anti-intellectual, cryptoreligious, business-oriented consensus about student interest and practicality that has become the hallmark of postprogressive educational policy making, be it of the Left or the Right.[66]

The abandonment of the values of liberal education may at first blush seem perfectly acceptable and even desirable to a country bent on egalitarianism in all things, but the principles of a watered-down Progressive education, adapted to the principles of scientific management, have perpetuated more hierarchy, more injustice, and the tacit acceptance of greater inequality in the heart of American educational institutions. Under the aegis of educational reform, the early twentieth century saw a massive expansion of the functions of schooling that were in turn underwritten by a reconception of educational administration. The expansion of the functions of schooling may have come out of John Dewey's exhortation that schools should address the needs of the "whole child," but Dewey's expansive definition of holism was eclipsed by the post–World War II movement to make vocational education a critical part of the American high school curriculum. The school would assume the task of preparing students for life itself, operating in loco parentis as a site of acculturation, assimilation, and transmission of modern values and attitudes. Beyond incorporating vocational education as a part of the secondary school curriculum, educational administrators allowed secondary schools to take on the tasks of teaching techniques of self-care, homemaking, grooming, and interacting with peers. Academic subjects like history, foreign languages, mathematics, and literature were not entirely eliminated, but they were squeezed uncomfortably in between "electives." Rather than focusing on teacher training in academic subjects, educational techniques such as standardized testing would focus on measuring the "aptitudes" of each student. The massive application of testing and intelligence testing in particular had important consequences for the rise of vocational education and the life-adjustment movement in American secondary schools. The life-adjustment movement of the 1940s situated a mass cultural personalism at the center of an educational philosophy and policy that were underwritten by a regime of testing. Testing made education look like a standardized, mass-reproducible product; it also convinced the public that curricular content could be calibrated and adjusted to each student's abilities. Eventually, it encouraged teaching to the test and learning for the test, abandoning the humanistic values of self-critique and self-cultivation that Bell's liberal education had once touted. Liberal education, however, has not disappeared. It has merely become a luxury good, accessible only to high scorers. Low scorers would have to be content with vocational preparation and a lesser lot in life, no longer determined by their birth or the stars but by their scores. Hofstadter's theory of American anti-intellectualism links popular resentment of pseudopersonalized education to the logic of administered inequality masquerading as the management of educational opportunity.

chapter three

the curious cult of religious practicality

American intellectuals and American people have traditionally viewed each other with distrust. From the millennial, cultural studies, cultural populist perspective, however, the 1950s were imagined to be an exceptional time: ordinary Americans were imagined to be extraordinarily deferential to intellectuals, and intellectuals were, in turn, condescending but generally well disposed toward the people and the nation. David Brooks and Andrew Ross both imagined that during the opening years of the Cold War, American society was dominated by "arrogant highbrows" who took advantage of popular trust in experts in order to cement positions of power in the liberal establishment. By 2000, Brooks had described the propitious transformation of a distinct intellectual class that valued its separateness into a hybrid entity, the bourgeois-bohemian, a new, well-educated class of elites who had fused hardheaded, high-achieving pragmatism with aesthetic education and consumerist sophistication. Their high standardized test scores and fine palates did not, however, prevent them from indulging in the mass cultural pleasures of popular consumption. Thus did Brooks distinguish the cosmopolitan values and tastes of this new meritocratic elite from those of Nicholas Lemann's reform-minded but parochial Episcopacy. Following in the footsteps of John Dewey and William James, Brooks urged intellectuals lagging behind to join the rest of the world: immersion in the unpredictable currents of everyday life and ordinary struggles could only benefit the thinking classes.

Intellectuals had entered the fray of commercial activity and the market; they had abandoned their volumes of Freud and left the "book-stuffed studio" on New York's Riverside Drive. Brooks writes: "We are right to be involved in the world, to climb and strive and experience the dumb superficialities of everyday life, just like everybody else."[1] The arrogant, commercial, culture-bashing *Partisan Review* types received rough treatment in Brooks's *Bobos in Paradise: The New Upper Class and How They Got There*, but as we have seen, 1950s intellectuals had already taken even harder hits in the hands of Left-leaning intellectuals like Andrew Ross. Ross's *No Respect* alleged that American intellectuals of the 1950s were no less than agents of Gramscian hegemony. They worked to extract submission from the masses to the liberal consensus by parading before them the benefits of the "postwar settlement." Ross saw intellectuals primarily as an intermediate class, representing state interests to the people by using their powers of rhetorical persuasion, cultural prestige, and political intimidation. In Ross's own words, intellectuals participated "in the hegemonic process of winning consent" by performing "operations of containment."[2] By producing distinction and containing irrationality, a group of entitled and empowered intellectuals engineered the liberal consensus. Moreover, according to Ross, they were "attracted to the mandarin prejudices of high German culture," as embodied by the exiled thinkers of the Frankfurt School.[3] While this representation of the 1950s has become the standard historical narrative in various cultural studies circles, it stands in stark contrast to Hofstadter's description of the bitterness among intellectuals after Adlai Stevenson's electoral defeat by Dwight D. Eisenhower in the 1952 and 1956 presidential elections. Hofstadter wrote that intellectuals tended to draw an overly pessimistic lesson about their place in American society after that election: "At a time when the McCarthyite pack was in full cry, it was hard to resist the conclusion that Stevenson's smashing defeat was also a repudiation by plebiscite of American intellectuals and of intellect itself."[4]

For Hofstadter, most intellectuals had overreacted to Stevenson's defeat. Arthur Schlesinger, Jr.'s essay "The Highbrow in Politics" was typical of this hyperbolic sense of public rejection. Schlesinger seemed to accept the conservatives' assessment that intellectuals had been repudiated by plebiscite during the 1952 election, and he deplored the results of this reactionary stance. When Schlesinger asserted that "anti-intellectualism has long been the anti-Semitism of the businessman," he was availing himself of the social-psychological critique of fascist tendencies found in Theodor Adorno's work on prejudice and the authoritarian personality.[5] For Schlesinger, the interests of the businessman had fully appropriated the perspective of the "people." This unlikely and unstable alliance had to find an enemy in order to maintain inner cohesion, and the intellectual proved to be a convenient scapegoat. On November 10, 1952, *Time* magazine's editorial on the election analyzed the results of the Eisenhower victory without even mentioning Adlai Stevenson. It lauded the victor's "revolutionary" ability to bring together a broad swathe of divergent interest groups, for once united in their support for the Republican Party. Yet Eisenhower's victory, it was alleged, revealed "a wide and unhealthy gap between intellectuals and the American people."[6] The dissent of the intellectuals was described by *Time* as an "egghead rebellion." *Time* magazine's editorial page had found a perfect target: the rebellious and out-of-touch class of "eggheads" who did not understand the temper of the times because they were soft on Communism and unaware of the danger that the nation faced.[7] There was, nevertheless, a critical segment of the population for whom Stevenson's intellectuality was a liability—and it was this group that Hofstadter hoped to identify as pseudoconservatives in revolt.

The concept of pseudoconservative revolt also owed a great deal to Adorno's *The Authoritarian Personality*, published in 1950 as part of a collaborative project called Studies in Prejudice funded by the American Jewish Council during the 1940s.[8] According to Rolf Wiggershaus's account of the project's inception, "A breathing-space in the world-historical persecution of the Jews was to be used to seek, with the support of scientific analysis, ways of preventing or weakening the next outbreak."[9] The authoritarian personality project was the culmination of years of collaborative social psychological research that sought to identify and isolate fascist proclivities in certain personality types or structures.

Between 1953 and 1954 a group of professors from various departments at Columbia University convened a special "Seminar on the State" that brought together thinkers preoccupied with antifascism from multidisciplinary perspectives. The seminar took place in 1953 and 1954, and it provided the hothouse, "Riverside Drive" atmosphere condemned by Brooks and Ross, but its participants experienced it as something extraordinarily productive, polemical, and experimental. In William Leuchtenberg's recollection of the seminar, participants "never strove for consensus. We would take up someone's idea, or listen to a paper, then weigh in with some thoughts, and when we felt we'd spent enough time on it, move on to something else."[10] Hofstadter's contribution to the seminar was called "Dissent and Non-conformity in the Twentieth Century." It was later published as "The Pseudo-Conservative Revolt" in *American Scholar* (1955) and reprinted in the edited collection *The New American Right* (1955). The essay was finally incorporated into *The Paranoid Style in American Politics* (1965). Hofstadter was concerned about the inflammatory rhetoric of the extreme Right during the Eisenhower/Stevenson campaign. For Hofstadter, men of intellectual capacity who aspired to high public office were vulnerable to accusations of treachery, elitism, and effeminacy. This suspicion of the intellect was not shared by a plurality of Americans; it was, however, a deeply ingrained set of reactionary attitudes that Hofstadter felt deserved close scrutiny.[11] While he was writing *Anti-intellectualism in American Life*, Hofstadter may have also been preoccupied with the election of 1952, the McCarthy Red Scare, and the general atmosphere of the early Cold War years, but by the first years of the 1960s, John F. Kennedy was wooing intellectuals in the White House and drawing upon a brain trust: this brief honeymoon was suddenly cut short by his assassination and the implementation of flawed expertise in the prosecution of the Vietnam War. Moreover, the 1958 launch of the Soviet satellite *Sputnik* had spurred unprecedented public support for federal funding for education, mostly inspired by fear of Communist takeover. The "ruling passion of the public . . . suggested that gifted children were to be regarded as resources in the Cold War. But the atmosphere did change notably. In 1952 only intellectuals seemed much disturbed by the specter of anti-intellectualism: by 1958 the idea that this might be an important and even dangerous national failing was persuasive to most thinking people."[12]

The national romance with intellectuals was extremely brief. After Kennedy's assassination, Lyndon Johnson's passage of the Civil Rights Act, and the failed Goldwater campaign of 1964, Hofstadter decided to expand upon his analysis of the extreme Right and its political imagination in *The Paranoid Style in American Politics*. Andrew Ross ignored the Goldwater backlash, however, and extrapolated from the three years of the Kennedy presidency that a durable alliance between American intellectuals and the state had become fixed and even normalized. Liberalism and its intellectual supporters had become mainstream. By the early 1960s, Arthur Schlesinger's plea for a robust, centrist politics in post–World War II America seemed to have been answered.

Ross imagined that the prestige of American intellectuals was so forbidding that it would take nothing less than a violent cultural revolution to unseat and subvert their authority over ordinary people. In 1967 Joan Didion reported from Haight-Ashbury in San Francisco, or ground zero in the countercultural rebellion, that "the center did not hold."[13] Most of the hippies she met were interested in experimentation with communal living, sex, and drugs, but a core of politically savvy activists saw in the youth revolt the seeds of a more consequential social and cultural revolution. Reportage from the Vietnam War made it more and more difficult for young people of conscience to support any kind of collaboration with institutions that supported a terrible war. The counterculture always had problems with organization, however, and most young people rejected Vladimir Lenin's question "What is to be done?" as too conservative. Andrew Ross saw this refusal as the dawn of a new kind of politics that responded to the "participatory" and "centerless" ethos of youth culture embodied by the exhortation, "Do it!"[14]

Ross's historiography could be roughly summarized in the following manner: Fifties bad. Intellectuals powerful. Sixties good. Intellectuals deposed. Young people empowered. For Ross, the advent of cultural studies was an institutional fulfillment of the promise of revolt of the counterculture. Because the 1960s saw an explosion of creativity and transgressive energy in the realms of popular culture, a new generation of academics and intellectuals abandoned the ivory tower values of their elders in order to participate fully and without reservation in the popular and subcultural milieus of their peers. Liberal skepticism about popular movements and mass culture espoused by Ross's intellectual and academic mentors and predecessors had to be soundly rejected in favor of an affirmation of popular disrespect for intellectual life and cultural hierarchy.

In Hofstadter's theory of American anti-intellectualism, resentment of the liberal concept of the mind had become a rhetorical weapon used by reactionary, progressive, and revolutionary political forces. Political and cultural adversaries who had struggled against each other (from poets to engineers, from farmers to bankers, from managers to labor union leaders) could find themselves in agreement on one thing: they were equally contemptuous of the scholar whose way of working seemed designed to separate him or her from "doing." The scholar's attachment to the past was considered suspect, since the action-oriented ethos of both businessman and political activist held debates about the significance of the past in high disdain. Hofstadter heard a common refrain in the language of both revolutionary and reactionary politics—the passionate denunciation of useless knowledge and its manipulation by "out of touch" elites whose hands had not been hardened by manual labor, whose characters had not been tested by material privation and hardship. Hofstadter cast a critical eye at the educated elites himself: the mugwumps of the last century, for example, showed a disdain of the often down and dirty political process. Their contempt for everyday struggles and compromise condemned them to condescension and withdrawal from the rough and tumble of nineteenth-century American life and politics. After the cultural upheavals of the late 1960s, detachment and objectivity as the grounds for robust dissent fell into disfavor for a large portion of the American Left. The liberal intellectual was seen as the conformist and establishmentarian par excellence. In 1962 Hofstadter seemed to believe that a comeback was in the making for his idea of the intellectual as a critical participant in the American political process.

Suspicion of learning and disrespect for the speculative mind emerged not as spontaneous expressions of popular sentiment but as a powerful rhetorical weapon in the heart of early American struggles for political legitimacy. This suspicion, once inflamed, was perhaps the mother of all wedge issues. Hofstadter traced its first exploits to struggles within the elites, especially in the

Federalist campaigns against Thomas Jefferson, when established clergy targeted him as a secular man of questionable morals. Because Jefferson had made a successful alliance with popular evangelical forces based on their "common hostility to established orthodoxy," his Federalist opponents such as William Loughton Smith of South Carolina published anonymous pamphlets casting Jefferson as a foolish philosopher, susceptible to foreign (especially French) influence. According to this history, it was a break within the elites and not the rise of popular democracy that produced the first demagogical convulsions within American politics. Hofstadter described the scene of struggle in 1796: "Political controversy, muddied by exaggerated charges of conspiracies with French agents or plots to subvert Christianity or schemes to restore monarchy and put it under the heel of Great Britain, degenerated into demagogy."[15] For Hofstadter, it was during political struggles for legitimacy within ruling elites that hostility to formal and liberal education became lodged within the American ideal of character itself. Although discipline, common sense, frugality, and perseverance were common traits for which early Americans professed almost universal admiration, these qualities were alleged by anti-Jeffersonian forces to be absent in a man of learning.

Early American self-made men such as Benjamin Franklin embodied the characteristics of sobriety, industry, craftsmanship, and a deep understanding of production processes that were the ostensible prerequisites for success in mercantile capitalism. Even today, his aphorisms and autobiography remain an oft-cited compendium of exemplary behavior that set a terrifyingly high standard of industry and rectitude for generations of young Americans. Politics, the study of science, the arts of diplomacy, social sophistication, and a tireless intellectual curiosity dominated the second half of Franklin's life after he secured his fortune. According to Hofstadter, during the time of the founding fathers, "leaders *were* the intellectuals" of American society. Hofstadter found that the liberal mind of mercantilism was oriented toward cultural and intellectual achievement. Although the nineteenth-century self-made man, like Franklin before him, often had little formal schooling, he had a healthy respect for education. Successful self-employment under the conditions of laissez-faire economic policy allowed the self-made man to act freely and independently in political, intellectual, and cultural realms. His sphere of action was circumscribed—a limited but passionate sphere of political agitation and spirited dissent—while his range of economic opportunity was a combination of production and speculation.

For Hofstadter, anti-intellectualism as a political symptom was made up of many movable parts: he described one of its most astonishing and important components as the "curious cult of religious practicality." The cult has changed over time, but Hofstadter originally saw it as a side effect of the process of American secularization. In the era of print culture, self-help and inspirational literature had evolved into a profitable and popular entire segment of the publishing industry that was geared toward producing a "long history of best-selling handbooks." For Hofstadter, this proved that the curious cult had secured its place as "one of the leading faiths of the American middle class."[16] Modern American inspirational literature was distinguished by a "practical motif" or a variant on the "this-worldliness" in Max Weber's analysis of Protestantism. Pragmatism and attention to worldly affairs made Protestantism the most spiritual underwriter for grace, work, and prosperity in a capitalism economy. Self-help and inspirational literature married the language of religion with the ethos of business, trying to replace religious practices with not simply a hardheaded atheistic materialism but a more rational and "down-to-earth" set of spiritual exercises. For Weber, *superstitio* was the Latin for the Greek term *ekstasis* and described the "Oriental" and Lower Empire practices of orgiastic, goddess-worshiping cults.[17] It is difficult to condemn or outlaw superstition on the grounds of rationality when a more reasonable set of religious practices designated the "world-conquering" ambitions of the Roman military-official nobility.[18] Weber drew a conceptual relationship between imperialist Rome's mandate of the Protestant ethos and a constant movement in human history toward rationalization not only in business but in religion. Self-help may have been a heretical form of Christianity, but it could also boast that its lack of doctrine and practicality made it eminently relevant to the everyday struggles of all believers, giving it a magical but down-to-earth quality.

Hofstadter followed Louis Schneider and Sanford Dornbusch's historicization of self-help literature in their *Popular Religion: Inspirational Books in America* (1958). Schneider and Dornbusch identified a historical change that occurred after the Second World War in inspirational literature: "Insistence upon churchgoing is considerably increased since the mid-forties, as is the stress on reading scriptures; and consulting a spiritual counselor, seldom recommended until the 1940s, has also been more and more emphasized since about 1945."[19] The advice in self-help literature had become increasingly concrete and the attitude increasingly pragmatic and optimistic: "efficiency," according to Schneider and Dornbusch, figured as one of spiritual technology's attainable goals. Spiritual life was oriented toward subjective experience, even as the spiritual world had become increasingly anthropocentric. Rather than revelation, the "reader of the literature looks for 'help.'"[20]

For Hofstadter, self-help literature and its concomitant "spiritual technologies" participated in refining and popularizing the cult of religious practicality.[21] As a genre of writing, it was intimately linked to the narrative of the self-made man and promised readers instructions on how to forge from spiritual technology a set of tools that would help people face the vicissitudes of everyday life. Moreover, it claimed to be able to harness the powers of religion for success in business. Hofstadter was struck by the fact that inspirational literature radicalized Protestant tendencies in its progressive weakening and eventual abolishment of the components of religious doctrine and ritual. Moreover, it was resolutely antitraditional. Hofstadter observed of this theology: "Nothing . . . is left but the subjective experience of the individual and even this is reduced . . . to an assertion of his will."[22] A subject-centered religion without history or doctrine would not demand the pain of sacrifice or the pleasure of communion from its experience of the sacred. Thus, Norman Vincent Peale's exhortations to mobilize the power of God to strengthen the believer's will appeared to secular intellectuals like Hofstadter as a form of blasphemy. Hofstadter wryly observed that academic criticism of Peale's abuse of religion could be mistaken for a defense of religion itself. The subject consumed spirituality rather than being consumed by it. Self-help's anti-intellectualism was "indirect" because it dismissed religion as a sphere of objective, shared doctrine in favor of personalized salvation, confirming Hofstadter's critique of Progressive education while supporting Adorno and Horkheimer's critique of pragmatism's subjective orientation. Their critique of the culture industry has often been denounced as monolithic and even paranoid, attributing to the power of popular media an impossible ability to coordinate and homogenize its products. In the case of midcentury inspirational literature as an arm of the culture industry, however, it would seem that there was a great deal of compatibility in its placement of subjective experience and individual interest at the center of both religion and the classroom. After all, both popular religion and educational theories legitimized their spiritual and curricular innovations with similar techniques of personalization.

As an example of the ways in which a blasphemous form of Christianity was peddled by Depression era self-improvement gurus, Hofstadter pointed to Henry C. Link's remarkable 1936 bestseller, *The Return to Religion*, with its prescriptive formulae for using church attendance to improve one's personality. "Jesus was an extrovert. . . . One of the functions of religion—and it would appear that Link considers it the main function—is to discipline the personality by developing extroversion."[23] Hofstadter called Link's book a "consummate manual of philistinism." Not only did Link promote dancing and socializing along with embracing Jesus as critical to extroversion, he encouraged skepticism about intellectuals and intellectual attitudes, both of which might lead to doubt and agnosticism. Link confesses, "I believe in God because I have found that without the belief in someone more important than themselves, people often fail to achieve their own potential importance."[24] Link's conception of spiritual life was shaped by his experience as an industrial psychologist and his expertise on employee testing, advertising, and publicity. In Link's thought, manifesting individual capacities became yoked to both religion and self-adjustment. Link claimed that religion could make manifest the latent divinity in all individuals, and he affirmed religion as both ends and means. Introversion and pessimism were spiritual failings. Link's religion was no longer concerned with a transcendent realm: authors of inspirational literature felt that the effects of religious belief had to be manifest and immanent. In this way, he was a critical precursor of Norman Vincent Peale's "power of positive thinking."

For C. Wright Mills, the "spiritual technologies" provided by twentieth-century motivational manuals could trace their origins to Puritan doctrine, but their durable popularity had something to do with the need for adjustment and motivation that the particular structures and pressures of work in twentieth-century American business required. If Hofstadter believed that self-help literature encouraged or flattered popular anti-intellectualism, for Mills, this literature was meant to quicken the consumerist appetites and quiet the ambitions of an increasingly well-educated but hemmed-in middle class. White-collar workers who found themselves employed in large organizations and bureaucracies were well educated, but their knowledge and expertise were either ignored or underused. American society, for Mills, had made a rocky transition from a population dominated by the entrepreneurialism of small producers and businessmen to one defined by salaried work and bureaucracy. He identified something he called a "literature of resignation" for those frustrated workers whose ambitions had run aground on the limitations of salaried employment: as examples, he offered James Conway's 1947 film *The Hucksters*, Charles Gorham's novel *The Gilded Hearse*, and Arthur Miller's play *Death of a Salesman*. The new literature "trie[d] to control goals and ways of life by lowering the level of ambition and by replacing older goals with more satisfying internal goals."[25] Inspirational literature from the early twentieth century, such as Russell H.

Conwell's *Acres of Diamonds*, prompted readers to action, while the more recent literature painted stark portraits of the ravages of frenzied ambition.[26] Mills felt that the new, midcentury vision of success and failure prompted readers to force an internalization of the values of success in order to escape from the reality of increasing stratification in American society. If ceaseless striving appeared to be increasingly futile and damaging, peace of mind could be cultivated as an antidote to the restless and distracted energies driving entrepreneurial capitalism. In their work on popular religion, Schneider and Dornbusch had discovered a blatant individualism embedded in all advice and counsel. Inspirational literature was exclusively focused on individual and interpersonal solutions to every problem, implying that "all social evil comes from some malevolence or misguided attitude on the part of individuals. In this mode . . . the only explanations of social difficulties are individual viciousness and individual shortcomings."[27] Mills felt that this turn inward contributed to the generalized sense of irresponsibility shared by all twentieth-century American white-collar workers: the inscrutability of social organization and networks encouraged individuals to seek a panacea of security instead of working toward forms of collective action. An internally adjusted sense of success or failure would compensate the individual for the objective conditions of his or her frustration, while dependency on government programs would prevent the worker from aspiring to other forms of action or solidarity. As Mills remarked, "In the amorphous twentieth-century world where manipulation replaces authority, the victim does not recognize his status."[28] Mills's theory of manipulation would eventually be construed as another terrible case of Left elitism; his critique of popular manipulation and victimization could be dismissed as intellectual condescension.

Like Mills and Schneider and Dornbusch, Hofstadter found the midcentury spiritual adepts experts of internalization: "In the old self-help system, faith led to character and character to a successful manipulation of the world: in the new system, faith leads directly to a capacity for self-manipulation."[29] He noted that the older self-help literature reflected some "organic relation to both the world of affairs and to the religious life," as a clear convergence could be identified between Protestant morality and classical economics. The newer literature was, for Hofstadter, distinguished by a blurring of the line between world and spirit, whereby the two become "vaguely fused" without the two halves being able to form a whole. Religion was supplanted by a vague belief in magic. In Schneider and Dornbusch's words, this fusionism led to a "magicalization of spiritual notions or principles" and offered believers concrete advice while allowing them an easy route of sinister withdrawal from reality into wishful thinking. Spiritual escapism seemed most damaging to those already marginalized by the economic and political situation. Hofstadter identified that "today's inspirational literature seems to be mainly read by 'defeated persons,' to use [Norman Vincent] Peale's words, and not as much by men as by women, who though affected by the practical code of business, do not actually enter business."[30] Peale was promoting with enormous success a particularly vivid example of inspirational literature. *The Power of Positive Thinking* remained on the bestseller lists for a year following its publication in 1952.[31] This manual for success married a highly reduced form of Christian gospel with relentless advice about maintaining a positive attitude, but its appeal must have had something to do with its direct confrontation with "the inferiority complex."

In Peale's teachings, the consequences of Protestantism's "attenuation" of ritual reached a kind of apex. He communicated an explicit message about the effectiveness of his techniques in mobilizing spirituality as a source of energy: "There is enough power in you to blow the city of New York to rubble. That, and nothing less, is what advanced physics tells us."[32] The image of God as an inexhaustible energy source could be traced back to the nineteenth-century popularization of Hermann Helmholtz's theories of the conservation of energy. His lecture "Über die Erhaltung der Kraft" (The conservation of energy), delivered in 1847 in Potsdam, proposed: "It is evident that the concepts of matter and force cannot be separately applied to nature."[33] The first law stated that the universe contained a stable amount of energy, which seemed to justify scientifically the idea of divine inexhaustibility. Helmholtz's work in mechanics inspired both materialists and Taylorists. Efficiency in production seemed only a question of controlling the amount of energy lost in its conversion from one form to another.[34] Helmholtz's first law of the conservation of energy also inspired nineteenth-century spiritualists because it gave scientific confirmation to the concept of an infinitely renewable source of power, setting into place one of inspirational literature's most seductive claims—that religion is a source of power and that scientific and technological knowledge can be harmoniously wedded to a highly personalized form of spirituality and spiritual growth. Readers who were anxious about lack of motivation could look to positive thinking as a spiritual technique for fostering and harnessing energy. Spiritual technologies promised to function as nothing less than morale boosters for depressed workers and demoralized students. It is not surprising that the "new" inspirational literature offered all sorts of advice about health and physical well-being as well, implying that readers needed help on almost every level to acquire the necessary "power for daily living." Religion was, therefore, not only a means of fitting in as an extrovert, it could help to create the conditions for efficient use of energy as a form of personal self-realization. In the cult of fusing religion with self-improvement, Hofstadter found something truly curious and uniquely American.

We saw how the institutionalization of advice was linked to the rise of statistics, standardized testing, and career counseling. We also saw how this process would have been impossible without the transformation of secondary schools into sorting mechanisms. According to C. Wright Mills, an increasing number of mid-twentieth century American youth could rely upon neither the inheritance of trades nor the "liberal" notion of choice in facing their career prospects. Instead, "educational institutions and vocational guidance experts would train and fit individuals of various abilities and class levels into pre-existing hierarchies."[35] An entire apparatus of persuasion had to be put into place in order to convince people of their fundamental inability to navigate the modern world without advice. Institutional anticipation of massive resistance could be discerned in its very insistence on the individual's incompetence in decision making. Theorists of "progressive" education insisted that "tests, measurements, placement services, and vocational guidance can at early ages select those who should go on via education to higher positions and those who should terminate their education, and hence their occupational chances, at lower levels."[36]

:: :: ::

In the fall of 1952 Adorno returned to California to do research on newspaper horoscopes just as Adlai Stevenson was defeated by Dwight D. Eisenhower at the polls, precipitating among American intellectuals a critical reevaluation of their place in the nation. A sense of defeat hung in the air of intellectual circles. They had made clear their allegiance to the defeated Democratic candidate. As we saw earlier, Stevenson's defeat was interpreted as popular repudiation of intellectual values in favor of military ones. Anti-Communist fervor had reached a fever pitch in Washington, D.C., with the inauguration of the McCarthy hearings. The material comforts of postwar prosperity had, it seemed, made Americans more anxious about enemies at home and abroad. Though the mood among American intellectuals was pessimistic in 1952, during the war there had been a sense that new scholarly tools of analysis provided by the integration of history, sociology, and psychoanalysis could provide ways for understanding and preventing the rise of fascism and right-wing reaction. As a result of this research, an integrated study of the authoritarian personality had been published as *The Authoritarian Personality: Studies in Prejudice*.[37] The researchers hoped

to isolate conditions for the emergence of prejudice, intolerance, and political extremism: the results would provide templates for public and social policy
in liberal and social democratic states. Authoritarianism's siren song had to be
interpreted in order to dismantle its appeal to large segments of the population whose interests were experienced as vastly unrepresented and whose psychic life was shaped by fear and anxiety about political, economic, and social
change. The psychosexual component of authoritarianism, with its stark views
of homosexuality as delinquency and the denigration of African Americans,
Jews, and "different" people, was measured by a series of questionnaires and
rated according to a controversial "F" scale, which measured the subject's authoritarian proclivities. It was in this study that Adorno identified the analysis
of the "irrational in culture" and superstition as a critical element of any critique of fascism and totalitarianism. The height of political irrationality would
be, of course, National Socialism.

It was under the undoubted influence of this collaborative research project
that Adorno decided to undertake a study of newspaper astrology columns,
which he described as a "fad" that encouraged the authoritarian personality's
repressive and reactionary proclivities. Adorno provided a striking and controversial metaphor for this study: "It should be possible to analyze the inner
structures of such movements ('fads which pride themselves on their irrationality') on a small, test-tube scale . . . and at a time when they do not yet manifest
themselves so directly and threateningly that there is no time left for objective
and detached research."[38] Irrationality as popular astrology is assumed to repli-
cate on an isolatable, smaller, and less dangerous scale the mass irrationality of
political reaction. The metaphor of the laboratory and the test tube sites of sociological study would seem to justify the cultural studies critique of the 1950s
as an era marked by worship of science accompanied by fear of contamination
and contagion. For Andrew Ross and other cultural studies scholars, intellectuals participated in the promotion of liberal and anti-Communist agendas by
acting as not-so-secret agents of containment. Adorno's critics have pointed to
his inability to engage closely with or understand the productions of a culture
industry that he condemned in hyperbolically sweeping terms. In fact, his critics argued, his own methodology was guilty of the reductive and homogenizing
effects of the industrial strength culture he spent a lifetime attacking. However,
his analyses of the 1953 *Los Angeles Times* horoscope and the broadcasts of radio
evangelist Martin Luther Thomas in "The Stars Down to Earth" and "The Psychological Technique of Martin Luther Thomas' Radio Addresses" prove that he did
have a feeling for the culture industry's audiences and consumers. He seemed

to feel closest to the thwarted, semi-erudite, lower-middle-class, white, *older* consumers, while early academic populists tended to avoid addressing this particular constituency. In these two studies, not only did Adorno enter into sustained and productive engagements with culture industry products, but, I would argue even further, he had a particular close identification with its consumers. He understood how cold and impersonal the well-intentioned liberal or leftist sounded to the isolated, dyspeptic individual. He seemed to feel particularly close to the experiences of everyday loneliness and isolation that would drive people to crave "contact" over the radio waves. He "listened" with the ear of Thomas's audiences, just as he read over the shoulder of the horoscope follower. I think what is particularly striking in the case of both the horoscope and Thomas's radio broadcast is that Adorno was able to identify with the projected audience of listeners, who were poor, who possessed little cultural capital, and whose physical bodies were well beyond the well-being of youth and its physical narcissism. The only place where Adorno seems to pull away from his mimetic immersion with these unhappy people was when he advised that counterpropaganda should point to the irrationality of fascism by showing that it offered no justification for the worship of leaders other than an admiration for power.[39] At this point, he called upon the power of the "cold" reason of objective interests to move unhappy and unhealthy newspaper readers and radio listeners.

In Ross's view, not only were intellectuals ready to denounce the pleasures of consuming "mass culture" as an undesirable contagion, but they also participated in the Cold War, the germ-phobic fear of the "spread" of Communism. Adorno's metaphor of analyzing test-tube irrationality dovetails neatly with Andrew Ross's version of the American 1950s as the heyday of intellectual panic about popular culture. Irrationality is likened here to a dangerous contagion that must be studied under laboratory conditions in order finally to be destroyed in complicity with state power and the liberal consensus.[40] Meanwhile, the West German government and the University of Frankfurt had made overtures to the exiled Institut für Sozialforschung, or Institute for Social Research, and Horkheimer was worn down by negotiating with granting agencies and university administrations for the continuation of the institute in the United States. Although it seemed that Americans and American academia were very enthusiastic about the new social sciences, concessions and compromises had to be made continually to satisfy the demands of university administration and private foundations. In 1950 Horkheimer and Adorno returned to Frankfurt. Adorno was struck by the enthusiasm for his work in German media and publishing: his warm reception no doubt had a powerful effect on his preference for his home country. Although Horkheimer was the only one offered a secure university post, possibilities in German academia seemed to emerge. According to Detlev Claussen, "Both men preferred the security of a life as public servants to the liberty of a market organized along the lines of the Culture Industry."[41] The experience of that somewhat ironic market-determined liberty would continue to color Adorno's thinking for the rest of his career. In this sense, both Adorno and Horkheimer chose the institutionally secure university positions that guaranteed them the kinds of autonomy and security that shaped liberal conceptions of the individual. Moreover, the attention they received from the German media was irresistible after the marginality and isolation of their American exile.[42]

Upon his return to Los Angeles in the winter of 1952, Adorno, who still did not have secure employment in Frankfurt and certainly no prospects of a university position in the United States, looked forward to a collaboration on a research project on violence with Austrian exile and Los Angeles–based psychoanalyst Frederick Hacker. It seemed that this collaboration did not work out, and it is not clear whether the study of popular astrology was related to it. There are many ways in which "The Stars Down to Earth" can be read as Adorno's attempt to write a sociological study of the state of insecurity that colored his professional and financial situation during the late 1940s and early 1950s. His fate, as well as the fate of the Frankfurt School for Social Research, seemed to depend all too much upon the waxing and waning of enthusiasm from conflicted funding agencies such as the American Jewish Council and the Rockefeller Foundation in addition to the needs of the evolving discipline of sociology itself. As Martin Jay has shown in his intellectual history of the Frankfurt School, in its inception, the fortunes of the institute and its autonomy had been guaranteed by a virtually no-strings-attached endowment from Felix Weil's family fortune. Weil wrote a doctoral dissertation in political science and was interested not just in writing about the implementation of socialism but in supporting radical organizations that might bring about massive social change.[43] With his considerable family wealth (his father, a grain merchant in Argentina, where he was born, exported Argentinean grain to Europe), Weil was determined to found an independent institute for Marxist-oriented research in the social sciences: the German universities were not hospitable to the ideas of secular, radical, and assimilated Jewish thinkers who had coalesced around Max Horkheimer and Friedrich Pollock. The institute would fund a group of loosely affiliated intellectual projects with the aim of producing rigorous and radical scholarship that would not be supported by mainstream German universities and research institutes. Thus was the Institute for Social Research in Frankfurt conceived and founded in 1923. Although Weil cherished the idea of intellectual independence, he also recognized the need for some kind of institutional recognition, and he entered into an agreement with both the Ministry of Education and the University of Frankfurt to house the institute at the university. The director of the institute had to be a full professor of the university. With the rise to power of the National Socialists, the institute went into exile first in Switzerland and then, during World War II, in the United States.

"The Stars Down to Earth" is one of Adorno's lesser-known works, but it is a highly condensed piece of writing that allows us to situate his methodologies and interests firmly within the context of American intellectual preoccupations of the 1950s. Furthermore, Adorno's ongoing and posthumous dialogue with Walter Benjamin's quasi-mystical description of the relationship between new media and the human sensorium may be found in his critique of newspaper horoscopes. In fact, Adorno worked on astrology because he wanted to continue Benjamin's thought experiment that astrology understood allegorically could be interpreted in its ancient forms as a mode of cognition, as a precursor of mathematical calculation, abstract thinking, astronomy, and physics. In a fragment entitled "On Astrology" unpublished in Benjamin's lifetime but probably written during his 1932 stay in Ibiza, Benjamin played with the idea that the origins of "scientific humanism" could be found in astrology, for which the activity of identifying "similarity" and "resemblance" was derived from our uniquely human "mimetic genius." In fact, astrological interpretation prefigured philosophical and materialist modes of interpretation: the stars and their celestial movement presented themselves to the human eye as a picture puzzle, or *Vexierbild*, that needed to be solved and demanded genuine cognitive effort. In their shared interest in astrology, Benjamin and Adorno demonstrated that they were both possessed by the critical notion of the "historical constellation."[44] Constellation was a figure for the work of thinking dialectically that Adorno shared with Benjamin. In his essay "The Actuality of Philosophy," Adorno was ill at ease with the astrological associations of the term *constellation*, even though he felt in the end that he could not abandon it—at one point, he wanted to replace it with the more scientific term *trial combination*. In any case, philosophical work was described as a process of putting "singular and dispersed elements" into "shifting constellations" and "trial combinations" until "they fall into a figure which can be read as an answer, while at the same time the question disappears."[45]

Astrology allegorized both what was lost and what could be overlooked when considering the enormous divide that separated modernity from antiquity. Taking a cue from independent scholar, collector, and pioneering German art historian Aby Warburg, Benjamin was interested in understanding how astrology might mediate the difference between modernity and antiquity. In Warburg's *Bildatlas Mnemosyne*, his unfinished pictorial atlas, a press photograph of a voyage of the *Graf Zeppelin* is juxtaposed with a diagram of the solar system from Johannes Kepler's cosmological text *Mysterium Cosmographicum* of 1596 alongside an image of Mars from a medieval astrological manuscript from Tübingen. Matthew Rampley has noted that Warburg felt that astrology could be seen as giving birth to astronomy, establishing a connection between ancient and modern worldviews.[46] Warburg's interest in astrology was not fleeting: his collection *Astrologica* constitutes one of the most important archives of printed material on astrology in Europe.[47] But if both Benjamin and Warburg were interested in identifying the difference between antiquity and modernity, they also showed how modernity was capable of regressing toward a remythologization of technology. After all, the New Age was ruled by the sign Aquarius, which encouraged networks, the counterculture, global telecommunications, *and* world-transforming individualism at the same time. The age of Pisces was the age of "groupthink" and rigidity, the age of the experts, the professors, the age of Adorno and of the university. Aquarius was the age of the individual.[48] The counterculture would use astrology to reestablish the cyclical time of mythology as the authentic alternative to the violent historical struggles announced by historical materialism.

But according to Benjamin, "If mimetic Genius really was a life-determining force in Antiquity, then it is more or less unavoidable that the full possession of this gift, the most consummate expression of cosmic meaning, should be given to the new born infant, who even today in the early years of his life will evidence the utmost mimetic genius by learning language." Benjamin's "new born infant" *even today* experienced the "full possession of the gift of ancient mimesis."[49] The infant mind is infinitely labile and takes on the shape of his or her environment: recent study of infant development has served as scientific corroboration of an expansive concept of the human subject's interaction with his or her environment, describing how the infant mind develops within a set of affective and linguistic conditions. This singular capacity for mimesis is life giving but also serves as the very condition of our ability to experience totality—and to master the methods and practices of philosophy. Benjamin wrote, "There is not a single one of [man's] higher functions in which his mimetic faculty does not play a decisive role."⁵⁰ Because pragmatism and idealism are unable to account fully for our mimetic relationship to the world, Adorno rejected their philosophical programs in the name of critical theory, which he understood as cognitively mimetic of all human attempts to understand our place and our work in a world that was both threatening and beautiful. Astrology may describe totality as cosmic, but for Benjamin and Adorno, our relationship to totality appears as an insoluble political, aesthetic, and social puzzle that can only be deciphered through critical experimentation on the order of the historical constellation. Adorno wrote, "Totality is the grotesque heir of manna."⁵¹ The sacred ancestor of totality shared similar qualities with astrology. Manna falls from the sky; the astrological message too comes from above as a puzzle that is addressed to our ability to perceive nonsensuous similarities between microcosmic and macrocosmic orders.

The mimetic faculty, however, was neither anthropological nor ahistorical. It has changed and is subject to further transformation. Benjamin's work on the perception of similarity and the importance of analogy in the premodern world anticipates Michel Foucault's own archaeology of knowledge and modes of classification. According to Benjamin, the mimetic faculty is withering away. While it was once constituted a cognitive disposition attitude or mode of comportment, it has now become merely a mode of perception. The mimetic faculty is an innately human capacity to respond to the world around us. Philosophy has traditionally deployed itself as the enemy of the mimetic capacity, but its ability to survive as that which is proper to all human beings actually undermines the very notions of propriety and property. The mimetic capacity for play and for learning survives intact in the child as that which is proper to all children. In children we see its persistence (ontogeny recapitulating phylogeny may be yet another mimetic mode of collective memorialization of that which has been lost): "Children's play is everywhere permeated by mimetic modes of behavior, and its realm is by no means limited to what one person can imitate in another. The child plays at being not only a shopkeeper or teacher, but also a windmill and a train."⁵² Benjamin, in fact, goes so far as to deduce a theory of cognition based upon child's play and the mimetic faculty that develops according to a child's ability to respond to the similarities he or she finds between disparate elements in the social and natural world. In other words, Adorno, following but revising Benjamin on mimesis, saw the necessity of articulating a satisfactory relationship between mimesis and reason itself.

Similarities in the world were "stimulants and awakeners of the mimetic faculty." The positive expressive power of mimesis within the artwork communicates the alterity of historical experience, both individual and collective.[53] As Robert Kaufman noted, "Following the early Benjamin, Adorno understands expression as semblance of mimesis, mimesis grasped not as transcription but as an attempt provisionally to know something of the otherness outside the subject."[54] In his or her mimetic and linguistic "genie," the infant's joyful accession to a linguistic heritage abolished the difference between modernity and antiquity: it was a moment of happiness and ahistoricity that was continuously renewed and renewable. Newly born children find themselves in full possession of a gift from a radically other time: it is a collective inheritance and one that is equally distributed among human children. It was this precious capacity for mimesis and the infinitely plastic playfulness upon which that linguistic mastery is based that was compromised by rationalism run amok. Mimesis was a way of being that was inherently democratic, transsexual, and transspecies because of its capacity for making links between the animate and the inanimate, the human and the animal, the large and the small. The young child who rumbled like an engine or cooed like a bird understood his body as an acoustic instrument that both imitated and incarnated the foreignness of the sonic world around him.

Strangely enough, however, for Benjamin, the mimetic faculty has made its deepest mark not upon human behavior but upon human language. A flash of similarity that accumulated like static electricity between what was said and what was meant, between what was said and what was written, allowed for the belief that language was a mode of communication between the radically dissimilar worlds of words and things. This imparting of qualities to words and things goes back to the magical and sacred quality of naming as it was related to a divine imparting of meaning to the world. The very possibility of reading is tied to a reading prior to all languages, to an occult act of "reading entrails, stars, or dances." Later, the mediating link of a new kind of reading, of runes and hieroglyphs, came into use. It seems fair to suppose that these were the stages by which the mimetic gift, formerly the foundation of occult practices, gained admittance to writing and language.[55] Language was both the "highest level" of mimetic activity and the greatest living archive of "nonsensuous similarity." Language as medium drew upon the powers of mimetic production so thoroughly that all traces of its magic have been "liquidated." An attempt to revive or restore to language and media this element of mimetic comportment, this intimate and intuitive relationality to the world, could only take place now through critical speculation that identified as historical apposites and even anachronisms. "Manna" and "totality" shared an intimate similarity. The philosopher, in his use of language, could not entirely escape the priest, but this was not to say that we had to accept the regime of piety when we "did" philosophy. Even as the Platonic demystification did a great deal to destroy an earlier relationship to improvisation and magic that was abhorrent to philosophical rationality, the philosopher retained something of the magical aura that he tried so hard to banish.

Roger Caillois described the mimetic relationship between organism and milieu as a primordial relationship between the animate and the inanimate.[56] Benjamin was fascinated by the exchange of qualities that could take place between the human and the nonhuman not in nature but in the jungles of the city. The temptations of the dream-space of the commodity and the deep feeling that the city-dweller would form for the most inanimate and obdurate of objects and gazes became part of those dense experiences. In fact, the relationship between the flâneur and the city streets he haunted could be described as mimetic. The flâneur or the dandy took on the deadpan but shiny flatness of the commodity and while styling himself according to the dreamscape of shop windows; he only spoke in the cryptic dialect of advertising. He offered himself up for display. He displayed a greater affective attachment to small variations in style than to great political changes. As Benjamin reminded us, Baudelaire, as exemplary flâneur, was distinguished by a highly charged susceptibility to inanimate, unresponsive objects that offered themselves up for sale to any comer. The mimetic faculty was a connection to the prerational world, and as a genie, it was also a minor demon.

In fact, despite his objections to Benjamin's affirmation of film and mass media, Adorno continued to be preoccupied by the concept of mimesis: "Anything that does not wish to wither should rather take on itself the stigma of the inauthentic. For it lives on the mimetic heritage. The human is indissolubly linked with imitation: a human being only becomes human at all by imitating other human beings. In such behavior, the primal form of love, the priests of authenticity scent traces of the utopia which could shake the structure of domination."[57] Our mimetic genius was threatened, as were all capacities that referred to a Utopia where becoming human is not a disciplinary or civilizing act that has been fully sanctified by a dominant class and its ethos. The "priests of authenticity" policed the very ground of a Utopian interrelatedness, a kind of erotic connection, "a primal form of love." This threat is parried, deferred, and held at bay in our capacity for play without end, a capacity most fully realized in the joyfulness of wordplay. "Even today," the fullness of this threatened genius in children persists and survives "vor alle Augen." It is "evidenced" in the English translation, "before our very eyes," which is already too biased toward empiricism. Imitation forms a vital link not only with the Other but with others: the mimetic relation allows for the possibility of solidarity founded on communicative, creative, and collective action. Jürgen Habermas decried Adorno's conceptualization of mimesis as yet another form of "irrationalism" that was immune to critique and theorization.[58] But mimesis named an expansive potentiality that could be understood as the medium of intersubjectivity: mimesis can be understood rationally as a primordial form of mediation. The scattered, unsystematic reference that Adorno made throughout his work to mimesis cannot be exhaustively summarized or totally explained away. Instead, as a concept that animated the Utopian reach of his work, it must be viewed "stereoscopically."[59]

According to historian Jack Lindsey,

> The main motive-force driving men to watch the stars was a hope of reducing their movements to regular patterns which could be understood and foreseen. Since this activity went on within cultural systems in which the notion of vital correspondences between heaven and earth was central, it at no time asserted itself as a disinterested and abstract search for knowledge. . . . This in itself was a valid enough attitude; what we now see as fantasy was the extremely oversimplified way in which correspondences were seen and treated. The reaction came in the sixteenth century with the slow foundation of scientific attitudes which totally excluded men from the world of natural phenomena.[60]

The exclusion of human beings as the measure of celestial movement and a concomitant rejection of anthropomorphism allowed for real progress to be made in astronomy. Scientific progress produced, however, a disorienting absence in the cognitive framework of the universe. How could nonscientists apprehend the scale of space and time without the anchoring presence of the human body? The horizon of scientific temporality had reduced the human being to terrifying insignificance. In premodern astrology, the fatality of the stars was experienced as total and totalizing. The relationship between the constellations and human fate, even if linked deterministically, still put human suffering and happiness in a meaningful relationship with the cosmos.

While Adorno's wild diagnoses of paranoia, anality, and the petit bourgeois personality will strike contemporary readers as heavy-handed and embarrassingly normative, his description of the psychic life of conservatism should strike us as familiar and ever so vital to understanding the conflicts gripping

American politics. Moreover, his speculations on the practicality and "down to earthness" of the *Los Angeles Times* astrology column dovetailed neatly with Hofstadter's historical presentation of the conceptual and political contradictions of twentieth-century American anti-intellectualism. For Adorno, the act of bringing stars down to earth embodied the oppressive philosophy of knowledge behind all forms of self-help and adjustment: everything in the world must be made useful to the interests of the individual, even the movements of the stars themselves. Beyond this critique of administered life and its ideological apparatus, Adorno recognized the promotion of elements of the authoritarian personality projected onto the presumptive reader of the column. He took the column seriously as a product of the culture industry's apparently innocuous influence on shaping of down-to-earth advice derived from celestial movement. The astrological "fad" exploited a "skeptical" but "insufficiently equipped" intellect in promoting "psychological defenses against instinctual urges" and in "strengthening the sense of fatality, dependence and obedience."[61] Carroll Righter was the author of the astrology column featured prominently in the politically conservative *Los Angeles Times*, which Adorno described as "far to the Right of the Republican Party."[62] Ronald Reagan mentions Righter in his 1965 autobiography, and it was rumored that Righter continued to advise both Reagans after Reagan's election as president. In any case, by 1953 Righter was well known in movie circles and was called the "astrologer to the stars." He began writing the astrology column for the *Los Angeles Times* in 1950, so it must have still appeared to newspaper readers as somewhat of a novelty in 1953.[63] The column was eventually syndicated in over 166 newspapers worldwide.

For Adorno, Righter's columns were remarkable for their appearance of reason and restraint: he presented a uniformly moderate mien with regard to both prediction and predetermination. In fact, what Adorno found most "paradoxical and challenging" about Righter's column was the "sobriety" and "over-realism of the material at the expense of anything reminiscent of the supernatural."[64] In the column, the animistic and magical thinking of "ancient humanity" seemed to have left few if any traces at all: it would appear that the newspaper horoscope scrubbed astrology clean of any hints of either primitivism or anachronism. The advice offered was resolutely modern in orientation: comments were restricted to familiar work and family situations that were both ostensibly populated by a banal cast of characters, including jealous coworkers, kind strangers, and demanding relatives. Accordingly, Righter's column promoted a psychological disposition with a sunny, apolitical attitude that disguised a deeply pessimistic and reactionary view of the world.

The magazines *Forecast*, *Astrology Guide*, *American Astrology*, and so on appealed to adepts with more specialized knowledge of astrology. These magazines, despite their range of content, assumed more esoteric knowledge on the part of their readers. Adorno found that the magazines were much more willing to predict worldwide catastrophes and vague, unnameable threats. They were directed at a more specialized audience, what would be called today a niche market or subculture, while the newspaper horoscope sought to address the widest possible audience, one in which direct experience with the occult could not be assumed. The newspaper astrology column represented, for Adorno, "secondary superstition," at one remove from folkways or esoteric traditions. Secondary superstitions offered a way for the ordinary person to believe that he could outwit the constraints of domination by committing himself to interpreting and negotiating with the most cruelly inexorable form of irrationality—destiny. Secondary superstitions represented a shortcut to a total world picture. It was for this reason that Adorno argued for the psychological rewards of identifying with the powerful. The world picture provided by secondary superstitions communicated to readers a temporary sense of "empowerment" before the puzzle of domination and exploitation in an increasingly complex and inscrutable world.[65] In 1975 Righter published *Dollar Signs*, an astrological guide to worldly success in which he explained that we can all follow our sun signs to the highest forms of personal and professional success. Righter was not content with giving advice to individuals: he cast the astrological chart of the World Bank, founded on December 27, 1945, and he rendered a "chart" for the United States based on the nation's birthday, July 4, 1776. Righter predicted the World Bank's failure to achieve its goals because of its horoscope. Furthermore, Righter predicted with twenty-twenty hindsight that the World Bank would experience a crisis from October 1972 to August 1975, coinciding with the double blow of the oil crisis and inflation on the global economy. The World Bank's birthday doomed it not only to failure but to corruption and opacity. According to Righter, the United States, on the other hand, was destined for success, since Gemini is its rising sign, and Gemini is "youthful, restless, changeable, idealistic, imaginative, hopeful and a little impulsive."[66]

Since the newspaper horoscope had to cast a wide net to reach the broadest audience, it appeared to be more democratic in its approach to converting esoteric knowledge into popular advice. The reader of the *Los Angeles Times* astrology column was no initiate of the occult and was assumed to be not very interested in the processes by which the calculations behind the predictions were made: the lightness with which the consumer of newspaper astrology took the results of astrological calculation reflected his or her secular and rational bent of mind. Neither outraged nor particularly drawn in, she was willing to countenance, for a fleeting moment, the truth value and usefulness of the horoscope's advice. This ambivalence betrayed one of the reified attitudes prepackaged by the culture industry for mass consumption, which Adorno called "lack of seriousness." The projection of individual fates onto celestial movements has a long tradition in hermeneutics, but the power of the modern superstition has been limited in today's Los Angeles Times by a disavowal of its utility: "This column should be read for entertainment only." The inclusion of such a caveat reflects the newspaper's acknowledgment of the column's unreliability as a purveyor of useful advice. The newspaper, however, still promises to deliver entertainment or cognitive relaxation. Readers are offered respite from "information" about the world in the horoscopes; instead, their personal interests seem to be directly and forthrightly addressed.

The horoscope appealed to readers as a mass while organizing them into twelve discrete sun signs that would provide useful and entertaining advice. The convergence of information and personalization was not only crucial to the culture industry's mass production of the "difference," it was also highly compatible with an educational philosophy that supported schools as sites of mass sorting and individualization.[67] In 1953 the newspaper horoscope had only two decades of history behind it. According to historian of astrology Ellic Howe, "The predictions published by a large number of European and North American mass-circulated newspapers and women's magazines have become such a commonplace feature of everyday life that the singular nature of the phenomenon has been obscured by its familiarity."[68] The Sunday Express of London was the first important newspaper in Great Britain to publicize astrology on a wide scale, and the horoscope's ability to sell papers was a highly accidental marketing discovery. The astrologer R. H. Naylor was invited by the newspaper to calculate the astrological chart of Princess Margaret Rose (sister of Queen Elizabeth II) immediately after she was born on August 21, 1930. The Sunday Express featuring Princess Margaret's chart sold beyond anyone's expectation. Thereafter the newspaper commissioned Naylor to do more work. The daily horoscope (calculated according to the individual's sun sign and lacking other planetary information) was "invented" by Naylor for the tabloid. Ever since, sun-sign astrology's popularity has proven quite unshakeable, despite the fact that sun-sign astrology stirs controversy within the astrological community itself for disseminating a simplified and vulgarized version of astrology.[69] Whatever the newspaper horoscope's failures as authentic astrology, it certainly enhanced and expanded print journalism's popular appeal.

On Sunday, October 5, 1930, Naylor's horoscope predicted that a British aircraft was in serious danger. The BBC reported later that afternoon that the R-101 airship on its maiden flight from Cardington to India had crashed in northern France. Suddenly, Naylor and astrology became famous. In Adorno's analysis of the *Los Angeles Times* astrology column, the threat of a possible car accident arouses the reader's anxiety while allowing for the column to leave intact her narcissism. With the proliferation of modern means of transport and the increasing chance of accidents, an astrological prediction in this vein could almost not go wrong: some reader somewhere would be involved in a misfortune of this sort.

In 1952 much of the news of the world was preoccupied with the threat of Communism and the rise of behavioral science. Adorno hoped to prove in his analysis that the down-to-earth nature of the *Los Angeles Times* horoscope strengthened the reduction of astrological irrationality to a "purely formal characteristic: abstract authority."[70] Acceptance of the administered life and an identification with our appropriate places within a hierarchical workplace formed the strongest underlying assumptions in the 1952–53 *Los Angeles Times* horoscope advice about proper behavior. The analysis focused on a projected or fictional reader, not an empirical one; in fact, Adorno warned against treating the "material dogmatically as a mirrored reflection of the reader's mind."[71] Without the time or resources to do a reception study of newspaper horoscopes, he performed a close textual analysis instead. As in his writings on jazz, his account of the newspaper column was rather short on history and failed to provide a critical context for advice and self-help offered by inspirational literature. As a work of cultural criticism, however, it provided a vivid glimpse of how deeply Adorno's thinking was in dialogue with the American situation. It offered a glimpse of his attempts to apply a theory of culture industry to a denigrated and marginal object and, in so doing, redeem and isolate its negative importance in the context of the culture at large. His criticism of the *Los Angeles Times* astrology column was able to demonstrate that the life-adjustment ethos of the postwar era had been metabolized by popular and mass media as they developed and packaged new forms of advice addressed to the struggles of average Americans. As we saw earlier, career counseling and the management of expectations and ambitions were developed alongside pedagogical theories that supported vocational education, standardized testing, and the life-adjustment movement. Having prepared students to internalize the directives of the soft coercion of career counseling in high school, the life-adjustment movement worked well as a form of indoctrination and discipline that masqueraded as popular forms of therapeutic "help" and "counseling."

"Adjustment" was a term that recurred often in the language of astrological advice, and Adorno tried to unpack the term's complexity and significance. He tried to clarify the ways in which "helpful" advice about "adjusting" to constellations always contained a coercive function and a veiled threat of disaster if the recommended adjustments were not made. Of course, astrologers would insist that there was room for choice, for the variables of character to allow the individual to deal with different situations differently; but freedom in this world is not freedom to question the setup but freedom to make the best of any given situation. In Righter's column, there are times when "it is quite frankly stated that the individual should adjust himself to certain constellations."[72] In this section of the essay, astrology, for all its pragmatism and down-to-earthness, might actually be a disguised "metaphysics of adjustment." The stars, representing an inexorable and unmovable fate, endowed determinism with a sense of mystery. "Life" in "life-adjustment" gave a false, organic sense of wholeness to insecurity, competition, exploitation, and disorientation. Behind Righter's concrete suggestions and common sense, incessant adjustment became the order of the day.[73] While Adorno engaged with Horkheimer in The Dialectic of Enlightenment in broad critiques of the philosophical assumptions behind pragmatism and its renunciation of objective reason in the name of subjective self-interest, he never directly criticized the life-adjustment movement.[74] It should be obvious by now, however, that just as the meritocracy and its sorting function were formed by concepts of individualized test results, "adjustment calls for individuality" as well: "He who wants to adjust himself to a competitive pattern of society or to its more hierarchical successor has to pursue his own particularistic individual interests rather ruthlessly in order to find recognition."[75]

Adorno's experience with the American secondary school would seem very limited indeed. He seemed aware, however, that the language of Progressive educational policies had permeated the language of the popular psychology scene, making terms like *maladjusted* and *overachiever* the common vocabulary of magazines and radio and television talk shows. Adorno's critique of adjustment should be read in the context of wider midcentury American intellectual concerns about life-adjustment and its contribution to popular anti-intellectualism. His concept of "semi-erudition" could be understood as an attempt to formulate a working description of the subjective psychology of an unintegrated theory of knowledge and, further, as an attempt to theorize the cognitive orientation of Prosser's student. If such a student were capable of keeping fit but denied knowledge of human physiology, he could live with the results of modernity and technological progress without knowing anything of the scientific method. The student had to accept forms of knowledge produced by scientific progress, but he did not have to grasp the process by which those results were reached; he would be particularly susceptible to believing reductive and simplified theories of the whole. Without any training in the history of philosophy, this student would be ignorant of the fact that thinkers, scientists, prophets, and gurus had been grappling with the problem of articulating and communicating an adequate descriptive, theoretical, and spiritual relationship of the individual to the whole, the subjective world to the objective world, the intimate to the distant for millennia in different contexts with different results. For Adorno, believing in the irrational connection between celestial bodies and one's personal fate represented a cognitive shortcut and a leap into the abyss of the mystical and magical systems that defied the out-of-touch experts and eggheads who did not, after all, know it all.

Adorno felt that secondary superstition was related to radical positivism: "Concomitantly with the ever increasing belief in 'facts,' information has a tendency to replace intellectual penetration and reflection. The element of synthesis in the classical philosophical sense seems to be more and more lacking." The deferral or even censorship of critical attempts to think synthetically exacts a psychic price on the thinker, just as the division of labor along the assembly line harms the craftsman and worker.[76] In Adorno's words, this cost is extracted as irrationality: "Astrology presents the bill for the neglect of interpretative thinking for the sake of fact gathering."[77] The *Los Angeles Times* astrology column encouraged in its readers a certain relaxation of the critical faculties. For Adorno, the readers enjoyed believing that distant, inscrutable powers controlled the details of their lives.[78] The modern culture of occultism promoted, as C. Wright Mills described it, manipulation as voluntary self-manipulation, along with the intensive internalization of limits. In "The Stars Down to Earth," the modern "belief" in astrology was based upon certain psychological elements necessary to the acceptance of fascist politics: (1) voluptuous passivity before absolute authority; (2) semi-erudition, a state of literacy that Adorno says affords its subjects a certain air of skepticism with regard to specialists and experts; and (3) willingness to accept the existence of a conspiracy of distant and mysterious forces that work together to determine every aspect of our lives. People inclined toward light or secondary superstition were also given to anti-intellectualism. They looked half-heartedly for advice from the spiritual world but rejected systematic, sustained critical and dialectical thinking. The constellation of conditions that determined our experience of everyday life presented itself as a puzzle that only the astrologer could decode. For the newspaper horoscope, there was only this world and no hope for a better one. "In as much as the social system is the 'fate' of most individuals independent of their will and interest, it is projected upon the stars in order to thus obtain a higher degree of dignity and justification in which the individuals hope to participate themselves."[79] Reading one's horoscope in the newspaper demanded little investment of belief, time, or energy. The reader was flattered as a cunning consumer who could gain an advantage over others not in the know without spending a dime or exerting much effort. In short, the horoscope held out to the reader the possibility that he was getting bargain basement insights.

The kinds of pseudobelief demanded by the newspaper horoscope are based upon a fantasy of "sex without consequences," which has come to be associated with countercultural emancipation of the instincts or at least Enlightenment era libertine behavior. Ostensibly, pursuit of sensual indulgence and nonrational hedonism would ensue from indulgence in this kind of fantasy. But for Adorno, sex without consequences represented a form of emancipation from sexual inhibition that allowed only the maintenance of Herbert Marcuse's "repressive desublimation" without any possibility of authentic sexual experience.[80] "Sex without consequences" described a fantasy of pleasurable submissiveness with regard to distant and all-powerful forces, but as sex, it always remained unconsummated, infinitely deferred, and safely virtual. It is polymorphous in nature, able to turn from homo-heterosexual encounter and back again. Adorno identified this fantasy as the masochistic core of the authoritarian personality: the social face of this perversion was often revealed as scrupulous conformity to rules, regulations, and requirements. The adherence to the rules seemed to be based upon the promise of some fantastic reward for our compliance, even though, practically speaking, compliance was the result of a coercive and veiled threat of imminent violence. Compliance and submission to a faceless power produced congealed pleasures, which then created a hard core of overdetermination in the authoritarian personality that blocked the subject's ability to tolerate ambiguity and complexity.

The semi-erudite person found in secondary superstitions an appealing shortcut to a sense of mastery of which "other people" were deprived. Rather than presenting a demanding course of critical reasoning, astrology presented a secret and esoteric form of knowledge that was not institutionally sanctioned.

In Righter's column Adorno found a more or less legible web of proscriptions, prohibitions, evidence of censorship, veiled threats, and vague compliments playing off against each other in a shadowy, internalized space in which the private and public lives of the readers were confused. For the semi-erudite, whose shaky grasp of the scientific method betrayed an admiration for and resentment of experts, inspirational literature and secondary superstitions provided a highly pragmatic orientation to life's biggest questions.

If in the eighteenth century Voltaire criticized religious extremism and superstition in the name of religious moderation, Adorno is critical of the *Los Angeles Times* astrology column's excessively moderate form of superstition. In his time, Voltaire may have identified religious fanaticism as the greatest threat to reason, but Adorno denounces the instrumentalization of superstition as a new adversary of enlightenment. Modern superstition cynically eliminated sacrifice in favor of an endless negotiation with the gods. This is the spirit of Odysseus, whose relation to the sacred is already distinguished by a combination of cunning and calculation. Odysseus is the primordial businessman who is ready to drive a hard bargain with the all too susceptible chthonic deities and demons. The negotiator's cunning is thus mythologized and narrativized across the ahistorical space-time continuum of the "adventure." As aspects of the dialectic of enlightenment, moderate religiosity and secondary superstition share this critical feature—the sacrifice of sacrifice. When Freud wrote that religion demanded our belief in the absurd eventuality that we would be saved by a higher power, that prayer would allow us to get what we need to survive, that self-denial would win us a place in the afterlife, he implied that the ordinary person would, in submitting to such an injunction, bridle at the sacrifice of his capacity for reason and his pleasures for specious promises of an unlikely redemption. With secondary superstition, however, even the sacrifice of reason was excluded, since the New Age seemed to be able to take advantage of scientific evidence at any moment to prove its legitimacy. As we will see in chapter 5, Andrew Ross would address New Age attitudes about science as part of a popular and ambivalent insurgency against dominant institutions.

Whereas Voltaire believed that an incorrect or extreme form of belief could be remedied by adopting a more "rational" approach to religion, Adorno showed that it was precisely this reasonable attitude to both religiosity and superstition that doomed the Enlightenment's critique of "compromised" secularization. We could take Adorno's critique further: it is with the rationalization of religion that the Enlightenment hoped to promote a moderate form of religious belief, or at least to substitute a more reasonable form of religious practice for fanaticism. This rationalization leads to a glaring contradiction of which ordinary believers are all too aware. The rise and fall of the charismatic sects of Protestantism that took hold in the United States are evidence of the spiritual restlessness that distinguishes the American believer, who is quick to leave institutionalized churches in search of less compromised forms of charismatic sovereignty.[81] The very concept of moderate religiosity betrays the essence of religion itself. Therefore, this moderate and "reasonable" religiosity is a compromise that will provoke greater reaction from believers who are justified in feeling that they are being deprived of something critical to religious experience in being offered this "modernized" form of religious experience. Those who embrace fundamentalism are in fact rejecting moderate religiosity and not scientific skepticism. Indeed, moderate religiosity is seen as a more dangerous adversary than outright secularization itself. The revolt against the calculating logic of modernization inflames the fundamentalist intensities of sacrifice and renunciation.

Moderation even in superstition was symptomatic of an age when the logic of self-preservation accepted all tools and all instruments as long as they did not tax our ability to think problems through. For Voltaire, moderation in belief was the sign of an enlightened and skeptical attitude: this was the foundation of a liberal orientation toward knowledge and the world. With the absolute triumph of instrumental reason, however, moderation became the principle of adaptation to the givenness of reality. On the other side of the dialectic of enlightenment, a mass-produced skepticism directed its suspicions against liberal education and formal knowledge in the name of common sense. According to J. M. Bernstein, "Secondary occultism involves a certain lack of seriousness; unlike serious religious belief it trades in a common sense rationality, it demands nothing from the believer, certainly nothing as demanding as faith, and often overtly concedes, in its advice, pride of place to its opposite; modern natural science. . . . [A]strology permits belief and obedience without demanding readers to overtly sacrifice the claims of rational evidence and reflection."[82] The semi-erudite person was perfectly willing to see herself as merely a set of aptitudes and capacities, personality assets and occasional resistances. Adorno grasped that this self-objectification was part of a larger impulse within the administered world, to make self-preservation the end that justifies all means, but his analysis also resonated on the level of an affective response to professional insecurity, which he seemed to have understood all too well. Adorno's essay could be read as an encrypted autobiography of his own professional and economic insecurity, especially during the period right after the war. His analysis addressed the problems of academic contract labor that he faced during his exile in the United States. For someone who abjured direct confession, who believed that the fullness of life was lived in defiance of direct memorialization, there are pieces of Adorno's work that can nevertheless be read for traces and fragments of an autobiographical mode of writing. *Minima Moralia*, a much more famous text by Adorno written at about the same time, interlaced philosophical speculation with encrypted autobiographical anecdotes. The same seems true for "The Stars Down to Earth," which can be understood as Adorno's testimony to his inability to adjust to the American academic scene as well as to a profound unease about his powerlessness before the shifting demands of his work situations in exile. His uncertainty about his personal and professional future during the late 1940s and early 1950s was intense: the Institute for Social Research had broken its collaboration with Columbia University after the latter moved toward a more empirical research model. Adorno's own position, unlike Horkheimer's in Germany, was extremely uncertain. Lorenz Jäger quotes Adorno, who was leaving Los Angeles in 1949 to return to Frankfurt, in his journal: "'I am sad to be traveling,' he wrote at this time. He had the feeling that he was 'the object of constellations, not really in control of myself.'"[83] In introducing his close analysis of astrological advice, Adorno chooses to focus on his own sun sign, Virgo, when he compares *Forecast* magazine's predictions to Righter's columns in the winter of 1953. (Adorno was born on September 11, 1903.) In the winter 1953 issue of *Forecast*, Virgos were urged to "relax; read a good book or do something that will occupy your mind and hands in a constructive manner. Retire early."[84]

A cluster of recent intellectual biographies of Adorno have explored personal and institutional archival materials that have shed more light on his experiences living and working in America. Ranging from the sympathetic (David Jenemann) to the outright hostile (Lorenz Jäger), these writers, along with Detlev Claussen, another Adorno biographer, concur on one point: Adorno had enormous difficulty adjusting to the American way of working.[85] This could be attributed to arrogance (Jäger) or a deeply ingrained sense of intellectual integrity (Jenemann). Either unwilling or incapable, Adorno seemed remarkably ill suited for adaptation to the requirements of holding down a job in the United States during the 1930s and 1940s. Jenemann's work in the Princeton Radio Project archives unearthed journals recording the grave reservations that Rockefeller Foundation grant officer David Marshall harbored about both Adorno's personality and his research findings. When the foundation eventually withdrew its funding for Adorno's position at the Princeton Radio Project, Marshall justified his decision by casting doubt on Adorno's ability to collaborate with the radio industry in order to improve the quality of broadcasts, which was, after all, the goal of the funded research. He wrote that the "tone of Adorno's paper leaves some doubt that Adorno would be able to collaborate in any such way. He seems psychologically engaged at the moment by his ability to recognize deficiencies in the broadcasting of music to an extent that makes questionable his own drive to find ways of remedying them."[86] In "Current of Music," his seven-hundred-page unpublished study of radio, Adorno theorized the ways in which radio functioned as a social technology and as one component on a wider network of the culture industry's matrix. Throughout, he rejected the foundation's desired statistical analysis for in-depth interviews. The contradictions of Adorno's position were succinctly theorized by Richard Hofstadter: "The position of the critical intellectual is a singularly uncomfortable one. The freedom of intellect and art is inevitably the freedom to criticize and disparage, to destroy and re-create; but the daily necessity of the intellectual and the artist is to be an employee, a protégé, or a man of business."[87]

Producing a half-educated student or at least a sense of docile but anxious ignorance may not have been Charles Prosser's explicit educational goal, but it did seem to be his assumption that students and job applicants were uniquely helpless when presented with the challenges of "fitting" themselves to appropriate work. Witness the 1947 guide he wrote advising the unemployed and returning World War II veterans on how to get a job and a promotion. After an unsuccessful interview, Prosser advised the applicant to undergo the following self-interrogation:

> Sit down and think over your experiences in your first attempt to sell your services and answer the following list of questions with *yes* or *no*: 1. Did I apply for a job for which I lacked the necessary qualifications? 2. Did I over-sell myself? 3. Did I under-sell myself? 4. Did I tell an untruth which was detected? 5. Did I make contact with the hiring official in the wrong way? 6. Did I select the wrong concern? 7. Did I lose my head or my temper in the interview? 8. Was I over-confident? 9. Did I fail to make out the application blank accurately or properly? 10. Did I prejudice my case by my personal appearance? 11. Did I prejudice it by a lack of ordinary good manners in dealing with the concern and its employing officials? 12. Did I show a lack of interest in anything else than getting the job? 13. Was it because I was unwilling to start in at the wage offered or for the position which was available? 14. Did I evade questions? 15. Did I fail to do justice to myself because of timidity? 16. Did I over-stay my welcome? 17. Did my statements in the interview agree with my answers on the application blank? 18. Did I insist on too detailed information or on direct promises of promotion?[88]

Prosser's rejected job candidate exists in the same social void as the subject of inspirational literature: all problems exist within individual responses to a situation. Prosser's implicit claim in his advice to job candidates is that rejection can be remedied through proper adjustment of the self, as in "personal appearance" or "lack of good manners." The radical focus on individual responsibility is mitigated by self-aggrandizement through self-interrogation. Everything would change if self-transformation and self-adjustment could be achieved. The most compliant employee or student would be the one most willing to accept a barrage of advice on fine-tuning his responses to the expectation of others. This indeed is an example of David Riesman's hollowed-out, other-directed person. To be susceptible to advice is also to be sensitive to the demands and standards external to oneself to the point of having no sense of autonomy or "inner direction" at all. Rather than being a gyroscopic monad, Prosser's job applicant had to direct the arrangement of the self completely toward the perception of others. In order to get his job, he would have to present an image of cooperativeness, a trait Adorno obviously lacked. In the eyes of his colleagues at the Princeton Radio Project and the Rockefeller Foundation, Adorno's uncompromising negativity and his inability to cooperate with colleagues presented themselves as difficulties of adjustment rather than differences of intellectual orientation.

If inner-directed and outer-directed personalities were dialectical concepts, meant by Riesman to be apprehended nonempirically, we could follow Norman Mailer's reading of Riesman's work as sociological fiction and understand Adorno's analysis of the semi-erudite in a similar manner.[89] The outer-directed, semi-erudite fictional character who reads the *Los Angeles Times* horoscope between 1952 and 1953 would have been educated under the life-adjustment curriculum; therefore, he would know little to nothing of American history but could "fit in" with his peer group and workplace. Adorno had diagnosed semi-erudition as a damaged state of the intellect. Although the semi-erudite had internalized the fragmentation of all knowledge, they still yearned for a privileged perspective, a superior if not secret key to an integrated and coherent worldview. Unlike the smug consumer of Dwight Macdonald's midcult pablum and kitsch, the semi-erudite person seemed much more anxious and much less confident about her relationship to leisure.[90] Carroll Righter imagined that she had to be reminded to make improvements on her home, wash her car, fix a household contraption, buy new gadgets, compromise with a spouse, and entertain the higher-ups. Under Adorno's scrutiny, Righter's pseudopersonalized advice reflected or was defined by the contours of objective, "insoluble situations of the present phase, impasses which threaten each individual and stimulate each individual's hopes for some effective interference from above."[91] The underlying psychology of the column revealed the necessity of submitting to a "magical authority." For Adorno, Righter's voice was that of the "homespun philosopher," a font of commonsense wisdom that was remarkably adept at flattering his reader's self-image while producing a sense of generalized anxiety. For Riesman, by the 1950s "the sphere of pleasure had become the sphere of cares."[92] In such a state of helplessness, the status-panicked reader of the column seemed to be in need of advice and guidance even about leisure time and pleasure.

According to Riesman's historical schema, the intellectual and the artist overcame the socially alienating separation of work and leisure of the inner-directed world and was able to revive the reconciliation of work and pleasure enjoyed by the craftsman of the traditional world. Adorno seemed to hail from a lost universe where inner direction and tradition kept in place both the separation and proper mixing of work and pleasure. The rigid distinction between pleasure and work-appropriate temporality struck Adorno as proscriptive and disciplinary. More often than not, daytime activities were characterized as necessary drudgery that Righter admonished readers to take care of as quickly as possible. The average worker not only experienced her interchangeability, she had to agree to the necessary suppression of "subjective urges" in white-collar work. This led Adorno to claim that the "columnist is very well aware of the drudgery of most subordinate functions in a hierarchical and bureaucratic setup." The column appeared to address the interests of the white-collar worker by encouraging the meticulous cultivation of an externally oriented image. "Self-promotion" and the manipulation of signs around the self were presumed to be the focus of a great deal of work itself. Nighttime was the time of leisure, but it was not imagined as a sphere of freedom: "It is one of the major tenets of the column, possibly the most important of all, that pleasure itself is permissible only if it serves ultimately some ulterior purpose of success and self-promotion."[93]

Although Righter's division of temporality into the "biphasic" spheres of work and leisure may at first glance appear to follow the Fordist template that required labor power's conversion into consumption power, there was already in the injunctions of the column a precise mixing of the two registers that would become another feature of the column's projected image of modern, idealized work conditions: "The semi-tolerant integration of pleasure into a rigid pattern of life is achieved by the ever-recurring promise that pleasure trips, sprees, parties, and similar events will lead to practical advantages."[94] In fact, mixing business and pleasure would emerge as the ideal form of leisure: for the most ambitious white-collar workers, concerns and interests of the daytime would cross into the land of the nighttime and dominate this world. Or at least nighttime pleasures and surprises could turn out very often to be magical rewards for daytime renunciations. In this way, the sphere of pleasure would take on the pressures of rationality and instrumentalization: the compulsion to consume radio and television seemed to Adorno, at least, to resemble the mobilization orders of constant social and professional networking. Righter's division of the day into two separate areas of activity—reason and pleasure, drudgery and freedom—tried to keep work and satisfaction apart. Daytime was the time to be "reasonable," while nighttime was the time to pursue the pleasure principle. The contradiction between reason and pleasure seemed to be resolved in the maintenance of an uneasy temporal divide between work and play: the reconciliation between the two spheres finally did take place as the subordination of the latter to the demands of the former.

In "The Image of the Addressee," Adorno speculated that the astrology column constructed an ostensible reader who was an ambitious young male protagonist. This young man was assumed to be a person of importance in a large organization: his rank is that of "vice president." He often had to make difficult and important decisions. If the column was in fact read by a middle-aged woman who, according to Adorno, lived in Los Angeles but could not afford a car and therefore did not participate in the automotive freedom of the 1950s freeway culture, she could still take delight in fantasizing about a life of significant eventfulness. She was reading over the shoulder, as it were, of the young executive, upon whose daily routine Righter lavished so much attention. As an escape from her own inconsequentiality, her reading of the column became a kind of mental transvestism, or cross-gender identification: she assumed the position of a dynamic and important young executive whose delicate relationships with his coworkers could often be marred by envy and jealousy while his relationships with "higher-ups" were mostly positive but demanded a great deal of care. Adorno used the term "penis-envy" to describe this particular sort of character. This rather bleak diagnosis should be contrasted with Adorno's criticism of Righter's flattery. "Follow up on that intuition of yours"; "display that keen mind of yours," Righter exhorts his reader. Powerlessness and its accompanying psychological vulnerabilities and proclivities gave shape to the superstitious personality, susceptible to this form of half-believed praise.[95] Adorno focuses particularly on the use of the article "that" in "*that* keen mind of yours," since it seemed to refer to specific knowledge that Righter possessed about the reader's secret qualities.

The keen-minded male protagonist was always facing decisive moments that loomed large on the horizon: these mysterious threats could be averted with the help of astrological advice in a series of parrying actions and self-adjustments. According to Adorno, the middle-aged woman was oppressed, and the identification with the column's projected subject prevented her from thinking about female emancipation: he theorized that her position could contribute to promoting a mass-produced response to penis envy and as a result promoted a rigidly normative sense of femininity.

The reader of Righter's column was imagined to be in a malleable relationship with powerful, if benign, higher-ups and sometimes helpful, sometimes envious friends or peers. The ethical assumptions behind the construction of the category "friend" revealed the column's entire philosophy of success-oriented social relationality. Adorno writes, "One has the feeling that the friend-foe dichotomy . . . has been subjected to some special censorship and that only friends have been allowed to survive."[96] If the enemy is suppressed, friends themselves acquire rather diluted and diffuse qualities: "A good friend bestows unique benefit" (November 10, 1952, Virgo). In fact, one of the things that Adorno found particularly galling was that Righter's "friends" were difficult to differentiate from mere acquaintances. "Friends" appeared almost exclusively as messengers of fate, bearing gifts and offering business "advice" or important connections: "Enjoying congenial amusement with serious comrade clears path for successful association."[97] Friends are instruments by which fate transmits to us its special gifts. The instrumentalization of human bonds and attachments gave license to the reader to devalue the question of her specific obligation to others. The reader's only responsibility was to deft self-preservation; her credo was therefore one of agile opportunism coupled with economic individualism. In this temporal logic, a new friend was always superior to an old friend, since he or she provided a new array of associations and connections. In the world of entrepreneurial individualism, the stranger as new friend represented new prospects, while the old friend was often the site of psychic conflict and resentment.

The gloss on friends that Adorno derived from advice to Virgos on November 10, 1952, should be contrasted with the news environment of that particular day. If Virgos had something particular to look forward to from "a good friend" on that day, the American intellectual class was reeling from Eisenhower's victory over Adlai Stevenson in that year's presidential elections. Eisenhower represented a proper, vigilant relationship to the Cold War enemy. As we saw earlier, Hofstadter argued that Stevenson's wit, eloquence, intelligence, and thought-fulness made him more popular with the general electorate at the same time that his intellectual orientation inspired sectarian doubt about his ability to govern the country in a time of war. Another world-consuming war was making itself felt as an imminent reality, but the column's suppression of the enemy in favor of the friend allowed Righter to eliminate and censor consideration of the political field itself. On November 10, 1952, the *Los Angeles Times* contained a full array of articles describing the threats posed by the Communist enemy. Articles dealt with the situations in not only the Soviet Union but also "Red" China, North Korea, and Czechoslovakia. In the article "An Escapee Warns of Red Men-ace," an unnamed Czech exile in Los Angeles wrote, "While your people watch the sky for an atom bomb, the Communists are working behind the scenes like a cancer in your government." Most notably, the anonymous escapee warned that the infiltration would take place through a network of Communist teach-ers and cadres who operated in the school system and labor unions. The escap-ee predicted that Communists, left unchecked, would engage the United States in a terrible war and then march in and enslave the country, just as they did to his or her homeland.[98] Adorno wrote:

> At times the ungrumbling attitude towards superiors takes the paradoxical aspect of bribery, but on November 10, 1952, almost all the star signs have to deal with unpleas-ant emotions and reactions to work situations, especially in relationship to the pow-erful. For Aries, "Urge to tell off official would alienate helpful partner, so keep calm despite irritation; later material benefits following making more co-operative deal at home." For Cancers, "Sulking over disappointing act of influential executive merely puts you in deeper disfavor; P.M. finds you can replace by adopting unthought, un-tried new plan. Be open-minded." For Capricorns, "You really want to tell off, force issue with one able to take away your present prestige, instead discuss with unusual associate the best way to placate."[99]

The weaker must placate the stronger: the subordinate has to amuse, entertain, and woo his superiors. Even though Righter acknowledged that the reader was plagued with negative feelings about his bosses, he was also urged "to take him out and to indulge in similar ventures in order to, as it is put euphemistically, achieve a satisfactory human relationship. . . . It is as though the notion of neo-feudalism which lurks in the back of the columnist's mind would carry with it-self the association of the serf paying tribute to the master."[100]

Ruthlessly pragmatic strategies for placating the powerful were masked as advice for cultivating effervescent sociability. Socializing with higher-ups allowed for both parties to participate in a fantasy of equality. Befriending someone was equivalent to impressing them; socializing became an arena of competition and display. In the 1952–53 astrology column, the coercive and threatening aspect of the friend/enemy dichotomy was evoked in the fantasy that, with the right moves, readers could force potential enemies to enlist as "friends." The most objectified relationships are personalized along the lines of a dangerous infantilism. Because the category of friend had been emptied of ethical, psychic, or emotional substance, friends themselves could be easily reshaped into different versions of higher-ups. The horoscopic friend was often the purveyor of "advice" and "help," but the altruism of this friend should be contrasted with the selfishness of the reader, who was never urged to spend energy or time without promise of a return. The various oppositions betrayed an overvaluation of the power of the "friend" as selfless benefactor who presumably had no thought but to help "the underling" as reader. The friend had become instrumental but was also strangely formless and fungible. Solidarity could not exist in this world except with the powerful. This was, after all, the great lesson of *The Authoritarian Personality*. All alliances and relationships gave off the whiff of either seduction or coercion. Adorno pointed out that the column tried to allay the anxieties and fears that such passivity and extreme dependency on the magical bounty of strangers might provoke: the narcissistic loss of autonomy was compensated for by an attitude of childish expectancy. The encouragement of an attitude of childlike passivity led both Adorno and Hofstadter to identify the readers of horoscopes and inspirational literature as predominantly feminine. The uncanny attitude of withdrawal from reality and the fusion of wish and reality were veils thrown over the anxiety and insecurity engendered by this extreme state of dependency.

Adorno did not quote the full forecast for Virgos on November 10, 1952: "Inability to solve annoyance quickly brings A.M. mental disturbance unless you realize time not yet ripe for completing. In P.M. a good friend extends unique benefit." Horkheimer, as a "good friend" and senior scholar, had intervened already on any number of occasions on Adorno's behalf during his early career. Righter's prediction, no matter how banal, must have struck Adorno as uncanny. Horkheimer had returned to Frankfurt with a solid job offer from the University of Frankfurt and the promise of a permanent home in the Institute for Social Research. Adorno was waiting for news of his appointment. In fact, he was hoping precisely for "a good friend" to extend the unique benefit of a job offer, this time more secure than anything he could have imagined possible in the history of his affiliation with the Institute for Social Research. Of course, Adorno and Horkheimer's friendship is legendary: the richness of their collaboration and the affection between the two men are well documented and preserved in their correspondence and in historical testimony about their comportment with each other. Their bond should stand in stark contrast to the shadowy associations and tepid relationships of Righter's horoscope. And yet it is certainly not an exaggeration to note that Adorno, from the very early days in his academic career, benefited from the patronage and mentorship of his more powerful and established friend. Adorno was content to remain Horkheimer's "deputy," and Horkheimer was willing to bestow and withhold professional and financial support and favors. In the winter of 1952–53, Adorno was waiting for his promotion to "regular extraordinary professor" in Frankfurt. Horkheimer had already been elected dean of the Faculty of Philosophy of Frankfurt University. He had secured funding for the reestablishment and reconstruction of the institute from both the U.S. high commissioner, John McCloy, and the city of Frankfurt.[101]

These kinds of relationships of mutual obligation are not uncommon in German academia: a powerful professor is expected to protect a circle of students and researchers with funding schemes, while junior or assistant professors are often committed to working on a research project designated by their superiors. These sticky relationships are personal and intellectual and would appear to the modern American academic as somewhat feudal and nepotistic. We are used to a much more rationalized and depersonalized process of selection in the distribution of jobs and benefits. In Lorenz Jäger's biography of Adorno, eyewitness accounts of the behavior of the older Horkheimer and Adorno toward each other gave the outlines of a cartoon of two foolish old men in a mutual admiration club that blinded them to the value of the work and the aspirations of their younger associates. Horkheimer and Adorno's deep intellectual bond lasted a lifetime for both men and was characteristic of the old middle class's valuation of friendship as a lifetime bond of passionate collaboration. For Adorno, an old friend like Horkheimer was infinitely better than any new acquaintance or stranger.

Finally, what is striking about Adorno's essay's musings about the *Los Angeles Times* astrology column and the curious cult of American practicality is his intensive close textual engagement with Righter's writing, which is particularly devoid of poetry or aesthetic value. Indeed, Adorno's analysis was thoroughly formal and theoretical. Sociologist of religion Paul Apostolidis understood this aspect of Adorno's aesthetic theory as fundamentally connected to reification and popular culture artifacts.[102] The symptom and the product of the culture industry contained within them the complexity of the artwork, albeit in a congealed and rigid form. Adorno's analysis made sense of the utopian aspirations of the commodity in its negative relationship to the artwork. The defects of the commodity, however, were not the defects of the artwork: Righter's horoscope envisioned a false reconciliation between subject and object wherein the individual was consigned to constant self-adjustment. However, as mentioned above, Adorno took Righter's column out of context: Adorno's qualitative analysis refers to nothing about the situation of its publication. On November 10, 1952, in addition to analysis of Eisenhower's victory and articles on the Communist threat, the *Los Angeles Times* contained a series of curious items on scientific reportage on educational theory and the benefits of expanding one's vocabulary, including one article, "Tension of Average Youngster Observed," in which child behavior experts described their allegedly scientific and objective observations of average children six to nine years of age. At six the average child displays an "overflow of tension at the mouth" that manifests itself as "tongue extension and mouthing, clicking, blowing through lips, biting lips. Throat clearing and throaty noises." Children this age were little in control of their appendages and orifices. Like Communists, children seemed utterly alien beings. Children, however, were redeemable through the efforts of behaviorism and discipline.

Far from being a "dope," the subject of popular astrology as the reader of the *Los Angeles Times* was a discontented product of mass education. She was not happy with her position in life. She was suspicious of academic authority figures. She may have wanted to criticize the irrationality of modern society, but it seemed a more acceptable path to attribute some organizational intention to higher powers. Her intelligence had of course been measured, and she had been tested, selected as average, and taught to adjust to the realities and limitations of her situation. There were, in fact, concrete reasons for the lacunae in her education: the domination of life-adjustment had provided students and citizens with minimal cultural literacy and neglected any serious training in critical thinking.[103] The life-adjustment curriculum prepared students for adaptation to a life of limited horizons. It taught them how to take advice but also to resent teachers, who, it seemed, exerted their authority by purposefully teaching things students could learn more efficiently "outside" of school. At the same time, the suspicion that more interesting materials were being withheld from the mass of "average" students and taught to an elite group was not unjustified. The privilege of high-scoring students was justified by the tests that had proven them to be "college material." Teachers had little status in American society to begin with, but when schooling became geared primarily toward future work, teachers seemed even more superfluous and suspicious since they appeared as relatively powerless stand-ins for future "bosses" or higher-ups. High schools became the breeding grounds of resentment and holding tanks for social triage. Education was despised by the authoritarian personality, but his or her hatred of the educator was part of the aggression against those who are, like the subject, powerless and victims of the betrayal of critical thinking in mass education. When citizens of industrialized democracies gained a certain amount of cultural and political literacy, they grasped that the "opaqueness and inscrutability" of contemporary society lay beyond any single person's total control. The temptation of popular astrology was that it seemed to confer a "higher degree of dignity" to the individual trying to understand her place in an increasingly administered world.[104] Astrology, like other "irrational creeds" such as racism and anti-Semitism, seduced us with a "shortcut" to being "in the know." Identification with a powerful authority, one whose (occult, divine, or military) authority could squash the contemptible learning of the impotent intellectual and destroy the fruits of educational privilege, became an accepted outlet for otherwise legitimate political resentments.

Freud's later essays on religion and civilization were concerned precisely with the mutilation and usurpation of the universal capacity for critical thinking by its uncanny doppelgänger, rationalization. Moderate belief, although it appeared perfectly compatible with reason, blocked critical thinking just as much as any form of fundamentalism. According to Freud, if we were not possessed of a universal capacity for reason, we would not have such massive, civilizational discontent. Discontent is a positive sign of potential emancipation. Adorno's critical analysis of newspaper astrological columns was neither exceptional nor eccentric to his project of articulating both the methods and the stakes of critical theory as the radicalization of the emancipatory potential of a damaged Enlightenment. Adorno's critical theory, in fact, extended Freud's critique of religion in the name of giving shape and form to a negative concept of everyday life.

For Adorno, the daily horoscope demanded a special form of pseudobelief the psychology of which promoted a fantasy of pleasurable submission to distant and all-powerful forces: what was repressed or excluded from this fantasy was the danger that such a relationship posed to the more vulnerable party. Adorno inherited the odd couple—authoritarianism and superstition—from the work done on *The Authoritarian Personality*. Assuming a passive and unquestioning position with regard to authority is rewarded by the promise of incalculable returns. The project had attempted to identify the "potentially fascistic individual" and discovered that both a proclivity to be superstitious and an "irrational" attitude toward the opposite sex were two of the strongest indicators for high scores on the "F" scale. The question of reason and its defense had social and political consequences, still fresh in the minds of researchers who had seen the world sundered in the devastating world war whose ashes still smoldered.

As we saw, "tests" were essential to the administered life: the test both justified and facilitated social triage. "Testing" for the capacity for reason could lead to the normalization of a dichotomy between the "irrational" fascist-leaning personality and the "rational" liberal. It could become yet another hierarchizing form of measurement. The capacity for reason may depend on the formation of personality structures, but Adorno never failed to emphasize that these structures of subjectivity were actually symptomatic expressions of objective social processes of domination and irrationality. In *The Dialectic of Enlightenment*, anti-Semitism was identified as a uniquely modern and European form of irrationality. The flawed project has been much criticized from many different points of view, but Paul Apostolidis's extraordinary study of James Dobson and the right-wing Christian organization Focus on the Family was able to use Adorno's theories in order to produce a fine analysis of evangelical grassroots movements.[105] Apostolidis would find that psychoanalytic theory had a way of pointing beyond the critical impasses reached in Frankfurt School critique. For instance, he found Adorno's description of the authoritarian personality much too "pat." Adorno followed the findings of a controversial study on the authoritarian personality sponsored by the American Jewish Council, first published in 1950. The study concluded that average people found the contemporary political and economic situations completely opaque: frustration caused them to regress to an allegedly infantile position before the status quo.[106] For Apostolidis, Dobson was able to fuse in his public persona a sense of deeply personalized care with spiritual redemption, in critical opposition to the images of the uncaring welfare state bureaucrat and doctor.

Adorno's critique of the "average" person as a degraded character, with all his or her retrogressive tendencies, was certainly deeply disturbing. But his critique contained a deep sense of theoretical, affective, and empirical identification with powerlessness. Adorno addressed the "uninformed" and the "confused," emphasizing their "rationalizations" and their inability to "overcome irrational mechanisms." Here the average person was reconstituted as a thwarted Everyman with whom criticism must build some kind of solidarity. The demand for coherence and transparency was shared by all political subjects, critics and average people alike. Its assumed universality provided the common ground that Adorno must share with his "average person." It was with him or her that he must forge a mimetic and "fraternal" relationship based upon reconciliation with the powerless that the authoritarian personality all too desperately rejected. Psychoanalysis always took discontentment seriously both objectively and subjectively; the authoritarian personality was not just the object of critique, he or she was also the subject of a universal experience. Adorno's brutal description of the average person should be contrasted with the idealization of "the people" that was constructed to fit the requirements of the political parties making a play, as Stuart Hall described it, for an "authoritarian populism."[107] In Hall's description of right-wing populism, the radical Right sought to reach the people and their affective discontents beyond and above political parties, processes, and reason by addressing the common experience of living with the contradictions of social democracy. Stuart Hall and Paul Apostolidis proposed provocatively that authoritarian populism and evangelical Christianity addressed profound problems experienced by the average person under social democracy and the welfare state.

If, as the Puritans believed, assiduous service to our earthly enterprises was service to the Deity and success in those enterprises a sign of his grace, then success in business or "grace" was available to everyone regardless of intellect, family background, or level of education. In fact, as the nineteenth century progressed, the value of success in business, which had once been considered a sign of one's exemplary fulfillment of godly duties, became more and more a value in and for itself. Hence, what did not serve those values could be safely held in contempt—"the school of hard knocks" became the only legitimate education, and "book learning" was the quicksand trap in which those little inclined for business found themselves foundering. Ironically, one could point to the book as the most important medium of transmission for the self-helpers, but self-help literature often presented itself as offering a kind of knowledge "not found in books," inaccessible to experts, and despised by the literature or psychology professor precisely because it dispensed with specialized knowledge. This genre continued the work of the Protestant Reformation, but the authority it sought to depose no longer emanated from the priest but was the purview of the hated specialist who wanted to monopolize a kind of knowledge not available to all.

Self-help literature also played a critical role in shaping popular American attitudes toward liberal education: it suggested that the only order of knowledge worth cultivating was practical knowledge and that the "character" necessary to succeeding in business was inimical to school learning. Like eighteenth-century religious pamphlets, each self-help book opened up to each reader the potential of a life-changing experience of conversion. As each manual for self-improvement indulged readers' skepticism about experts, it proposed to offer a "secret" way of becoming expert at outwitting the odds and succeeding where others failed.

The critique of irrationality could all too easily become an imperious and imperial project, but the attempt to identify with the travails and failings of the average person could be transformed into a fetishization of antielitism. The unbearable complexity and ambiguity of the present situation appeared to everyone, including cultural critics, as a demand for interpretation and analysis. Truncated forms of thought, however, were deeply tied to the enjoyment of powerlessness before the status quo. The ideology of life-adjustment depended upon the censorship of critique. What critical theory demanded was an effort to think through the "opacity of the present," for it often failed to account for the contingency and inventiveness of the culture industry it sought to denounce. It is difficult to deny, however, that mass-produced shortcuts to a total world picture were both repressive and sterile. The authoritarian personality and the reader of newspaper horoscopes were both symptomatic products of the culture industry at midcentury. These "characters" were not empirical or phenomenological, nor were they simply structuralist or semiotic projections of the texts that addressed them. The authoritarian personality, like the reader of newspaper horoscopes, rebelled against the system of state-sponsored triage that had identified him or her as "average": the mystical shortcut to a theory of the world that defied scientific and institutional explanations was his or her reward for the renunciation of reason itself.

David Riesman, C. Wright Mills, Theodor Adorno, and Richard Hofstadter looked upon the American entrepreneur/craftsman with different degrees of nostalgia. In Philip Roth's *American Pastoral*, Lou and Seymour Levov are fictionalized versions of this mythical American character. Lou Levov worked his way up from the putrid Newark tanneries of the early twentieth century to become owner of Newark Maid, a glove-making company that would fund his son Seymour's American pastoral. Lou began working with skins and hides in conditions where workers were "driven like animals through the laborious storm that was a twelve-hour shift—a filthy stinking place awash with water dyed red and black and blue and green with hunks of skin all over the floor, everywhere pits of grease, hills of salt, barrels of solvent—this was Lou Levov's high school and college."[108] Lou gets his degree in every single stage of glove making, from the skinning of animals to the tanning of hides. In fact, Lou never quite leaves the cloacal cave that is his pitiless schoolroom. The rage and energy that propel him forward are fed by his having been reduced to little more than a beast during his youth in the Newark tanneries. By his twenties he has founded Newark Maid, a small glove-making company that is catapulted into prosperity in 1942 when he receives a commission from the military corps for women's uniform dress gloves.

Lou's son, Seymour, known as "the Swede," sacrifices himself at the altar of his father's love of this family business but in doing so becomes a millionaire in love with America and its promise of physical ease and beauty, which is consummated in the Swede's own Apollonian grace. The Swede is a natural athlete and legendary figure in the narrator, Nathan Zuckerman's high school.[109] For a Jewish community that worships educational achievement and abhors the abuse of physical strength and violence, the Swede was a natural aristocrat but also an aberration. He is blessed with an almost pagan gift of athletic prowess and Nordic good looks: he accepts his community's idolatry with a kind of quiet stoicism. At the end of World War II, Seymour Levov is the living incarnation of American valor for Weequahic High School. He represents for that immigrant community "the emboldened valor that would prevail to return our high school's servicemen home unscathed from Midway, Salerno, Cherbourg, the Solomons, the Aleutians, Tarawa."[110] In the end, he sacrifices a career in professional sports in order to join Newark Maid and learn every aspect of the craft and business of glove making. He inherits the business from his father, and he presides over its expansion after the war. While Lou seems never to have completely left the stink and filth of his alma mater, Seymour serves the business with aplomb and love. He has even bought a farm in rural New Jersey. He works hard, but he and his former-beauty-queen wife aspire to the pleasures of the gentleman farmer. Dawn is the daughter of Irish immigrants, afflicted with all the working-class immigrant resentments of her hometown of Elizabeth. When she decides to use her husband's money to start raising beef cattle, Levov's American dream is ironically consummated. The two urban, ethnic Americans have achieved the flinty independence of pioneer woman and Early Republic gentleman farmer. The Newark Maid millions will now support a new generation of Americans whose cramped, urban, immigrant childhoods will be redeemed in the vigorous physical labor of the Jeffersonian enterprise.

Seymour Levov's business success allows him to re-create the Jeffersonian American pastoral in rural New Jersey, located within commuting distance of the Newark factories.

Seymour and Dawn's daughter, Meredith or Merry Levov, is supposed to inherit not only the farm and her parents' dreams but the entrepreneurial, democratic ethos upon which Seymour's dream house is built. The love of this country that nourished and elevated her father from the floor of the tannery to the stone farmhouse with a tree swing outside is measured in Seymour's simple-minded capitulation to family, to tradition, to service, to loyalty, and to prosperity. Late in his own life, after facing down his own physical limitations, Nathan Zuckerman confronts the mystery of Seymour Levov and in the process reveals the unraveling of this handsome, successful, and hyperbolically ordinary Jewish American man at the hands of his demonically vengeful daughter, Merry. Merry is Roth's monstrous child of the 1960s. Zuckerman, with his artful literary mind, fills in for the culture and ease from struggle that Levov aspires to. Zuckerman as artist and Levov as craftsman/entrepreneur are the two sides of the mercantile, essentially liberal mind. The achievements of the nineteenth-century autonomous individual as Hofstadter's mercantile capitalist allowed him to exercise a maximum amount of sovereignty and freedom with regard to his leisure time—all in the name of non-business-related pursuits. Education and sensibility were the qualities that he could allegedly provide for his immediate family. They were carefully sequestered from ugly competitiveness and brutal exploitation of the working world: the domestic world was supposed to be the enchanted site of genteel cultural cultivation and consumption. The successful businessman was sophisticated and proudly advertised his cosmopolitanism and culture as badges of his financial success.

Seymour Levov is resolutely apolitical, naively trusting in the consumerist hedonism that allows him to provide for his family in the highest form of class ascension. From working-class Jewish Newark he ascends to WASP rural farm country, where he can become a gentleman farmer surrounded by bucolic luxury. In this world, he and his wife raise their only child, a stuttering and awkward girl who becomes a demon seed, a young woman whose hatred of everything ordinary, everything American, in the name of an impossible politics distilled for Roth the essence of the counterculture. Merry is animated by a world-destroying hatred of bourgeois humanism and the liberal institutions it built. In America's democratic ambitions, she can only see hypocrisy, abuse, patriarchy, imperialism, the war in Vietnam, and racial violence. In such an ugly country, everyday life must be purged of aspirations to the ordinary happiness and comforts in the name of ideological purity and radicalism. Before she has even graduated high school Merry goes underground after she bombs the gas station and post office in Old Rimrock and inadvertently kills the village doctor. She has thus succeeded in bringing a piece of the violence of the Vietnam War into the center of her father's American pastoral. Roth imagines her underground as a particularly repellent place: she has returned to the dark, putrid, death-filled space that her grandfather Lou worked in. But her squalor is completely nonproductive and sterile. There is no craft to learn, no productive labor to perform, no association with others, no collective enterprise, no future that would be secured by her labors. She is in the black hole of interiority, of self-aggrandizing debasement.

This demonically angry young woman embodies the countercultural hatred of her father's America: her whole life has become a refutation of her father's values. The Swede's great physical strength has not been able to protect her from being sexually abused during her fugitive existence, but his principled liberalism prevents him from violently extracting her from the excremental squalor that she has chosen. Completely on her own, she has embraced her own radical version of the Indian religion of Jainism and adopts a regime of radical nonviolence taken to an extreme. She wears a stocking over her face so that her breath does no harm to the microorganisms in the air. She will not bathe because this does harm to the creatures in the water. She will soon no longer eat even vegetables because that does harm to plant life. Her teeth are rotting, her body is emaciated and debased. She makes a mockery of nonviolence, since she embarks upon a mystical path without communion or community with her fellow human beings. From Roth's point of view, this regressive, perverse mysticism and Orientalism abuses religion and ritual by making of it a radically personal, noncommunicative set of self-purgative practices. Merry picks up what she knows of Jainism from reading in public libraries. Hers is a bookish radicalism that strains for a metaphysical purity. She is a living affront to the casual physical well-being of her handsome father. Her extreme self-deprivation married to a lust for self-abasement pulls her father into an underworld that utterly destroys him. Merry adds an absurdly hateful footnote to the ravages of race, war, and globalization that have consumed Newark and the life and work of generations of Levovs. The destruction of Newark as a city in the riots of 1967 and the deindustrialization of its vibrant core are directly linked to the masochistic, perverse, self-destructive, and exultant daughter.

Roth imagines Levov's biblical suffering as emanating from the senseless evil of radical politics. Roth's own reaction against the 1960s is staged as a denunciation of youth culture's disdain for craft and industry. His detailed and loving description of the craft of glove making, the source of Levov's wealth and immigrant stability, immerses the reader in one of the most vital American myths. The American entrepreneur was once also the American craftsman. Glove making is a craft and process that a generation of Levov's employees— Italian, Jewish, and African American—preserved and revered as much as he and his father did. In Levov's deep and sensual knowledge of the craft of glove making, he is one with his business and his workers. He is not an exploiter or a boss. He is as familiar with the demands of this labor as his most subaltern employee. The smells of glove making and its sensuous tactility are described in laborious detail: from the cutting of the finest leather to the expert sewing of each finger, a sense of solidarity with craft, material, worker, and wearer is forged forever. In Roth's mind, after the racial tensions sparked by the Newark riots, Levov's workers hold him and their craft in contempt, soldiering at work, refusing to produce the quality product and participate in the economic activity that once gave meaning to the Levovs and their lives. This, in turn, paves the way for the outsourcing of glove making first to Ponce in Puerto Rico and then to the distant sweatshops of Asia. The liberated informality of post-1960s life makes glove wearing itself a sign of a bygone era. The demand for immediacy and satisfaction is cast by Roth as a critical part of the cultish radicalism of the antiliberal mind.

Roth's version of Jainism and Merry's embrace of its worship of animal life represent the utter demolition of liberal humanism and its values. The bestial existence of poverty and back-breaking labor that Lou Levov tried to keep at bay through industry and craft has returned full force upon the American pastoral as the revenge of the daughter against the father.

Hofstadter opened *The Paranoid Style in American Politics* with the following assertion about the nature of political conflict in the United States: "Although American political life has rarely been touched by the most acute varieties of class conflict, it has served again and again as an arena for uncommonly angry minds."[111] He was talking about the Right. What Philip Roth memorialized in his version of 1960s counterculture captured something of the uncommon anger against American civilization, its institutions and way of "life as learning" embodied by the uncommonly angry Merry Levov. The uncompromising extremism of Merry's political logic has lived on in the hothouse atmosphere of campus radicalism. The angry minds of the Right, however, forged the weapons of its renewed war on Johnson's Great Society and Roosevelt's New Deal, fueled by a sense of disgust at the counterculture and its grandiosity. The bitterness of the Right fed into a radical reconfiguration of conservative politics: the Goldwater campaign secured victories on a party and national level that were not limited to the presidencies of Richard Nixon and Ronald Reagan. Hofstadter studied fringe and radical groups of right-wing, conspiracy-minded extremists; when they were wedded to religious fundamentalism, the views they espoused began to move into the mainstream. But there was also a left-wing revolt against experts that makes it very difficult for us to attribute a simple anti-intellectualism to the American Right. In Roth's novel, the Vietnam War has made Merry unable to see anything of value in the hard-won Jewish immigrant version of the American pastoral. In this passage, her radicalism is expressed in a particularly condensed manner: "Well sometimes you have to fucking go to the extreme. What do you think war is? War is an extreme. It isn't life out here in little Rimrock. . . . I don't know if I'm going to go to college. Look at the administration of those colleges. Look what they do to their students who are against the war. How can I want to be going to college? Higher education. It's what I call lower education."[112]

chapter four

against all experts

In April 1969 a group of young women, leaders of the Women's Council of the Sozialistischer deutscher Studentenbund (SDS), or German Socialist Students Party, entered Theodor Adorno's lecture hall in Frankfurt, where he was giving a lecture called "Introduction to Dialectical Thinking."[1] They surrounded Professor Adorno and threw flowers at him while performing a "pantomime" that culminated in the baring of their breasts. Flowers and breasts were cast in the face of a professor attached to the dialectic, and the display of beauty and eros was designed to stop both dead in their tracks. The public exposure of the breast was a gesture that contained both a promise of pleasure and a threat of punishment or humiliation. Before the demonstrations, the women had distributed leaflets printed with the words "Adorno as an Institution is Dead."[2] Three months later, in July of that same year, Adorno as a man was indeed dead: the young women's prophecy or wish seemed to have been miraculously fulfilled. Adorno's response to the German student movement has thus acquired many of the qualities of a mythical and fatal confrontation. Detlev Claussen writes, "To this day it is widely rumored that Adorno was destroyed by the conflict with his students."[3]

Adorno's sudden and fatal heart attack has been attributed to the shock he received in his classroom that fateful spring day: the rising tensions between students and faculty in Frankfurt had become quite intense. Adorno had been at the forefront of a number of confrontations among administration, faculty, and students. The Women's Council wanted to confront the professor and authority that he represented with a performative and political problem. They did it in a playful but aggressively personal manner. Flower power versus professor power: here was a disarmingly graphic face-off with patriarchal and institutional authority. Why was Adorno its target? Because, as many of his biographers have noted, even though he was the official and unofficial inspiration for the antiauthoritarian leaders of many radical student groups, he refused to endorse without reservation any of their actions. His work represented a compelling, unorthodox, and antiauthoritarian critique of domination, and yet, as a person, he came to embody many of the insular and patriarchal qualities of the German academic. In that moment of performative confrontation, the Women's Council successfully cast Adorno as the representative of technocratic and patriarchal authoritarianism. For decades afterward, his thought and his reputation would be associated with professorial arrogance and cultural elitism.

Adorno's relationship to the student radicals was more complicated than the myth of his cryptoauthoritarianism could ever account for. Hans-Jürgen Krahl, the charismatic leader of the Frankfurt SDS, was his advisee, as was Hans Immhof, provocateur and action artist. Until the end of his life, Adorno had always been connected to the most radical factions through Krahl, who was, according to Claussen's account, the "outstanding representative" of Frankfurt's SDS. Herbert Marcuse's return to Germany from California in 1967 opened the possibility of a solid alliance between critical theory and student radicalism. Marcuse's lectures about total revolution and Third World solidarity won the sympathies of radical student groups. Following Marcuse's logic, Krahl urged SDS to pursue a line of escalation. Yet Adorno remained critical of and distant from direct action activism. He guarded his intellectual autonomy jealously and, unlike Marcuse, refused to give students anything that resembled positive reinforcement or direct encouragement. It was, of course, no small irony that pirated copies of Adorno and Horkheimer's *Dialectic of Enlightenment* had been an inspiration to the campus insurgencies across Europe. But Horkheimer had opposed its republication in part because he had no sympathy for the radicals' short historical memory, so *The Dialectic of Enlightenment* circulated in student milieus in the form of pirated copies published in Amsterdam. Horkheimer was skeptical of the students' virulent anti-Americanism. Their reaction against American imperialism struck him as containing a latent anti-Semitism or, as Russell Berman called it, a "Left Fascism."[4] Habermas identified in the student movement an ardent desire for an absolute moralization of political conflict. Finally, it was Horkheimer who horrified the German Left by denouncing its anti-Americanism at a lecture at the Amerika Haus. To his audience he was endorsing the war in Vietnam and the policies of Lyndon Johnson.

In a 1959 public lecture entitled "The Meaning of Working Through the Past," Adorno had publicly stated that there was something unbearable about the West German status quo. He was sympathetic to the younger generation's sense that things could not go on as before—that the dark German past had to be unearthed and worked through. Public silence and collective guilt about the Nazi past were wearing thin in the DDR. Adorno's lecture had been published in 1959 in the major media and was broadcast on the radio: "I once wrote in a scholarly dispute: in the house of the hangman one should not speak of the noose, otherwise one might seem to harbor resentment. . . . One wants to break free of the past: rightly, because nothing at all can live in its shadow, and because there will be no end to the terror as long as guilt and violence are repaid with guilt and violence; wrongly because the past that one would like to evade is still very much alive."[5] In 1959 and 1960 Adorno had anticipated the aggressive questions that the postwar generation of young Germans would start asking about their parents' lives before and during the war years: a collective working through of the past was both politically and personally necessary in order to produce what Adorno believed would be a truly democratic society. "Enlightenment about what has happened must work against a forgetfulness": civic and public education about National Socialism and the extermination of Jews and other minorities, even if imperfect, had to address the past in all of its ignominy.[6] Adorno recognized and confronted the lingering sense of German resentment against reeducation. The threat of fascism could not be dispelled as long as objective conditions that allowed for its popular appeal persisted. For Adorno, persist they did. Modern "economic organization . . . now as then renders the majority of people dependent upon conditions beyond their control." Given an experience of objective powerlessness that was accompanied by an imperative to adapt to the status quo, a popular sense of rage against and resentment of democracy would continue to simmer.[7] A decade later, the rising sense of discontent would explode among German youth who demanded a clear reckoning with history.

Despite the German SDS's confrontations with Adorno and Horkheimer throughout 1967 over the question of the Vietnam War and the American military presence in West Germany, both professors felt it was important that the "contact was not broken off. In particular, the spokespeople of the antiauthoritarian faction of the SDS thought of themselves as pupils of Adorno."[8] The Women's Council's actions followed Immhof's earlier disruption of one of Adorno's lectures in the spring of 1969, when Immhof and Arno Widmann (now editor in chief of the *Berliner Zeitung*) interrupted Adorno's lecture to discuss the right of order.[9] The women's action had, of course, a particularly sharp edge: marginalized by the male-dominated student movement, which still depended upon women to perform the household duties and childcare, feminism as a social movement had a difficult time gaining traction in West Germany. Lorenz Jäger described the women's actions as "tasteless," but a direct assault on taste was perhaps the very point. Jäger placed this "direct action" in relation to the early and mid-1960s convergence of theory and practice, students and artists, Marxism and the avant-garde, intellectual life and youth culture. Such a convergence precipitated the great confrontations with power that were taking place in universities all over the industrialized world during the late 1960s. In the shadow of the Cold War front, the specific forms of self-censorship and inhibition under which Germans lived had produced a certain political evasiveness on the part of all intellectuals. Adorno felt his obsession with completing *Aesthetic Theory* to be a symptom of this innervating depoliticization. During the 1960s, the German situation had other particularities: despite radicalization and ceaseless mobilization, the students had failed to produce significant reforms in German universities or win significant support from outside the university, much less inspire a revolution that would overturn the social democratic complacency of West Germany. The situation abroad in France and the United States, in Beijing and Mexico City, seemed to indicate that something monumental was happening and that German students, even on the front lines of the Cold War, with the ever-present threat of Communism and the East, had to rise to the occasion.

Conceptually, the baring of breasts and the throwing of flowers could be traced as gestural inheritors of the power of Dadaist and Surrealist performances. In the late 1960s this sensibility was married to the budding counterculture's sense of youthful rebellion and confrontation. The Women's Council obviously took advantage of the destruction of shame in its performative intervention. To act without shame was to be like a child: this return to childishness and its values was pivotal to Walter Benjamin's ideas about critical thinking. The Women's Council of the SDS could be understood as referring to something that exceeded the limits of the lecture hall: their refusal of language and Adorno's consternation brought them closer together, and a hoped-for confrontation was precipitated in the name of the power of silence and the intensity of remembering. If art and life were to be fused by the avant-garde into the political economy of performance, the Women's Council did indeed produce a puzzling silent spectacle of flowers and breasts meant to unsettle and disarm the authority of the eloquent philosopher/professor.

On June 2, 1967, German students had participated en masse in street demonstrations against the presence of the shah of Iran. The shah was on a state visit to Berlin and had been attending a performance of Mozart's *Magic Flute* at the Deutsche Oper. He was seen by the Left as an autocratic puppet-ruler installed by the United States after the CIA-sponsored coup against Iran's democratically elected prime minister, Mohammed Mossadeq. As students in the Western world increasingly understood their struggle in terms of the Third World's anti-imperialism, they were repulsed by the tactics of the British and American secret service in disrupting popular democratic movements during the Cold War standoff with Communism. The shah's human rights record was appalling: he was seen as acting in complicity with the worst forms of Western imperialism. Students and protestors gathered outside the Opera House. As the demonstrations were breaking up, Benno Ohnesorg, a twenty-six-year-old student protestor, was shot and killed on a side street by a plainclothes policeman, Karl-Heinz Kurras. Later, Kurras was acquitted of all wrongdoing in the affair. Ohnesorg's death has been understood as a critical moment in the radicalization of the German student movement. For many, the murder of the unarmed young man revealed that the orderly, social democratic West Germany concealed an ugly underbelly of police violence and repressive authoritarianism. The significance of Ohnesorg's murder has to be reappraised, since in May 2009 researchers discovered in the Stasi archives records confirming that Karl-Heinz Kurras was a member of the East German secret police, the Stasi, as well as a member of the East German Communist Party.[10] Although there is no archival evidence that Stasi or the East German Communist Party gave Kurras direct orders to kill protestors as an agent provocateur, it is no secret that the GDR and the Soviet Union hoped for nothing less than the destabilization of the West German political order. Ohnesorg's murder radicalized university students and faculty members and polarized German public opinion. Reflecting upon that heated moment in history, Mike Ely, American leftist blogger, likened it to the events at Kent State: it "divided the country between those orderly Germans who thought the society should crack down, and those rising in just rebellion. And it helped harden emerging radical movements, making people consider serious revolutionary politics against the West German state and capitalist society."[11] After the archival confirmation of Kurras's role as an undercover agent provocateur, the Left's romanticization of radicalization must be completely abandoned. Russell Berman's analysis of the situation seems more apt: we must see the degeneration of "progressive politics" in West Germany as a direct consequence of East German secret police tactics.[12]

Unfortunately for both the student radicals and the GDR conspirators, West Germany did not fall, but Ohnesorg's death accelerated the radicalization of certain segments of the student population for whom the continuation of business as usual was declared unbearable. On June 7, 1967, Adorno had the unfortunate privilege of giving a lecture titled "Classicism in Goethe's Iphigenia." The lecture was disrupted by the distribution of gummy bears in reference to Adorno's nickname, Teddy. Lorenz Jäger found in Adorno's papers in Frankfurt the leaflet distributed at his lecture, which read, "The big cheese of science is coming! What's old Adorno to us? Why should we care about a theory that disgusts us because it does not say how we can best set fire to this shitty university and a few America Houses with it?"[13] A few days later, Ohnesorg was buried in his hometown of Hanover, and his funeral was followed by a conference, "The University and Democracy: Conditions and Organization of Resistance," during which student leaders Rudi Dutschke and Hans-Jürgen Krahl denounced Jürgen Habermas's reservations about direct action as counterrevolutionary. In the words of Dutschke, "The material preconditions for the possibility of making history are given. Everything now depends on the conscious human will, to finally become conscious of the history it has always made, to control, and to command it, which means, Professor Habermas, that your objectivity devoid of concept is crushing the subject of emancipation."[14] Habermas was pushed to the breaking point and responded that the student movement had become the inheritors of "Fascism," albeit of the Left.

Berman emphasizes the fact that while Habermas felt sympathy with the general current of the student movement, he was in the end repelled by its pure voluntarism, "its triumphalism of the will," and its contempt for reason, democracy, and the still-nascent liberal institutions of West Germany. Berman's article, "From 'Left Fascism' to Campus Anti-Semitism," traced a genealogical relationship between contemporary political and intellectual conditions and the ghosts of student radicalism past. Although some of the claims he made were hyperbolic, he wrote passionately about the decline of vigorous and reasoned debate in intellectual life, which, for him, had arisen out of progressive/ Left anti-intellectualism and its censorship of robust forms of dissent. Berman described the student radicals as distinguished by "a contemptuous disregard for democratic institutions and processes; and an adventurist willingness to engage in violence, precisely in order to provoke crises inimical to liberal democracy."[15] Their contempt for institutions came to be articulated as impatience for a general emancipation from liberalism in general. In his studies of the authoritarian personality, Adorno demonstrated again and again that a desire for irrational accession to some extralegal sphere of action and satisfaction was connected to the latent fantasy of violent solutions in the arena of political struggle.

A year and a half after these events in Berlin, a sense of crisis simmered in West Germany; despite the student radicals' "exercise of the conscious human will," their much hoped for revolution seemed difficult to consummate. In 1969 the Frankfurt SDS sought to spark a significant confrontation with university authorities. According to Claussen, it "tried to revive the flagging enthusiasm for political activities by bringing demonstrations back into the universities. . . . With the occupation of the Institute for Social Research, the SDS wished to provoke a further intervention on the part of the police so as to mobilize the students to resist the University authorities without regard to eventual casualties."[16] On February 1, 1969, Hans-Jürgen Krahl entered the Institute for Social Research with seventy-six students and refused to leave. Adorno later testified that when he saw from his window "several dozen students" walking at great speed into the institute, he thought that the police had to be called.[17] Along with Ludwig von Friedeberg, a young sociologist of Habermas's generation who was an institute researcher, Adorno summoned the police. After refusing to leave the premises when requested, Krahl and the "occupying" students were arrested. All the others were immediately released, but Krahl was charged with breaking and entering. During his hearing, Krahl "cross-examined his supervisor [Adorno] and asked him what made him think the Institute was being occupied." Adorno replied quite simply that after being asked three times to leave, Krahl refused. There followed a calm discussion of the phenomenology of occupation.[18] Adorno stayed true to his opposition to escalation and remained remarkably pragmatic in his responses to the student actions.

Krahl was famous in the antiauthoritarian branches of the SDS for his thrilling but esoteric speeches. However, when he stepped into the leadership vacuum left by the assassination of Rudi Dutschke, he occupied this place with uneasiness. Adorno was struck by the contradiction between Krahl's political charisma and the intellectual and personal deference Krahl displayed toward him as a mentor and advisor. In February 1970 Krahl was killed in a car accident, and the SDS splintered into even more radical subgroups. So significant was the attempted occupation and subsequent intervention of the German police in the annals of the Left that Fredric Jameson felt compelled to condemn Adorno's participation in calling "the police to the University" as a "deathless shame." Only after condemning Adorno's act did Jameson feel he could embark upon the redemption of what was properly Marxist in Adorno's thought.[19] For decades after those turbulent years, it was difficult in academia to criticize or express skepticism about the international student movement of the 1960s without being accused of being a reactionary. In *Late Marxism*, Jameson parried anticipated hostility about his engagement with Adorno's work by conceding that the German professor's actions in 1969 were unforgivable, simplifying the situation quite a bit for generations to come, since he condemned the German professor for a moral failure suffused with sexual iniquity. Indeed, Adorno's reputation was to bear the scarlet letter of elitism for the next four decades. In this sense, despite Jameson's redemption of Adorno's thinking for 1990, he seems to be confirming Berman's assertion that Left conformity has inhibited full discussion of the significance of Adorno's thinking and the fate of critical theory.

In *American Pastoral,* Philip Roth created a particularly vicious version of enraged feminist radicalism married to performative exhibitionism in the character of Rita Cohen, Merry Levov's alleged lover and co-conspirator. In one harrowing scene, Cohen has lured Seymour Levov into a hotel room for a money drop. In return for $5,000 in cash, Cohen makes the vague promise of guaranteeing Merry's safety and perhaps eventually taking Levov to her. This act of extortion is complicated by Cohen's sexual demands. She propositions Levov in the name of his daughter, telling him that if he does not fuck her, she will not take the money. If he does comply, Cohen promises that she will take him to his prodigal daughter. Her act of extortion is designed to force Seymour, the perfect liberal bourgeois father, to abase himself and become violent, to break his own codes of behavior and be transformed into the physically threatening male that his strength will underwrite. Ever the decent man, even in a situation where decency is no longer commensurate as a response, Levov is rendered both speechless and sexless before this mythically angry woman: disgusted, turned on, and paralyzed at the same time, he rushes out of the room and leaves behind $10,000 in cash—he had brought an extra $5,000 just in case. Roth's female characters have always been treacherous, and Cohen is a particularly despicable incarnation of female fury and depravity. When Rita asks Levov to look inside her exposed sex, he replies with astonishment, "You are subjugating no one by this. Only yourself."[20] But Levov is terribly mistaken: Rita has debased the Swede as a father and a human being. She tells Seymour that her pussy smells like his daughter's. Paternal love has become hopelessly entangled in a deadly mix of incest and aggression. Levov's liberal, secular Jewish love for his daughter, the crown jewel of a successful bourgeois family, has been so thoroughly violated that he is destroyed as a man. Years later, Cohen reappears in Levov's life to tip him off as to his daughter's whereabouts. Merry is working at an animal hospital in Newark. Merry's do-it-yourself Jainism has convinced her that she must harm no life, even microscopic life, so she is starving herself to death while ministering to abandoned animals: a modern-day mystic, Merry makes a mockery of her parents' liberal, bourgeois values. Roth has created a countercultural demon, possessed by a fanaticism designed to offend and destroy every humanist impulse toward reason and self-preservation.

Rita Cohen may be dismissed as a misogynistic male fantasy of feminist provocation, and she is such a disturbing, unresolved character that Roth as a novelist is completely unable to decide how to deal with her. In terms of pure plot, it remains unclear whether or not Cohen is a figment of Levov's anguished imagination or a "real" character who has profited from Merry's situation. As a provocateur, Cohen is obviously inspired by historical characters. She is Roth's cartoon of radical, antiestablishmentarian feminism. In the groundbreaking 2007 show of feminist art from the 1970s and 1980s, WACK! (at the Museum of Contemporary Art in Los Angeles), curated by Cornelia Butler, we see a particularly striking preponderance of naked female bodies, including bare breasts and hirsute genitalia. From Carolee Schneeman, to Eleanor Antin, to Lynda Bengalis, to Valie Export, to Cosey Fanni Tutti, to Hannah Wilke, feminist artists were pushing against the limits of feminine modesty by defiantly exposing themselves in artworks and performances. During the 1970s, feminist artists could not keep their clothes on. Much of the artists' work is humorous and sensual, two qualities Rita Cohen notably lacks. It is not, however, an exaggeration to say that the women's movement, as was quite evident by the late 1960s and 1970s, had an aggressively performative and obscene intent: feminist self-exposure, both literary and literal, was supposed to be empowering for women and humiliating for the male spectator.[21] Roth's Levov was supposed to be aroused and emasculated all at the same time: the striptease was reappropriated for feminist purposes. If the female nude was both fetishized and objectified by the male gaze throughout the history of art, what better way to demystify it than to make oneself the author of its total exposure and objectification?

Performance studies professor Peggy Phelan placed feminist art of the 1970s in a direct genealogical relationship with the politics of the 1960s: "Inspired by the civil rights and antiwar movements in the United States, protests against military dictatorships in South America, student revolutions in Western Europe, and political unrest in Eastern Europe, feminist art emerged unevenly, but persistently in various international locations during the 1960s as a political and aesthetic movement simultaneously."[22] According to Phelan, a common theme ran through the work of a diverse group of women artists after World War II: they evoked tactility only to make touching impossible. The works of Atsuko Tanaka, who made a dress composed of light bulbs, and Louise Bourgeois, who created a latex dress that "seemed to render the artist all breast," evoke an untouchable female body. In Roth's novel, Rita Cohen performs an act of self-exposure for Seymour Levov alone that seems entirely personal: Roth would like feminist performances to be stripped of political content. But Cohen's gesture owes a great deal to feminist artists and the breast-baring students of Adorno's seminar. Roth's idea of radical politics and feminist performance may in some sense historically resonate, but it is a poor conceptualization of the politicization of the female body. Merry's precocious political radicalization takes place before the television set, during the nightmarish broadcasts from the Vietnam War. Traumatized by the spectacle of the self-immolating South Vietnamese monk, Merry can no longer see anything redeemable in her parents' comfortable, middle-class lives. Merry's and Levov's paralysis allegorizes the radical loss of self caused by witnessing a traumatic image. One is destroyed by a broadcast image, the other by a provocative and devastating act of striptease.

Even as the Red Army Faction took to violence in Germany, many middle-class Western European and American students were rejecting Western traditions and norms in more peaceful ways: an idealization of Eastern wisdom provided many with a compelling vision of alternative philosophies of being-in-the-world. While Philip Roth's antiheroine performed a hyperbolic and caricatural appropriation of Jainism to justify her martyrdom and self-abnegation, many more 1960s activists participated in moderate refusals of empire, objectivity, and technocracy.[23] The cultivation of the inner journey produced an antinormative and therapeutic consensus that was anticipated in Theodor Roszak's *The Making of a Counter Culture*, published in 1969. Roszak speculated that youth rebellion and countercultures were primarily animated by "Left" disgust with the heartless, pseudo-objectivity of technocracy and the experts who served it: "In the technocracy everything aspires to become purely technical, the subject of professional attention. The technocracy is the regime of experts—or of those who can employ the experts."[24] Roszak imagines that experts who are guardians of a secret knowledge have become latter-day priests of a power-hungry cult, exploiting the innocent and serving the powerful. The technocrats have become a special protected class, shielded from the anxieties of the ordinary person. Within the postwar corporate state, experts and technocrats could exist behind the high walls of large organizations and self-reproducing bureaucracies. Expertise seemed to give technocrats protection from economic forces even as it allowed them to collude with the powers that be in order to perpetuate the status quo.

In "The Meaning of Working Through the Past," Adorno wrote that "the majority of people" found themselves forced "to submit to the given conditions; they must negate precisely that autonomous subjectivity to which the idea of democracy appeals. . . . [T]o see through this nexus of deception, they would need to make precisely that painful intellectual effort that the organization of everyday life, and not least of all a culture industry inflated to the point of totality, prevents."[25] As we saw in his essay "The Stars Down to Earth," Adorno felt that everyday life had become inscrutable: it appeared as historical traumas and Utopian dreams condensed into a desire for material comfort and personal survival. Conformity appeared as an ostensibly voluntary adaptation to the increasing compartmentalization and unfreedom of "administered life." In "The Meaning of Working Through the Past," Adorno addressed the problem in West Germany of a banalized and administratively correct relationship to the Nazi past. For Adorno, public discourse in West Germany was dominated by clichés of remembering and working through fascist history. The official line on the past actually allowed for its repression: "National Socialism lives on, and even today we still do not know whether it is merely the ghost of what was so monstrous that it lingers on after its own death, or whether it has not yet died at all."[26] In the shadow of this ghost, Adorno overheard Germans talking about the present, noting that "one often hears Germans among themselves making the peculiar remark, that they are not yet mature enough for democracy." The "dominant ideology" at work here for Adorno had to do with the subjectivization of "objective constellations." Germans identified something constitutionally unchangeable about themselves that was incompatible with democracy: their resignation allowed for the reification and internalization of objective conditions over which individuals seemed entirely powerless.

"Objective constellation" is a phrase that condensed two different sets of analytic tools that critical theory used: the one has to do with the objective and material conditions by which a totality could be apprehended and communicated—and therefore transformed; the other derived from Benjamin's use of astrology—an interpretive and imaginative relationship with the stars—as one image of historical materialism's predecessors that was always at risk of making its objects into false idols and gods. For Adorno, objective constellation provided a highly condensed concept that could be used to denounce the irrational acceptance of the status quo as both unchanging and unforgiving as the stars themselves. His critical concept aimed at unsettling received ideas about popular superstition: it allowed for the transformation of subjective experiences of the limits of destiny into a historical and communicable spectacle of subjugation. The ancient ability to identify with and interpret the arrangement of the stars was both preserved and abused in the twentieth century, and a certain set of popular attitudes reinforced a sense of hopelessness and inevitability, which absolved individuals of responsibility for the historical and political conditions of their resistance to democracy as such. Astrology had represented a historical mode of apprehending the world picture or cosmos: the projection of our fates onto the stars allowed us to grasp an immanently magical relationship to distance, scale, and difference. What Adorno denounced in the newspaper horoscope was not its pre-Enlightened superstitious attitude toward the cosmos. The irrationality of the daily horoscopes for Adorno "[was] not necessarily a force operating outside the range of rationality: secondary superstition supported the ethos of rational self-preservation 'run amuck.'"[27] Modern occultism and modern astrology delivered an ancient worldview to the coercive imperatives of "adaptation" and adjustment. The hyperrational astrology of contemporary horoscopic advice made a mockery of the "primal form of love" that Adorno and Benjamin called our mimetic heritage. Secondary superstitions evoked the pleasures of mimetic thinking in order to enslave mimetic capacities to adjustment. According to Adorno, Benjamin "viewed the modern world as archaic not in order to conserve the traces of a purportedly eternal truth, but rather to escape the trance-like captivity of bourgeois immanence."[28] Although Adorno was as skeptical about Benjamin's newspaper delivery boys turned experts as he was of Charlie Chaplin fans transformed into "members of the avant-garde," he obviously shared Benjamin's critical investments in thinking about experience and emancipation as key terms in the same constellation.[29]

It would seem that Roszak and Adorno could agree on the need to overturn the rule of the technocracy with its "influence over even the most seemingly personal aspect of life," but their critiques are not really compatible at all. For Roszak, "Western tradition" was characterized by a crippling "scientific world-view" that alienated Western people from nature, feeling, intuition, and spirituality. Roszak argued that "scientific consciousness depreciates our capacity for wonder by progressively estranging us from the magic of our environment."[30] Rather than working through this blighted past, the counterculture would discard it and appropriate non-Western traditions as its own. If Roszak opposed objectivity in all its forms, Adorno sought to preserve what was redemptive about objectivity and reason. He did not believe that a return to magic or eclectic irrationalism would necessarily lead us to a better world. According to Roszak's account of countercultural revolt, however, the Western past had to be abandoned if we wanted to achieve a better world. For Adorno, the German student revolt was a demand that the older generation work through the past, but the rejection of European modernity had to be understood against a backdrop of liberal democracy's contradictions—its high ideals of autonomy and self-determination, on the one hand, and the consolidation of corporate state administration, on the other. Once again, a higher form of reason, the dialectic itself, had to be invoked in order to break the hieratic domination of instrumental reason.

While Adorno and Horkheimer refused the outright rejection of reason as such, the hatred of the expert as a representative of the technocratic order appeared as an irresistibly powerful weapon in an arsenal of a politics of revolt that spanned the political spectrum. While the Left reacted against professors, the Right was also mobilizing an antielitist revolt of its own. When Stuart Hall coined the term "authoritarian populism" to describe the rise of the radical Right in England during the 1970s, he related its politics directly to reaction against social democracy: "The expansion of the state machine, under the management of state servants and experts, has often been defined [by Fabian collectivism] . . . as synonymous with socialism itself."[31] Hall's analysis of the Right in Great Britain has not been examined alongside Adorno's and the Frankfurt School's preoccupations with reactionary politics and the authoritarian personality: later developments in cultural studies would emphasize an affirmative engagement with popular culture against Frankfurt School negativity and elitism and prevent any positive association between the two bodies of work.

By the 1960s, Adorno and Horkheimer had achieved the kind of academic freedom in Frankfurt that was guaranteed by the social democratic state. To the younger generation of Germans, it appeared as if the two intellectuals had enjoyed state-sponsored institutional protections throughout their academic careers. We have seen that this was far from the case. The fortunes of the institute were tied to Weil's personal philanthropy, Horkheimer's institutional and organizational survival instincts, and the political necessity of rebuilding West German universities after de-Nazification. Under social democracy, the "streamlining" of the state had made it resemble a gigantic business enterprise: "Those whose real powerlessness shows no sign of ceasing cannot tolerate even the semblance of what would be better; they would prefer to get rid of the obligation of autonomy, which they suspect cannot be a model for their lives."[32] Social democracy and its discontents could produce a form of reactionary politics that would condemn autonomy, be it intellectual or aesthetic. Autonomy itself became an object of resentment, especially when the knowledge and experience it produced could not be translated into practice. The value of autonomy would be seen as both a burden and a proscription, in short, an additional "obligation" from which the people yearned to be free. For the present generations, "working through the past" must entail the task of dealing with the institutional successes and fantasmatic failures of 1960s radicalism.

In the post-1960s academy, one of Benjamin's most often cited concepts, historicism, communicated empathy for the victors and became an inspiration to new scholars and new scholarship. For Walter Benjamin, film and sport created a place for the expert without experience: film and sport could conjure up the pagan and prerational world of magical skill and sudden transformation. Benjamin's attitude could be understood as more compatible with Roszak's countercultural rejection of "Western" science and his embrace of non-Western alternatives to our modern social organizations. It is not hard to see why the Anglo-American countercultural youth who emerged as intellectuals and academics during the 1970s embraced Walter Benjamin's work as more and more of it was translated into English. "The Work of Art in the Age of Mechanical Reproducibility" would emerge as a user's manual for a new generation of cultural theorists. Its influence has been almost immeasurable. Benjamin's concepts have become critical in thinking about politics and aesthetics: *aura, constellation, flâneur,* and *arcades* were terms that became reinvested with a new theoretical force. Benjamin's tricky, dense, aphoristic, and inherently interdisciplinary writing was interdisciplinarity *avant la lettre,* antiacademic yet erudite, dilettantish, yet critical and historical. It constructed a rigorous theory of culture without sacrificing a poignant lyricism for lost worlds and shattered dreams. In a snow globe he could perceive all the principles of late nineteenth-century bourgeois aspirations for exoticism and containment, wonder and degradation, crystallized as a mass-produced porcelain tchotchke cherished by an aging aunt. He was the ultimate hashish-smoking, dreamy dropout compared to Adorno's and Horkheimer's imagoes as postwar "organization men." Benjamin, the prototype for a countercultural outsider, was therefore entirely attractive to restless academics hoping to find a new paradigm for the study of both culture and history.

Benjamin's work has become so important for Anglo-American academia that it has become difficult to grasp the basic ways in which his thinking and language have inspired a massive reappraisal of what we think of as academic research and intellectual life, even if the disposition of educational institutions as guardians of professional identity has remained largely untouched by the core of his thinking. *Constellation* was one of the critical terms that Adorno borrowed from Benjamin to provide an image for critical theory's methodology. As a metaphor and a critical concept, it was vital to Adorno's and Benjamin's understanding of the apprehension of historical experience. Constellation offered a multidimensional allegory of historical imagery where the flash or shock illuminated only a partial field of the past, and the configuration of images rendered visible was spread out against the darkness of the night sky. In a fragment written probably in 1932, Benjamin expanded on what he had already alluded to in *The Origin of German Mourning Play* and in the fragment "On Astrology": in a world without transcendence, astrology was a melancholic and mimetic epistemology that offered a way of apprehending a primal relation to both history and language. Adorno wrote of his late friend Walter Benjamin: "He viewed the modern world as archaic not in order to conserve the traces of a purportedly eternal truth, but rather to escape the trance-like captivity of bourgeois immanence."[33] For Benjamin, the modern subject had lost her ability to perceive mimetic resemblances: astrology preserved, as a ruin, a link to antiquity, or to that which had been rendered unintelligible to the present. Astrology was significant insofar as it allowed us to apprehend a premodern concept of a perfect micro- and macrocosmic harmony that distinguished the world of Western medieval mysticism. Benjamin observed, "As students of ancient traditions, we have to reckon with the possibility that manifest configurations, mimetic resemblances, may once have existed where today we are no longer in a position even to guess at them. For example, in the constellation of the stars. The horoscope must above all be understood as the primitive image of totality that astrological interpretation merely subjects to analysis."[34]

The "primitive image of totality" persisted, however deformed, in the modern imagination. According to Aby Warburg, astrology was a key term in the "pure aesthetics" of the ancient and premodern world. Astrology had provided a critical link between human beings and the natural world. According to Richard Wolin, "What has been lost in the species' inexorable drive toward rational self-assertion was the capacity to view nature *mimetically* or *fraternally*. The solution to this dilemma hinged upon the capacity for remembrance of nature in the subject."[35] While it may be tempting to apprehend nature as an image of an untouched natural landscape, Benjamin's understanding of our inner nature was deeply implicated in a psychoanalytic and anthropological apprehension of psychic wildness that modernity had sought to domesticate and subjugate.

In Benjamin's "Work of Art" essay, athletic and expert "recruitment" was crystallized in a brief anecdote about overhearing Berlin paperboys arguing heatedly over the results of the latest cycling races. Benjamin remarked that it was primarily newspaper companies that were sponsoring professional cycling competitions: the newspapers wanted to dignify the work of their delivery boys with an epic or heroic aspect and to give to the improvement of work performance a new dimension. What struck Benjamin about the overheard conversation was its passionate tone, the investment in the sporting spectacle. He wrote,

"It is inherent in the technology of film, as of sports, that everyone who witnesses these performances does so as a quasi-expert."[36] In fact, for Walter Benjamin, film would be the people's medium par excellence, as it laid the groundwork for a mass-produced feeling of easily accessed expert knowledge about spectacle itself. "Jeder Mann ein Fachmann." Every man an expert. More precisely, the *Jedermann*, or "Everyman," was supposed to possess a special kind of knowledge not accessible to the "official" experts. As schools and universities oversaw the intensive processes of credentialization and professionalization—alongside the proliferation of rackets and mafia-like enclaves—technological advances also laid the groundwork and rhetoric for popular openness, an immediacy and immanence that promised direct access that would make every man an expert. Today a delivery boy, tomorrow a champion. These manufactured fantasies appealed to restless, childish, and feverish daydreams about awards, prizes, and trophies, not to mention the magical stage upon which drudgery could become prowess and employees heroes. The spectacle of professional sports, communicated by the very papers the boys were carrying, allowed for mass access to serious debate about the merits of star athletes, their chances at winning or losing, the nature of competition, and the risk of cheating. If newspaper delivery boys played at being both experts and champions, they did so by purloining the authority of experts on the sporting event. This intense interest fueled a dream of rising from child laborer to sports journalist *and* professional racer. The delivery boy, like every enthusiastic spectator of film and sport, felt immediately entitled to pronounce judgment on what he saw. The newspaper boy's simultaneous identification with both sports critic and athlete expanded the scope of his workaday drudgery in two ways: first, by elevating the activity of delivering newspapers into the field of athleticism and honor, and second, by attempting to destroy the barriers that restricted knowledge about heroic activities and performances to the chosen few. Hence new vistas of mastery, both imagined and real, were opened by the new media and its organs of dissemination. The passionate pride of the newspaper boy/sports fan stood in stark contrast to the false humility of the Victorian scientist or scholar. If the society of discipline, control, and asceticism engineered by the nineteenth-century elite was crumbling to dust under the scorn of the mass media skeptic, the passions of the fan as deposer of the expert projected a Utopia of fair play, joy in athletic prowess, a just competition with clear winners and losers—all in stark contrast to the secret and shadowy dealings of the meritocracy and educational institutions, whose regimes of testing destroyed the collective and cathartic aspects of physical competition.

Benjamin referred to the "Letters to the Editor" function of newspapers as offering the promise that each reader could "write back" and had the potential to become an author. As a generalized sense of expertise was made available to an ever-wider public, popular suspicion of inaccessible forms of expertise would simultaneously emerge as a by-product of the rise of the new mass media. Although there was nothing inherently progressive about popular skepticism, it did point toward the radical democratization of knowledge and open access as critical components of a new media Utopia. The "Work of Art" essay had a prophetic power about how the everyday experience of new technologies would remake the ways in which cultural value and political prestige were intertwined. Benjamin understood that during the first decades of the twentieth century, just as administration and rationalization of research were dividing academic knowledge into ever more tightly bounded forms of specialization, mass media such as film and newspaper communicated to spectators and readers the critical idea that each one of them could instantaneously be transformed into cultural producer and expert.

One of Walter Benjamin's most salient insights in "The Work of Art" could be summarized in this way: the invention of cinema promoted the expertise of the Everyman or the Everyman as expert. This essay has been canonized in cultural criticism as one of the most important critical texts of progressive academic methodologies. In *Window Shopping: Cinema and the Postmodern*, Anne Friedberg provided a fully fleshed out, interdisciplinary understanding of the historical conditions of cinema's emergence through intensive engagement with Walter Benjamin's work on the flâneur, the arcade, and the city.[37] For Anson Rabinbach, Benjamin's intellectual historical project aimed at nothing less than the redemption of the Enlightenment through the expansion of a new concept of experience and culture that could take into account the magic of the "prerational." Rather than decrying the nullification of accumulated experience in favor of a pure engagement with the present, Benjamin hoped to articulate the positive qualities of "imaginative improvisation" made possible by the visual experiences of cinema, arcades, and city streets. The forms of mass-mediated expertise produced by both cinema and sports encouraged a new form of intimacy with spectacle and power. Both cinema and sports were forms of recruitment that demanded a newly configured concept of "experience." This new experience would be expansive enough to contain *Erfahrung*'s reflection on *Erlebnis*. According to Rabinbach, for Walter Benjamin, "enlightenment could only be redeemed through a 'higher concept of experience,' one that could take into account the prerational, the magical and even madness."[38] If the German Roman-

tics had rebelled against the Enlightenment in the previous century by calling
for a rebirth of mythology, Benjamin demonstrated over and over again that
industrial culture had generated its own forms of "mythic power for a 'universal symbolism.'"[39] While this was neither an inherently positive nor a negative
development, the effects of industrialization and administration on culture in
particular and aesthetic experience in general could no longer be ignored. Ironically, the oppressive somnolence of nineteenth-century bourgeois fantasies of
progress also rushed headlong into the future with the hastily stitched together
traditions, values, and emblems of a phony and entirely trumped up past.[40]
Benjamin seemed to have had the gift of perceiving history itself as a landscape,
but under his powers of reflection, the details of everyday life revealed the ruins
and traces of the archaic, the anarchic, the outdated, the ruined, the childish,
the unassimilable. His own writing captured both the unpredictable flashes of
insight and intense obsessiveness characteristic of children whose empathetic imagination was made up of both mimetic and competitive impulses. This
imaginative and empathetic engagement with the world was both a cultural
and an anthropological legacy: it was able to contain the human capacity for
both play and innovation.

Adorno saw a darker side to the diffusion of expertise and the easily assumed,
mass-produced skepticism that it produced. In fact, for Adorno, the reader of
the *Los Angeles Times* horoscope, like the newspaper reader in general, expected
to be provided with a ready-made relationship of intimacy with the total world
picture. Adorno's analysis of the psychology of secondary superstitions provided a darker vision of modern irrationality. For demagogues intent on inflaming
the deep feelings of powerlessness and discontentment in imperfect democracies, calling for the destruction of the expert appeared as a convenient tool
of political mobilization. In Adorno's analysis of right-wing propaganda, the
expert was to appear as the very incarnation of technocratic bureaucracy. His
punishment at the hands of justice-seeking people would be one of the crucial
scenes of instinctual release for those seeking revenge against technobureau-
cratic modernity and its administrative solutions. For Adorno, administration
possessed an "immanent tendency" toward expansion. Like French sociologist
Pierre Bourdieu, who was another close reader of Max Weber, Adorno understood the principles of institutional rationalization as primarily oriented toward self-reproduction. What was once an apparatus for resolving social contradiction and mitigating injustice had become a condition of the world: what
was once means became end. If Stuart Hall became interested in the rise of a
radical Right, Adorno had been interested during his years of exile in the United

States in studying the emergence of the psychological techniques of reactionary demagogues. His work on the Princeton Radio Project was controversial,
but it offered a powerful, qualitative interpretation of reactionary politics and
its use of broadcast media. Hall criticized the Left for its lack of political imagination and will while remaining dumbstruck by the Right's ability to appropriate media vehicles to transmit its critique of the corporate state. In the end, it
was Antonio Gramsci and not Theodor Adorno who provided Hall with the concept of hegemony to describe the ways in which reactionary powers were able
to extract consent from a disparate group of class actors.

For Apostolidis, returning to Adorno's study of the now-forgotten right-
wing radio agitator, Martin Luther Thomas, allowed him to understand the
appeal of James Dobson's Focus on the Family and Christian broadcasting in
general. Adorno's analysis is what permitted Apostolidis to isolate the negative Utopia of broadcast intimacy that made up the reactionary responses to
the "ambiguous coexistence of an official ideology of utopian mission with a
concrete set of elite responses to economic and political crisis that were defensive, discriminatory, and incrementalist."[41] Michael Kazin's analysis of Father
Coughlin, the Catholic radio priest who became an anti–New Deal anti-Semite,
followed Coughlin's fascinating political itinerary: newly empowered American
Catholics adopted Populist themes while rejecting their Protestant brethren's
prejudice against the Roman Catholic Church. According to Kazin, "Like the
Populists in the 1890s, Catholic activists wanted to pull down the rich and raise
the spiritual state of the nation."[42] Father Charles Coughlin began broadcasting
sermons from the Shrine of the Little Flower in Royal Oak, Michigan, in 1926:
Kazin cites a network estimate that at the height of his appeal, Coughlin had
30 million Americans tuning in to his show on Sunday afternoons.[43] Following
the papal endorsement of Catholic social doctrine, Coughlin became one of the
most vocal critics of what was once called "the money power." He was an avid
supporter of Roosevelt during the campaign of 1932 but became increasingly
impatient with the ruling party and its New Deal institutions. As Kazin notes,
"According to Coughlin, the New Deal, the Soviets, and modern capitalism had
one essential quality in common: the drive to centralize power in the hands of
a privileged few—whether liberal bureaucrats, international bankers, or atheistic tyrants."[44]

Like Father Coughlin, his more famous Catholic counterpart, Martin Luther
Thomas was a radio priest whose popularity peaked in the 1930s. Adorno's analysis emphasized the rhetorical sleights of hand that allowed Thomas to connect
with listeners. He claimed that Thomas was uniquely skilled at aggravating the

sense of grievance experienced by the ordinary radio listener. The radio evangelist's appeal to a "higher law" actually masked a call to "nonlegalistic rule," absolute domination, exploitation, and violence toward the weak.[45] The destruction of the democratic and fundamentally abstract principle of political equality lay behind the demagogue's personal and intimate "anti-institutionality." Thomas's appeal was deeply affective: he was able to establish a sense of intimacy with his listeners. He revealed his weaknesses and his own neediness, making endless appeals for financial support. Although at first blush this may have seemed unholy in a man of the church, Thomas's self-exposure produced in his listeners a sense of immediate connection to his honesty and apparent lack of guile. His appeal to personal experience was a tried-and-true technique of the "fascist leader" that, according to Adorno, left-wing propagandists were unable to master: leaders on the left tended to speak rationally to "objective interests" that were inherent in the "objective argumentation." Transmitted across the airwaves, left-wing rationality "intensifie[d] the feeling of despair, isolation and loneliness under which virtually each individual today suffer[ed]." The right-wing propagandist avoided the alienating appeal to reason and reasoned argument because he understood that his listeners wanted to escape the impersonality of everyday life: he satisfied this need for intimacy and irrationality by appearing to take his listeners into "his confidence and to bridge the gap between person and person."[46]

Franklin Delano Roosevelt used the radio skillfully to communicate his own messages about New Deal government policies. His personal warmth and charisma shaped the federal government's message of compassion and concern, but Thomas's radio broadcasts had the aura of a transgressive intimacy. He was able to admit to financial need and beg his listeners to send him money; his style of speech was fragmented and associational. Thomas's grasp of the techniques of fascist propaganda seemed more intuitive than fully calculated. According to Adorno, he was so deeply connected to the powerlessness of his aging, struggling, lower-middle-class constituency that he was able to reproduce their private logic and broadcast it on the airwaves. He gave voice to their frustrations and their sense of marginality. Thomas possessed, finally, a mimetic relationship to the inner landscape of frustration and aspiration. Here is one of the examples that Adorno analyzed: "Christ says, 'by their fruits ye shall know them,' now that is the only way that I have of testing whether a man or woman belongs to God, it is what you do. My friend, one of the best things in the world that you can do to demonstrate that you are a child of God—work on your neighbor; send for all of this vital literature."[47] The word "neighbor" was the associational link between Christian theology and the logic of the door-to-door salesman, for whom a neighbor is someone to "be worked on." Good works (charity) were thus associated with "working on" someone. Throughout the study, Adorno studied Thomas's sermons in detail while he puzzled over the incoherence of Thomas's rhetorical techniques. Adorno emphasized the repetitive nature of Thomas's rhetorical sleights of hand: God and Thomas were bound together by a series of irrational associations. The sheer number of confusing links between God and Thomas undermined in his listeners "any element of resistance implied in responsible thinking as such."[48] It was just this kind of criticism that would make Adorno appear to be offering normative and judgmental sanctions on popular forms of media consumption. For Apostolidis, Adorno's critique of the culture industry and authoritarian personalities always contained within it a negative account of popular aspirations for Utopia. A desire for redemption and connection could be seen in the rhetoric of Thomas's sermons. Both Thomas and Coughlin criticized the proliferation of (New Deal) institutions and government legislation as dangerous secular instruments that threatened their listeners' independence and capacity for self-reliance. Adorno saw in Thomas's attacks against "institutionalized" religion and unjust laws a thinly veiled call for the lifting of all legal and institutional protections for the rights of the weak.

The rise of the expert accompanied the hegemony of administration and the streamlined state: both were made possible by the Enlightenment, which taught us to aspire to "dissolve the injustice of the old inequality—unmediated lordship and masters—but at the same time perpetuates it in universal mediation, in the relation of any one existent to another."[49] Abstraction functioned as a tool of the Enlightenment, which separated intellectual labor and expertise in order to facilitate its organization: this was the degeneration of *Vernunft* into *Verstand*, of reason into instrumental reason. Adorno wrote that "administration through blind ordering processes actually prevents negative coincidence, blind control over others, nepotism and favoritism."[50] While modern administration attempted to manage individuals as equals, it also turned them into exchangeable equivalents: the ability to make valuable distinctions seemed to be worn away and dissolved in the bureaucratic tendency to reproduce its own systems of surveillance and rationalization. And yet this bureaucracy was supposed to be an improvement upon the feudal court system, where an ever-present threat of violence in the forms of physical domination and apprehension cast its shadow upon the subjugated. Dependency on the whim, intelligence, and probity of the sovereign oriented all relations. The dialectical nature of historical "progress" was made palpable when Max Weber showed that the most modern and rational of institutions have not been able to eradicate the fear of the "overlord" who based his authority not on rule of law or administrative hierarchy but on the threat of physical violence.[51] But if the Enlightenment proclaimed to free us from fear, it also subjected us to administrative oversight and surveillance under the principles of scientific management, which produced a new experience of oppression. In the new world of work, lack of compliance was no longer punishable by physical domination, and yet, in the modern world, one found that distinction and legitimization backed by force were still operational. New forms of dependency had been created that were producing new forms of revolt. Mass media repudiation of the expert contained the same structural features of anti-Semitism (conspiratorial thinking, worship of physical force, contempt for reflection) that formed one of the wellsprings of potentially violent reaction against modernity and modernization. Explicit anti-Semitism and fascist sympathies were much more obvious in the rhetoric of Father Coughlin, but both he and Thomas were adept at inflaming a popular sense of suspicion about not only New Deal initiatives but the Roosevelt government in general. Having pinned his hopes on Roosevelt's promises to make economic reforms his priority, Coughlin's sense of betrayal turned him inexorably against the president he once supported, but it also drove him to embrace extreme, hard-line positions against "liberal elites" and the Left liberal intellectuals who conspired against the common man. In his sermons and in his journal, *Social Justice*, "the shift away from skewering the financial elite to bludgeoning alleged Communists brought out a fierce ethnic antipathy that had only been hinted at before." In order to differentiate himself from the fascist regimes of Europe, for which he had nevertheless expressed a degree of sympathy, Coughlin tried to insist that there were two kinds of Jews: the good religious Jew and the atheistic Bolshevik Jew.[52]

While the world of administration rationalized and abstracted workers and their labor processes, making not only objects of labor but subjects of experience entirely fungible, the culture industry compensated with fantasies of individual survival and sovereignty. Protest against bureaucracy appeared at first glance to be part of a progressive movement, supporting the common people in their daily struggle against the impersonality of contemporary governmental institutions. And since bureaucracy was not perfect at preventing "nepotism and favoritism," it appeared that to destroy "blind ordering processes" and to replace them with the flawed but at least seemingly human eyes of the leader or despot would be one way of remedying the faulty organizational structures of rationalized systems of management. The expert was no less than an anthropomorphization of the massive technorational organizations of the postwar era. As sociologist Steven Brint has shown, expertise has always been a thwarted and imperfect form of authority.[53] Those who wielded true political power were those who could ignore the experts. Experts may have operated in the service of power elites, but the sovereign elites had no obligation to obey or respect the findings of their advisors. The popular confusion of experts with the powerful and expertise with the exercise of power had become a convenient populist shorthand for oppositionality: like everyone else, the expert had to follow the iron logic of instrumentalization and division of labor. A thwarted aggression against experts masked an unconscious complicity with the despot or tyrant, who was imagined to be free from all rules. During the twentieth century, rage against experts hardened as anti-intellectualism. It was an appropriate response to a constellation of objective conditions, including lack of transparency and authoritarianism, that haunted liberal democracy and made it fertile ground for the percolation of fascism: the material conditions of economic coercion married to the high ideals of autonomy in a democracy represented a most terrible psychological contradiction for ordinary citizens.

If Martin Luther Thomas sought to connect across the airwaves with his listeners in an unusually direct, personal, and forceful manner, intellectuals of the Left were also preoccupied with bridging the gap between writers and readers, teachers and students, intellectuals and workers. In fact, we could say that intellectual activity of the 1930s seemed particularly preoccupied with establishing both a mimetic and a fraternal (sic) relationship among the child, the "Everyman," and the "average person." From Dewey to Benjamin, thinking was reengaged with doing while being conjugated with popular experience. A philosophical sympathy with the ordinary struggles and dilemmas of everyday life aimed to restore to cultural criticism a vital relationship to modernity. As Adorno repeatedly reminded us during the postwar period, an inability to have new experiences was one of the most striking features of the authoritarian personality. Experience, so central to both Benjamin's and Dewey's philosophy, reemerged on the other side of the war as a crucial element of the politics of critical theory's engagement with its contemporary situation. Dewey's pragmatism, ostensibly so difficult to reconcile with Adorno's dialectic, was as deeply preoccupied with philosophy's estrangement from ordinary experience and common struggles. The restoration of a mimetic relationship to nature had to take place collectively, as a radical reconstruction of the whole notion of experience. The experience of the Everyman or average person had also begun to stand in metonymically for an otherwise qualitatively unrepresentable collective experience. It would not be too much to say that for Benjamin as for Dewey, restoring a strong sense of solidarity and mimetic sympathy with the Everyman had become the most important task of criticism itself. To protect this ordinary person from being deceived by experts, charlatans, conmen, and grifters could have been one of the critical goals of the new pedagogy: if experts seemed to collude with the state in the perpetuation of rackets and impenetrable networks of shadowy elite, then popular education would give the people the tools by which to dissolve the veil of obscurity surrounding the operations of power.

In Benjamin's history, the very experience of early cinema would be able to oppose the hegemonic attempts of cultural experts and elites to make aesthetic experience a mirror for political and economic hierarchy.[54] Benjamin's optimistic point of view produced a new optic on culture and history. The "quasi-expert" (*Fachmann*, or "expert," in German) was someone with an institutional address—*Fach* refers to a mail slot; thus, a *Fachmann* was the receiver of memos and processor of papers, an expert by virtue of his access to information. Yet, as discussed above, film and sport produced a sense of immediate contact with expertise. Every spectator could feel as if the spectacle were addressed directly to her. If the salaried masses could only live from moment to moment without being able to accumulate either capital or experience, film created a space where the attitudes of distraction encouraged by the medium itself created a temporary sanctuary where the rhythms of both recreation and work for the new urban population would be valorized.[55] It was a theory of new media that promised the breakdown of compartmentalized, jealously guarded forms of knowledge by offering to the Everyman a sense of immediate, mass access to expertise. Benjamin saw in film's generalization of cultural expertise a Utopia of amateur enthusiasm, worker empowerment, and proletarian self-representation. While Lawrence Levine demonstrated that the nineteenth-century American elites struggled to appropriate "high culture" and urban spaces of recreation for their own, Benjamin's proposal that cinema would rearm the working-class forces with a new cultural confidence seemed to open new fronts in the culture wars of the 1980s and 1990s in the United States. Levine's analysis of the 1849 riots in Astor Place defending American actor Edwin Forrest's interpretation of Shakespeare against that of the British actor William Charles Macready painted a portrait of unruly popular theater-going practices that the gentrification of the dramatic arts tried to contain. The riots in front of the now-demolished Astor Place Opera House left twenty-five people dead and hundreds injured: the state militia was called out to put an end to the violent protests. Participants were working-class New Yorkers rebelling against elite Anglophilia. Levine was explicit in his intention in writing *Highbrow, Lowbrow*: he hoped to undo the reification of cultural hierarchy by showing that the hierarchical divisions between high and low culture were historical and contingent.

The spectator of film felt immediately that he or she was an expert and qualified to give an opinion or judge a film's qualities; because of this, she was awakened from the premodern and feudal awe before cultic and aesthetic objects. Expertise and authority had something to do with the happiness of demystification: "I can see that!" allowed the film spectator to judge with expertise. The encounter with the art object was much more disorienting, especially since, after the age of mechanical reproduction, high art images were widely disseminated and yet still entirely cryptic. Aesthetic experience seemed to demand contemplative patience as well as submission to an authoritative voice of knowledge and taste: the art historian and the connoisseur seemed to lecture from every corner of every museum. How could the ordinary person escape such proscriptive viewing regimes? Film offered a sense of "empowerment" or authority that arose from the ordinary person's close identification with the cinematic apparatus: the camera was the instrument of the screen test, and every spectator felt that he or she was administering the test. Every actor's performance was always being "judged" or "evaluated." This generalized sense of expertise or "accessibility" inherent in film then structured a certain way of encountering the world and confronting "education." Film schooled the spectator in the habits of the apparatus, and it was, without a doubt, a powerful and disturbing form of "materialist pedagogy": after the advent of film, all education would take place in the shadow of the fantasy of cinematic immediacy.

Benjamin became a theorist of education in his 1929 essay, "On Communist Pedagogy." Benjamin believed the Soviets were creating a "new, nonhumanist and noncontemplative but active and practical universality."[56] This kind of education was allegedly both practical and universal: it created a collective reconciliation between practice and theory. Revolutionary education emphasized an immersive, active relationship to the present. Its universality was practical, not vocational. Rather than isolate humanist education from the polytechnic (with students sorted by way of tests, class self-selection, and teacher assessment), Soviet schools would offer a humanistically oriented, polytechnical education for the proletarian child, who represented the ordinary working people of the twentieth century. In allowing children to engage with the material conditions of technology, education would awaken them to its emancipatory and poetic potentiality while conferring dignity upon labor and the experience of work. A properly materialist pedagogy would allow modern children to grasp the room for play made available by new technologies. During the height of his love affair with the Soviet Union, Asja Lācis (a Bolshevik actress and theater director), and film, Benjamin wrote, "Work itself is given a voice" by film. Benjamin set his sights on a new form of Communist education that would allow children to understand this in a theoretical and practical manner.

Children would learn to enter into a positive mimetic relationship with media. Education would give children the ability to resist the swindle of recruitment and ceaseless, spectacular forms of pseudocompetition. For Benjamin, the universal readiness to engage in class struggle would be the direct consequence of antibourgeois, proletarian education. We could say that the student movements of the late 1960s emerged out of a generational rejection of the technocratic rationale for university education. For radical students who longed for a better world, free of domination and exploitation, the university was the place to begin to make their demands. Direct action, such as that undertaken by the SDS in Frankfurt, embodied the performative politics of 1960s youth rebellion. The Women's Council performance set into place a certain series of oppositions that would function as a political template for struggles over intellectual and political legitimacy within the university for decades to come. The protestors were supposed to be on the side of creativity, spontaneity, youth, pleasure, antiauthoritarianism, and the immodest and youthful body of rock and roll; the professor was on the side of erudition, specialization, credentialism, elitism, privilege, high culture, the dialectic, and classical music. Henceforth, Theodor Adorno would be seen as a cartoonish version of the stuffy and slightly nutty professor, while his friend Walter Benjamin would be embraced as the hashish-smoking flower child. In between them would stand Herbert Marcuse, sympathetic to the students in ways that Adorno was not and yet deeply steeped in the dialectical thinking of his Frankfurt School collaborators.

Benjamin and Adorno disagreed on the emancipatory powers of film, but neither one felt that cultural critique could avoid confronting its effects on our apprehension of the place of experience and cognition. In fact, they would agree that the new technologies of spectatorship had disturbed the disposition of knowledge and specialization as such. For Benjamin as well as for Adorno, the processes particular to critique and theorization were still invested with raw powers of redemption. In the new technologically mediated sensorium of the twentieth century, the expert's expertise would be negated in the name of a different, if not higher, order of experience. In working life under capitalism, experience, like expertise, was actualized and nullified at the same time. In the fragmentation of manual labor along the assembly line and at the cash register, mastery of job performance required less and less experience. Workers did not accumulate experience; instead, their capacity for work was simply used up. Increasingly, work experience became a liability, especially, as we have seen, in the temporality of the meritocracy, which is entirely future oriented.[57] A destabilized, fragmented, and insecure workforce emerged in late capitalism in desperate need of diversion. Benjamin offered a more optimistic view of the reconfigured set of skills and capacities that modernity and its technologies offered.

Benjamin's work was profitably mined in the 1980s and 1990s by Anglo-American scholars for a new theory of play and a new theory of history and culture. His engagement with popular culture, pedestrian and everyday life, as well as the cinematic apparatus provided a rich source of inventive, playful theories about the immersive media and symbolic ecology in which post-1960s intellectuals found themselves. His gnomic works were fusions of critical and creative invention: he had, in the space of his own thinking, collapsed the distance between theory and creative spontaneity. For Benjamin, the neoclassical revival of the Olympic Games in general and the 1936 Berlin Olympic Games in particular was reactionary because they suppressed the pleasure of play. Benjamin saw in the games the spectacularization of "the industrial science of Taylorism" because, as in scientific management, measuring an athlete's performance depended upon "the stopwatch to analyze minutely the bodily actions of workers for the purpose of setting norms for worker productivity. . . . [W]hereas these tests themselves cannot be displayed, the Olympics provide for them a representational form."[58] In Benjamin's view, the mask of ancient Greek culture and competition disguised the ubiquity of the test. The modern Olympic Games spectacularized the triumph of measurement as the final arbiter of competition—and play. Competition was always linked to play and the ludic aspect of all games contained within its apparatus, but with technological advances in capturing speed and pace, it could be reduced to discrete, measurable "performances." As Benjamin scholar and professor of German Miriam Bratu Hansen reminded us, Benjamin's use of *Spiel*, or "play," was intimately related to *Schein*, or "semblance." In every act of playing there was also an element of risk, because *Spiel* also means "gambling."[59] Benjamin decided to play with the idea that film would fundamentally rearrange the ways in which we apprehended the world: he speculated upon its theoretical efficacy. Hansen understood Benjamin's reading of film as a dangerous gamble: he refrained from denouncing the mass spectatorship of either film or sport as fundamentally regressive or reactionary. He speculated that film would have a revolutionary effect on the human sensorium, creating new, collective forms of experience and an improved form of "human" nature that was capable of taking apart the bourgeois hegemony on cultural production.

Adorno's take on the sporting spectacle was extremely harsh: "Sport itself is not play, but a ritual in which the subjected celebrate their subjection."[60] He denounced the structure of sports as fundamentally sadomasochistic and as participating in the culture industry's destruction of "semblance" for imageless competition. The aesthetic, along with its narrow band of hard-won autonomy, was also "sportified"—remade by prizes and competitions into a brutal regime that justified competition and survival of the fittest. But it was perhaps the positive aspect of cultural barbarism that Adorno was unable to accept. Hansen pointed out that even Max Horkheimer saw something positive about sports and sporting competition, namely, that these activities have something to do with a reconciliation between pleasure and effort and that "mass culture had grasped play."[61] Could cultural barbarianism promote happy, hedonistic philistinism? Did it have to degenerate into the most regressive forms of anti-intellectualism and support the most violent forms of reaction? Would this happy barbarian inevitably turn out to be the executioner of the expert? For Adorno, the newspaper delivery boys were initiated as consumers of sporting events: they were reproduced as "screaming fans." But it was their passionate discussion that Benjamin overheard, not their senseless screams. As fans and workers, the boys were undergoing a dual form of recruitment: one as collective dreamers, the other as atomized, competitive workers. If this motivated them to ride harder against each other in order to deliver more newspapers, it was because they had been taught to dream at work, that is, play at being champions while doing their jobs. Better employee performance could be the final but not entirely predictable outcome of the newspapers' sports sponsorships.

In order to redeem "recruitment," Benjamin emphasized the radical potential of film: the documentary newsreel could make of Everyman and anyone a worthy subject of representation. We were therefore all potential recruits of the film industry. According to Benjamin, every ordinary person "can lay claim to being filmed."[62] Our lives, our experiences, our skills could be redeemed, represented, and communicated by cinema. The new technologies and media promised both greater participation and creative cultural productivity from which the great masses of humanity had hitherto been barred. The fungibility of reader/writer, viewer/actor, spectator/athlete was therefore a crucial aspect of the new media situation in the history of twentieth-century popular culture and new media technology.[63] According to Benjamin's optimistic view of labor and media, if everyone deserved to be filmed, and each viewer could make a claim to becoming the subject of film, it was because we all knew some special piece of the labor process to which only we could give voice. For Benjamin, the democratization of expertise also participated in the liberation of "literary competence" from the realm of private property and training in the liberal arts or human sciences. A new form of literary training would entail the cultivation of an ability to describe one's own line of work. For Benjamin, most critically, the democratization of expertise would break the monopoly on the human sciences and make the humanities available to students in the "polytechnic training." Instead of proclaiming the triumph of technological vocationalism in education, Benjamin hailed the new media as the triumphant liberators of humanistic knowledge that could no longer be monopolized by elites. If the masses rejected Picasso and embraced Charlie Chaplin, it was because film produces its own progressive reception "characterized by the direct intimate fusion of visual and emotional enjoyment with the orientation of the expert."[64]

For Benjamin, the new media promised a relationship of reciprocity with the apparatus. Before the screen, mass and expert could become one. Solidarity with the expert would be reciprocated as solidarity with the people. If "every man" could expect to be an expert, the expert was demoted to Everyman. How we recognize the real expert was as vexed a problem as our identification of the true "Everyman." Mass media recruitment could not be controlled by enclaves of authorities: beginning with the printing press, new media would lead to an absorption of the expert by the "viewing and reading public." While John Dewey advocated for professorial control over academic issues—and in this sense created the grounds for the doctorate as university credential and tenure as the foundation of academic freedom—Benjamin saw in new technologies an anti-institutional means by which expert and amateur could be reconciled or even fused. As literary critic Jeffrey Mehlman has pointed out, in one of the radio broadcasts Benjamin recorded for a children's show in Berlin, he was preoccupied by the difficulty of identifying counterfeit stamps. In the broadcast, which was called "Briefmarkenschwindel," or "Counterfeit Stamps," he suggested that since it was impossible to control the counterfeiting of stamps, we should do away with stamps altogether and replace them with postmarks. Then stamp collectors could shift to postmark collection.[65] This whimsical solution to identification of the counterfeit defused the fear of being deceived: it offered a childlike solution to the problem of authentication by abolishing the significance of the original. Benjamin's proposal to abolish stamps because of the possibilities of the counterfeit bore a negative resemblance to his affirmation of the decay of the aura. An affirmative identification with the passionate and obsessive engagements of childhood added a different dimension to Benjamin's understanding of the industrially produced spectacles of success and happiness. Benjamin scholar and professor of political philosophy Susan Buck-Morss has insisted upon the revolutionary potential of both the "dream world of mass culture" and the modern childhood that it both addresses and produces.[66] Modern children could find within the new conditions of modernity more room for play: material comforts provided a prolongation of childhood itself, but modern children were also more tested, more observed, more measured, and therefore more disciplined and better trained under the ubiquitous regime of "testing" (*Leistung*).

For Benjamin, film and sport gave audiences the feeling that every fan could immediately possess meaningful "expert" opinion: sheer enthusiasm and self-education were the only credentials that counted. The sports fan sought what John Fiske called "peaks of intense experience" located in the body when it felt itself to be escaping the "social control" and forming its own "identity." Sociologist of sports Eric Dunning somewhat deflated Fiske's hyperbolic praise of popular enjoyment by identifying the peaks of a sports fan's excitement as "pleasurable de-routinization."[67] When Dunning described the role of modern sports as cultic, its communal celebrations replacing the peak experiences of early religious life, the arousal of powerful emotions was central to his conceptualization of modern sports culture. The power of those emotions was, for Dunning, inseparable from the promise of an escape from everyday life and its increasing routinization. Radical sociologists Henri Lefebvre, Raoul Vaneigem, and Michel de Certeau theorized everyday life as a privileged site of both critique and rebellion, just as ordinary culture was for Raymond Williams a site of transmission for working-class traditions and experiences.[68] For a group of leftist thinkers hoping to escape from the aridity of materialist dogma, everyday life had replaced the shop floor and the factory as the privileged places where both discontent and subversion could be galvanized.

The corporate/state streamlining that Adorno described in the late 1950s was deeply dependent on the promotion of expertise. For the corporate state, the bureaucrat and the expert were called upon to play critical roles in the production of consent, or Gramscian hegemony. During the Cold War, bureaucracy and expertise would find themselves increasingly intertwined and interdependent. Ironically, this particular configuration also allowed for the protection of certain kinds of intellectual, aesthetic, and scientific freedom from the "free market." Research and development could be supported by Keynesian economics, since its institutions could tolerate areas of non-market-driven, specialized activity. It was in this new atmosphere of relative economic and intellectual freedom that Adorno defended the strong concept of aesthetic autonomy in his *Aesthetic Theory*. The principles of modernism and the postwar corporate state could therefore find themselves sharing common principles. The student movement was in fact not so wrong about identifying professors with a military-industrial complex of shared intellectual and political interests. In arguing that aesthetic questions should not be decided by plebiscite and should be protected from the "barbarism of the common will," Adorno appeared to affirm the fact that culture would always have to call on the "ignominious figure of the expert" to protect itself from popular opinion.[69] Adorno's idea that cultural expertise had an extremely high barrier to entry would make him appear as an elitist for which the post-1968 generation of Left critics would have to atone. For him, a truly enlightened, radically democratic culture could tolerate recourse to the expert, but only if administration respected the autonomy of the aesthetic. The relation between administration and expert was not only a matter of necessity, it could be a virtue as well. It opened up a perspective for "the protection of cultural matters from the realm of control by the market, which today unhesitatingly mutilates culture."[70] The cultural sphere needed to be protected from both the plebiscite and the demands of the market: Adorno struggled to justify the maintenance of an autonomous zone that would be protected from market consensus. He was haunted by fascism's cultural agenda, which encouraged the mobilization of both antidemocratic and anti-intellectual sentiments in the name of resentment and incomprehension. Unleashing resentment against aesthetic experimentation and intellectual autonomy was critical to totalitarian regimes. Cultural and academic freedom required certain forms of structural and state protections that depended upon the liberal, "postwar settlement's" institutional structures.

Richard Hofstadter shared Adorno's affirmation of a liberal notion of intellectual autonomy, especially in his critique of the paranoid style in American politics. The "uncommonly angry mind" was one that Hofstadter felt no compunctions about condemning: for him, the People's Party's demands for greater democratic participation and financial reorganization at the end of the nineteenth century had given way to the white supremacist, nativist, anti-immigrant, and anti-intellectual sentiments of the twentieth century. In the post-1960s political climate, Hofstadter's and Adorno's positions would appear deeply compromised by their investments in postwar liberalism, which had, in the wake of the Second World War and in the shadow of the Cold War, agreed temporarily to protect academic freedom and intellectual autonomy from the vicissitudes of the marketplace. In fact, both Hofstadter and Adorno would be accused of the unforgivable sin of elitism in the decades after the 1960s. By 1992, in cultural studies scholar Jim McGuigan's essentially sympathetic critique of "cultural populism," elitism had revealed itself as a vice to which no one would confess: "Being thought an 'elitist' is just as bad as being a 'populist' if not worse." For McGuigan, "elitist" is "used occasionally as convenient shorthand for ideological positions that are disrespectful of ordinary people's tastes."[71] From McGuigan's point of view, Adorno and Horkheimer represented "neo-aristocratic," crypto-Nietzschean positions regarding mass culture and the "culture industry" that Raymond Williams had been able to correct and overcome. In order to connect with the power of the people, the monopoly of knowledge and expertise had to be broken. For twentieth-century purposes, the politics of a cultural populism identified modernism as an adversary armed with continental European cultural condescension, ready to perpetrate an outrage upon "ordinariness." Although McGuigan is critical of knee-jerk cultural populism, he praises its attempts to forge "solidarity with ordinary people's capacity to win space from below."[72]

One of the most serious engagements with the new configurations of culture and politics in relationship to populism could be found in Stuart Hall's work on the rise of Thatcherism in Great Britain during the late 1970s and early 1980s. *The Hard Road to Renewal: Thatcherism and the Crisis of the Left* is one of the best polemical engagements with populism and populist discontent in post-1960s Great Britain. For Hall, the base/superstructure model of analysis had failed to galvanize support or produce creative engagements with working-class interests or popular culture. Hall's anguished testimony to the failure of a post-1960s Left to articulate a program of socialism led him to coin the term "authoritarian populism" to describe Margaret Thatcher's rise to power. Hall sought to account for Thatcher's success in the dual policies of brutal union busting and propagandistic appeal to British nationalism and insecurity. He criticized the Labour Party for failing to address the cultural discontent and malaise with social democracy. Labour oversaw the expansion of the social democratic state, with its Fabian solutions to social problems and its deployment of a technocratic, bureaucratic apparatus to deal with ordinary people. An authoritarian populism emerged that appealed affectively to the experience of everyday life in economically besieged, deindustrializing England. While the Labour Left stood on the side of the experts and the state, it appeared that only Thatcher was able to give voice to "real problems and real and lived experiences, real contradictions." In the area of education, the Right gained a great deal of ground by stoking, in conjunction with the popular press such as the *Mail*, the *Sun*, and the *Express*, the flames of a crisis of "falling standards." Hall's assessment was trenchant: in a time of economic recession, the Left simply caved in to right-wing criticisms about falling standards and social anomie. According to Hall, Labour was caught between viewing education either as a means of "improving chances for working-class children" or as a means of improving the "economic and efficiency needs of the productive system itself." When the Labour Left happily accepted the formula "success in education = meeting the needs of industry," it betrayed any notion of democratic or socialist reorganization that could result in a truly progressive concept of collective life.[73] In conceiving of education as a tool of industrial expansion, Labour demonstrated that it had sold out the people's interests to business needs. In the midst of a recession and general economic anxiety, it turned out that the Right was able to embody and articulate working-class and petit bourgeois discontent, all the while reshaping the political parameters of the education problem so that popular sentiment could be turned in favor of competition, free markets, and nationalist, anti-immigrant sentiments. An anti-intellectualism that despised the autonomy of noninstrumentalized knowledge was also a critical piece of the authoritarian populism that became the political and cultural arm of an ascendant Right in British politics.

Hall's cultural and academic program inspired an antieducational street-smart embrace of the people that had emerged as a magical weapon wielded by the Right against the mystifications of both the high culture–loving Arts Council and the leaders of Labour.[74] If Thatcher could consolidate her powers by speaking directly to petit bourgeois fears of chaos and cultural disorder, it was imagined that a culturally reconfigured Left could rally the discontented and the marginal to an oppositional stance based upon allegiances with the struggle for autonomy and "for space from below." A specifically working-class worship of pure style emerged in the 1970s that drew the attention of Dick Hebdige, who received an MA at the Centre for Cultural Studies in Birmingham. Hebdige saw that punks, mods, and rockers as well as other working-class street-smart dandies attacked the well-meaning hyperrationalism of administered society. Punk and other counter-countercultural street styles caught British academics off guard when they married the stylish imperturbability of the nineteenth-century dandy to a smartly turned out, defiant nihilism of a disenchanted white working class. Punk and its predecessors expressed a hatred for meritocracy, social democratic institutions, and the compromises of the Labour Party. Hebdige's work on subcultures was groundbreaking in cultural criticism insofar as he did seem to address quite directly the lived experience of social contradictions in 1970s and 1980s Great Britain. Using the work of Roland Barthes to interpret British street style, Hebdige was able to reframe the cultural and social world with new tools, endowing the defiant styles of punks, mods, and rockers with structuralist and semiotic significance. A working-class generational rebellion was at hand, and the pioneering cultural studies theorist saw in the disturbing and imperturbable dandyishness of street culture a critical break with parental loyalties to Labour and social democracy.[75] This Left-inflected subcultural populism, based on an immersion in styles of popular consumption habits, may have been pioneered in Great Britain, but it emerged renewed and reconfigured as a powerful rubric for new scholarship challenging the disposition of academic knowledge in the United States. Any attack on the elites and elitism, whether or not it was grounded on the principles of a long and historical struggle against corporate capitalism and monopoly forms, resonated deeply with Americans. The antielitist animus of the cultural studies agenda spoke to powerful strains of historical populism in the American political imagination. Cultural populism demonstrated an unremitting suspicion of elites, who more often than not were associated with aristocratic, effete, manipulative, non-American thinkers, critics, and artists whose intellectual aspirations disguised a more nefarious form of will to power. In Hofstadter's analyses, anti-intellectualism appeared to be antiauthoritarian in its inspiration, but when pressed for political solutions, it devolved almost immediately into a nativist resentment of intellectual and aesthetic freedoms. The assertion of individual sovereignty against the institutionalization and fragmentation of knowledge was reflected in the populist belief in the basic integrity of the ordinary person, the common man, the forgotten man, the small business owner as modern yeoman who had become the best twentieth-century representative of "the people." The mythologization of the ordinary thus replaced the American pastoral.

In 1990 Larry Grossberg, Paula Treichler, and Cary Nelson hosted an epoch-making conference at the University of Illinois at Urbana-Champaign. The conference was the second ever official gathering of cultural studies scholars, the first having taken place in 1988, when it was still preoccupied with Marxist themes. According to Chris Rojek's recent introduction to the history of cultural studies, the 1990 conference was marked by growing confidence and a distinctive note of "professionalization."[76] The conference proceedings were published two years later by Routledge. Under the directorship of Bill Germano, a publishing visionary, Routledge became one of the preeminent publishers of the new scholarship. *Cultural Studies*, the collected volume of conference proceedings, went on to become one of the cornerstones of the new American field of cultural studies. In the introduction to the 1992 volume, editors Grossberg, Treichler, and Nelson described the "unprecedented" international boom of this new academic movement.[77]

The success of cultural studies was so complete that a new anxiety had arisen. Many authors included in the collection gave voice to a set of worries about the routinization of the race/class/gender critical matrix, but the inclusion of these critical points of view seemed only to make the academic movement appear more robust. Cultural studies emerged as a robust and eclectic form of academic self-criticism. In the volume, certain marked tendencies and points of agreement could be found. The Frankfurt School remained the obscure enemy: despite the pleas for relevance and engagement, there was little discussion about the end of the Cold War but a great deal of worry about elitism. Foucault was the most frequently cited French theorist. Contributions were wide-ranging: if an intellectual spectrum could be measured, we would have to put Homi Bhabha's essay, "Postcolonial Authority and Postmodern Guilt," a peripatetic rumination on postcolonialism, South Asian situations and thinkers, the musings of Barthes in Tangiers, Frantz Fanon, Rushdie, Lacan, Freud, and Toni Morrison's *Beloved* on one end and Jan Zita Grover's "AIDS, Keywords and Cultural Work," a deeply personal testimony to her work in AIDS activism, on the other. Bhabha's famous invocation of the "third space" of hybrid identities gave form to his attempts to produce a lyrical, theoretical, informal, barely argued form of the essay. The stylistic innovations that Bhabha attempted to invoke also distinguished him as one of the purveyors of "high theory" within a volume that was at best ambivalent about the intellectual nexus that Bhabha sought to occupy.[78]

Douglas Crimp's "Portraits of People with AIDS" and Jan Zita Grover's contribution were most striking in their condemnation of academic scholarship in general and with regard to the AIDS crisis in particular. Both Crimp and Grover described their increasing disillusionment with academia and academics while articulating the greater satisfactions provided by social movement activism. In Grover's essay, academics appeared as a by now familiar group of stodgy literary formalists who remained stubbornly out of touch with the struggles of their students and "the people." Grover's essay was short but affecting: it used powers of populist persuasion to give voice to one of the most important "structures" of academic populist feeling in the late 1980s and 1990s. Many could sympathize with Grover's feelings of being "hemmed in" by the formal study of literature. For Grover, "people outside the academy read and use many of the same materials that scholars do, although often their style of dealing with them is more direct, blunt, and emotional. These, I think are virtues rather than defects at any level of discourse."[79] Professors, especially literature professors, were in some way always pretentious. When she compared ordinary people with professors, the professors looked ridiculous as well as superfluous. From this point of view, Adorno trying to give his talk "Dialectical Thinking" in 1969 would have embodied succinctly for the new generation of scholars and academics the vanity of the elitist and the academic. The people appeared heroic, emotionally connected, hardworking, practical, and besieged on all sides by communities of experts and professionals who were ready to exploit their probity. In Grover's analysis, academic research and expert knowledge were essentially and substantively flawed. For Crimp, the highly mediated academic interventions on AIDS took place when "people are dying in the street." The opposition between the authentic knowledge and suffering that took place on the street and the pretension and falseness that were staged in classrooms and lecture halls could not have been more stark. The grounds of Crimp's and Grover's discontentment with academia were absolutely legitimate.

The publication of *Social Text*'s 1984 special issue on the 1960s and Fredric Jameson's "Postmodernism, or the Cultural Logic of Late Capitalism" in the *New Left Review* was critical for shaping debates about cultural politics within academia during this period.[80] Also in 1984, Michel de Certeau's *Practice of Everyday Life* was published in English, and its ideas about ordinary people would point to a new direction in the study of fandom and star worship as everyday life.[81] The translation of Certeau's work into English would define the direction of popular culture and media studies in the decades that followed: his influence was especially evident in the work of new media scholar Henry Jenkins.[82] The late 1980s saw the countercultural Left consummate its student radicalism in the form of self- and institutional critique: the publication of Andrew Ross's *No Respect* was a critical academic and intellectual event. *No Respect* was favorably reviewed by Robert Christgau (in the *Village Voice*) and Jon Wiener (in the *Nation*) and seemed to signal that British cultural studies was carving out a new space in the public sphere about the "central role cultural politics should play in a revived left."[83] In affirming popular culture and its deep engagement with "the feelings, desires, aspirations, and pleasures of ordinary people," Ross gave voice to an ardent ambition to fuse the interests of popular culture and the cultivation of "populist self-esteem."[84]

In 1990 Stuart Hall's "The Emergence of Cultural Studies and the Crisis in the Humanities" appeared in the journal *October* as part of a special issue on the humanities as a social technology. Hall suggested that the humanities were merely a social technology of oppression whose usefulness had expired: their weaknesses had been revealed by the emergence of cultural studies. In fact, in the face of real contestation and rejuvenation of their dry-as-dust methods, the humanities as a set of practices and interests were distinctly hostile to the birth of cultural studies. In his account, the old, hidebound humanities were jealous of the youth and vigor of the new interdisciplinary matrix of oppositional practices and methods known as cultural studies. For Hall, the humanities were clearly on the side of the reactionary politics that had prevented Great Britain from actually entering the modern world. Popular culture and new media, with all their suppleness and fluidity, had disturbed cultural hierarchies and powers. The Centre for Cultural Studies at Birmingham became a place where the humanities would witness the emergence and dissemination of their unruly and unwanted stepchild.

While Hall refused the "populist intellectual" aspect of the cultural studies project, he attacked the elitism of British national culture, of literary study, and made fun of Leavisite seriousness for being terribly inadequate in solving the pressing problem of culture and politics. F. R. Leavis was an influential literary critic of the 1950s whose formalist approach was directed at modern poetry and novels. Hall framed the pedagogical questions that he might pose to a potential cultural studies graduate student in this way: "What do you really think is a problem you don't understand out there in the terrible interconnection between culture and politics? What is it about the way in which British culture is now living through its kind of postcolonial, post-hegemonic crisis that really bites into your experience?"[85] In his history of the Birmingham Centre for Cultural Studies, Hall maintained a critical attitude about the disciplinary configuration of any form of knowledge. Hall's keen sense of marginality gave urgency to the imperative to translate intellectual knowledge "into the battle of culture." The journal *October* was and still is one of the most active interdisciplinary journals of its time, taking a critical view of the New York art world and the academic and disciplinary state of art history. During the theoretical efflorescence of the late 1980s and early 1990s, it set the terms for many of the most important intellectual debates taking place between artists and academics.

In the transcribed discussion of Andrew Ross's paper on the New Age, which became a long chapter in his book *Strange Weather: Culture, Science and Technology in the Age of Limits*, Jennifer Daryl Slack criticized him in the following manner: "You don't sound like a fan [of the New Age]." She reminded him of Donna Haraway's assertion that she never undertook the study of something to which she was not "vulnerable." Ross welcomed her question with gratitude but sagely cautioned against allowing the "intellectual as fan" to become a "new kind of credentialism." Ross's clever reminder not to go too far in imposing a "fan" requirement on intellectuals implied that with academic affirmations of our vulnerabilities, all that was needed was a bit of moderation. As if to undercut his own admonition, Ross had recourse to a self-revealing gesture. More specifically, he confessed to a cryptoautobiographical investment in the New Age: "All such research is deeply autobiographical."[86] Even Jameson in his review of *Cultural Studies*, the enormous edited volume of the 1990 cultural studies conference proceedings, could not resist this demand when he rather tendentiously identified James Clifford and himself as "white males."[87] Such was the temper of the times. And so academic autobiography and self-location became gestures of solidarity with a politics of difference that no well-intentioned scholar would dare to forgo for fear of appearing aloof from his or her object of research and critique. The professor would have to bare his soul, if not his breast, in a gesture of reciprocated exhibitionism: Jameson speculated that the 1980s would be a decade of reckoning for "the inflationary expectations of [the] 1960s and its overvaluation of the world-changing, revolutionary potential of the student movement." Jameson predicted that the 1980s would be "characterized by an effort on a world scale, to proletarianize all those unbound social forces that gave the 1970s their energy, by an extension of class struggle, in other words, into the farthest reaches of the globe as well as the most minute configurations of local institutions (such as the university system)."[88]

In other words, whereas the German SDS Women's Council bared their breasts to a speechless professor in 1969, garrulous professors of the 1980s were ready to pay tribute to feminist social movements with an aspirationally equivalent gesture of rhetorical self-exposure. Performative self-revealing had become not only intellectually acceptable but ethically and politically necessary: the reticence of the elites had to be broken. The self-contained WASP reticence of an aspiring child of immigrants like Seymour Levov was portrayed as obsolete: Levov was crippled by his sheer propriety, his lack of imagination, and his belief in craftsmanship and liberal humanist principles. Merry Levov was Roth's hyperbolic countercultural villainess, an ungrateful daughter who had tasted and rejected all the fruits of the American dream. Embracing instead an idiosyncratic, cobbled-together, and extreme version of a South Asian religious sect, Merry Levov stood in for the self-aggrandizing generation's rejection of American liberalism and its democratic potential. From the counterculture's point of view, we had Theodor Adorno, a culture villain for the Left who allegedly proved himself a frightened and weak man and called the police when he saw students readying themselves to occupy his office building. Adorno appeared as an out-of-touch elitist who was unable to engage with women in an institutional environment, an old cad made speechless by a vision of Amazonian shamelessness. From within the professoriate, Marshall McLuhan had predicted in 1964 that bureaucracies and hierarchies were being smashed by the power of electronic media and the "person-to-person" relationships that they facilitated. Indeed, the lecture and the lecturer were disappearing before our very eyes.[89]

the new age of cultural studies

A vast spiritual restlessness animated the counterculture in the wake of the civil and social unrest of the 1960s. The dark ferment of youth in rebellion and its feral potentiality haunted those who came of age at the end of the turbulent decade. Joan Didion had reported with some trepidation from Haight-Ashbury in 1967: "The center was not holding." Less than twenty years after Arthur M. Schlesinger's eloquent declaration that "the hope of the future surely lies in the revival of the Center," his vigorous defense of moderation and centrism— "Neither fascism nor communism can win so long as there remains a democratic middle way, which unites hopes of freedom and of economic abundance"— appeared to be no different from complicity and hypocritical compromise with the domination and violence of bigotry and imperialism.[1] Schlesinger's middle way seemed to lead to the soulless conformity and callow consumerism condemned by the authors of the Port Huron Statement of 1962. The youthful rebels were a generation born into a prosperity that began to repel them: "Some would have us believe that Americans feel contentment amidst prosperity— but might it not better be called a glaze above deeply felt anxieties about their role in the new world? And if these anxieties produce a developed indifference to human affairs, do they not as well produce a yearning to believe there is an alternative to the present, that something can be done to change circumstances in the school, the workplaces, the bureaucracies, the government?"[2] The American center seemed to keel under the accumulated discontent of its best and brightest: there was an urgent sense that the past needed to be destroyed in order for the future to be born. The counterculture welcomed the anarchy evoked by Joan Didion in her reportage from San Francisco when she cited William Butler Yeats's "The Second Coming."[3] Schlesinger's center seemed sullied by its association with the political stalemate of the Cold War and the material blandishments of a smug, middle-class suburban life. There had to be an alternative politics, an alternative culture, an alternative economy that the young themselves would have to create, since the older generation had abandoned them to the disastrous inevitability of the present. Whereas Michael Young described a parodic and violent populist revolt of the underclass against meritocratic selection, it was the middle-class youth of the 1960s who rose up against "mainstream culture."[4]

In the recent cultural history of the United States, antielitist populist animus has taken the form of a revolt against reason in both religious and radical circles: one of the most unpredictable sites of rebellion took place within academia itself. In the 1950s and 1960s Hofstadter grappled with the political and intellectual import of anti-intellectualism, taking it for granted that his academic readers would agree with him that the cultivation of reasoned detachment necessary for the discipline of an autonomous, liberal intellect was worthy of defense. That consensus in fact did not hold, and, most strikingly, it has not held among academics and intellectuals. The conditions of Fordist modernism that supported the work of Hofstadter and Daniel Bell would eventually give way to modes of production dominated by "flexibility." In this new world of post-Fordist work and management, workers had to be trained to be cybernetically responsive to ever-changing job market demands. It may, in fact, be true that liberal education, with its insistence on reason, difficulty, intellectual history, and tradition, has seen its day. The forms and practices of critique that have come to replace it understand themselves as inherently transgressive and emancipatory. Antielitist academic criticism espouses solidarity with the plebiscitary judgment of popular opinion. Mark Fenster condemned Hofstadter's *Anti-intellectualism in American Life* for its dark vision of popular democracy and labeled both Hofstadter and Bell neoconservative because they condemned forms of popular extremism.[5] "Extremism" became the denigrated pole of the famous "binary oppositions"; "centrism," its opposite, had been incorrectly "privileged" by "liberal" critics. Extremism called out for redemption. For cultural studies, the difference between extremist and moderate had to be "deconstructed," "disrupted," "complicated," and "subverted."

Haight-Ashbury, more than any other place in the United States, seemed as if it could be the new Bethlehem, or at least an infernal crucible where the savior was to be born: it was there that hippies and heads sought the fierceness of the beast, the innocence of the newborn child, and the flat, clean desert from which to create a new and better world. In *Slouching towards Bethlehem*, Didion described the United States in 1967 as "a country of bankruptcy notices and public-auction announcements and commonplace reports of casual killings and misplaced children and vandals who misplaced even the four-letter words they scrawled. . . . People were missing. Children were missing. Parents were missing."[6] Didion was, by her own admission, a nervous and imperfect witness to a feeling of incipient revelation and catastrophe in the cradle of American counterculture:

Haight-Ashbury, 1967, ground zero of the explosion of creative destruction that had been launched by dreams of world-changing, countercultural messianism. From Ken Kesey's retreat in La Honda in San Mateo County, a vision of an alternative future swept out and through the hills of San Francisco, wafting incense, marijuana, and manure across a country starved for something new, reaching far across the Atlantic, blowing through the imagination of millions of young people who one day would wake up and discard their button-downs and pearls and twinsets and penny loafers in order to don the velvets, ruffles, feathers, and soft boots of pirates and gypsies. The year before Didion published her astonishing essay, the psychedelic bomb that launched the countercultural revolution had already gone off in northern California when Ken Kesey and the Merry Pranksters decided to run the first of what Kesey called Acid Tests.

The Trips Festival, which took place from January 21 to 23, 1966, in the Longshoreman's Hall in San Francisco, was going to be an Acid Test on a bigger scale, thoroughly wired and psychedelic. It would simulate the LSD experience, since the drug had been recently outlawed. Stewart Brand, who first had the idea to rent a large space and throw open its doors, brought to the event his peyote and avant-garde-infused sense of performance and multimedia installation art. Bill Graham, a New York impresario and then a member of the San Francisco Mime Troupe, helped to organize the three-day festival of multimedia installations, music, and immersive experiences. The Grateful Dead and Big Brother and the Holding Company supplied the music. Describing the festival, Fred Turner wrote: "Brand and some friends performed his multimedia piece, 'America Needs Indians,' which consisted of soundtracks, three slide projectors and four Native American dancers. Brand thought of it as an immersive experience."[7] Two days before the festival, Kesey was arrested for possession of marijuana, giving the festival even greater publicity and notoriety. Thousands of curious young people ended up attending Trips: the festival gave shape and form to a vision of a different America, a youthful, warped Utopia of drugs, music, and art. It was so successful that Graham began offering weekly Trips festivals at the Fillmore West. Turner observed that "within a year, teenagers from across America would be streaming into Haight Ashbury, looking for the sort of Utopia Graham was marketing. Reporters for *Time* and *Life* were not far behind."[8] News of the "dread LSD" spread like wildfire through all of San Francisco's various interlocking bohemian, intellectual, and social circles. For Tom Wolfe, the festival "was the first national convention of an underground movement that had existed on a hush-hush cell-by-cell basis. . . . Haight-Ashbury Era began that weekend."[9]

A year later, there was already, from Didion's point of view, an uneasy sense of anticipation and anticlimax on the streets of San Francisco: activists tried to organize all that youthful energy into a revolution, but the Utopian yearnings of the counterculture were not so easily channeled into a streamlined political program. According to Didion, "Of course, the activists—not those whose thinking had become rigid, but those whose approach to revolution was imaginatively anarchic—had long ago seen the reality which still eluded the press: we were seeing something important. We were seeing the desperate attempt of a handful of pathetically unequipped children to create a community in a social vacuum."[10] Didion described the various political actors as vacillating between paranoia and cold-blooded realpolitik. Almost all her informants promised her that something big was about to happen. She befriended young heads like Mark and Sharon, who spent their days cooking health food, smoking pot, and planning their next LSD trip. Didion also sought out community organizers like Arthur Lisch and Chester Anderson. They were very hard to pin down, and despite Didion's most earnest attempts to find them, they eluded her journalistic grasp. She may have seen the hippies and flower children as fatefully ill equipped for the impending cataclysm and rebirth, but the movement's informal leaders and impresarios turned out to be remarkably adept at forming, marketing, and shaping the energies of the countercultural revolution. Bill Graham and Stewart Brand went on to make a great deal of money from their various enterprises, Graham as a rock-and-roll promoter and Brand as a completely new sort of northern California entrepreneur. Stewart Brand, a midwesterner, was educated at Philips Exeter and Stanford. He grew up dreading both nuclear apocalypse and "the organization man": torn between these two fates—incineration by nuclear fire or living a life of white-collar dissatisfaction—he was determined to be an artist. Brand found that creative self-sufficiency was the most important value. Ken Kesey possessed the full range of necessary qualities to be an energetic leader and frontiersman of the early republic. Faye, his wife, could have been one of the long-suffering pioneer women, braving harsh prairie winters to cook and sew for her adventurous husband and gaggle of tow-headed children. In his *Electric Kool-Aid Acid Test*, Wolfe quotes Kesey as saying, "Don't stop plunging into the forest." Kesey insisted he was going to lead his tribe into the unexplored wilds of psychedelic consciousness and that he was tasked with leaving tracks for others to follow.[11] The Merry Pranksters were dreaming the American dreams: their countercultural imagination was shaped by acid and the myths of the American frontier. In Kesey's words,

> In Manzanillo, I took some acid and I threw the I Ching. And the I Ching—the great thing about the I Ching is . . . it slaps you in the face when you need it—and it said

we had reached the end of something, we weren't going anywhere any longer, it was time for a new direction—and I went outside and there was an electrical storm, and there was lightning everywhere and I pointed to the sky and lightning flashed all of a sudden I had a second skin, of lightning, electricity, like a suit of electricity, and I knew it was in us to be superheroes and that we could become superheroes or nothing.[12]

This electrical dream of the superhuman potential in every enlightened mortal being may have seemed self-indulgent and excessive, but Christopher Lasch failed to see its creative energies. Like Adorno, he became the square audience who could not "get on the bus" and be a part of the enormous cultural and evolutionary upheaval that Kesey envisioned.

Shaped by postwar prosperity and its particular set of comforts and anxieties, children of the middle class entered American universities in unprecedented numbers during the 1960s. Endowed with a growing sense of self-consciousness and self-confidence, a generation of Americans weaned on the counterculture, television, and rock-and-roll defiantly claimed their place in the academic professions during the 1970s and 1980s. They gave voice to a deep impatience with the humanistic and liberal values of their professors and participated in a redefinition of both politics and critique: their politics were defined by cultural struggles rather than by the "class-reductionist" methods of their forebears. Rock-and-roll and the youth-centered counterculture fueled their zeal to supplant the cultural values of the Old Left.[13] Christopher Lasch remarked drily, "In the seventies, the most common criticism of higher education revolves around the charge of cultural elitism."[14] Didion's very reference to the Yeats poem would seem an affront to countercultural youth for whom the future and not the past vibrated with meaning and possibility. For progressive sociologist of the 1960s and 1970s Herbert J. Gans, cultural conservatives and radicals from T. S. Eliot to the thinkers of the Frankfurt School were united by a fear of popular culture "and felt impelled to defend high culture against what they deemed to be a serious threat from popular culture, the industries that provide it, and its publics."[15] New York intellectuals of Left and Right Irving Howe and Irving Kristol had proven equally deaf to the siren song of rock-and-roll and deconstruction. Despite their modest origins in New York City's teeming Jewish ghettos and tenements, to the young and the impatient they appeared as "aristocrats" and "patricians." Whereas the Old Left saw themselves as a class of intellectuals who had an ethical obligation to act as Socratic "legislators," the New Left saw themselves as participants in and "interpreters" of a diverse array of cultural and political struggles and conflicts.[16]

Consequently, the 1980s bore witness to a sense of institutional and intellectual optimism for the countercultural New Left academics. A generation of increasingly empowered scholars who had cut their teeth on post-1968 struggles defined an aggressive new attitude toward the Old Left. Theorists and cultural studies scholars participated shoulder to shoulder in defending themselves against attacks coming from dyspeptic conservatives and dogmatic Old Left holdouts. Sophisticated, cosmopolitan, and antiauthoritarian, this new generation of academics was extremely critical of what they saw as the Cold War complicity of their institutional and academic predecessors. The most vanguardist members of the academic Left had experimented with communal life, had taken mind-expanding drugs, had multiple sexual partners of both sexes, sometimes in the same bed, and were inclined toward countercultural forms of existence that promised alternative ways of being and working together. They entered the professions while retaining their Utopian investments for these alternative forms of collective and communal coexistence. Not only did their generational quest for self-determination shape popular culture and mass aspirations in the 1970s and 1980s, but their ambitions remade academia as well. Like Stewart Brand, they feared becoming a small cog in a large, impersonal "machine." Small-scale technologies and Eastern spirituality galvanized the Utopian aspirations of these countercultural men and women. New forms of being together, new forms of work, new forms of sex, and new forms of connectivity could be fostered and cultivated with minimal interference from centralized powers like the state. For Sarah Pike, a religious studies scholar who wrote about New Age religions, "weekend retreat centers like Esalen were to some extent a withdrawal from the political scene. . . . Countercultural men and women envisioned communes as model alternatives to the society they had rejected, and alternative spiritual practices were part of their vision."[17] Countercultural enclaves existed as autonomous zones, peopled by like-minded participants in experiments in communal living: most communes shunned contact or affiliation with local or national politics.

In *No Respect: Intellectuals and Popular Culture*, Andrew Ross identified the uncomfortable coexistence of two contradictory attitudes toward intellectual life as incarnated by high culture and professional expertise: popular feeling vacillated between submissiveness and indifference. Ross claimed, like Stuart Hall and Dick Hebdige, that powerful, politically resonant meanings could be extracted from the popular indifference to intellectual life. If high culture and liberal consensus were the tools of hegemony that worked to extract cultural and political deference from the people, popular rejection of taste and judgment could be reforged as tools of insurgent antiauthoritarianism. Having honed his analytical skills on popular ambivalence toward professionals and intellectuals in the postwar era, he was ready to take on contemporary confrontations between scientists and mystics, experts and laymen, Cold War liberals and countercultural radicals. A scant two years after *No Respect*, Ross published *Strange Weather: Culture, Science and Technology in the Age of Limits*. In this book he analyzed the significance of New Age, science fiction, and hacker subcultures in the context of what he called "technoculture." His work on hackers was one of the earliest academic engagements with this important field of activity and activism. In his investigation of the New Age subculture, he found that its adherents held deeply contradictory attitudes about scientific expertise and scientific legitimacy: they simultaneously sought robust alternatives to and affirmation from mainstream science. New Age medicine was implicitly critical of Western, allopathic attitudes toward the body. Its practices sought to revive allegedly "gentler" forms of intuitive, hands-on folk healing and remedies that the professionalization of medicine had suppressed or eliminated from the healing arts. Most important for Ross, New Age people were looking for empowerment and self-control through their exploration of alternative healing practices that were marginalized by mainstream medicine because of fear and prejudice.

Ross praised "non-class reductionism" and "lack of systematicity" as desirable qualities in cultural studies methodology, and he put his commitment to those values to practice in his study of the New Age technoculture. In the first chapter, "A Kinder, Gentler Science," concerned with the New Age's aspirations for an expanded notion of human capacity, he enthused that the convergence of counterculture and technology posed a fundamental challenge to the ways we thought about the relationship between life, work, play, consciousness, and knowledge. The combination of "kinder, gentler" was certainly an allusion to George H. W. Bush's "kinder, gentler" nation, but it was not at all clear what, if any, political meaning Ross derived from the president's appeal to establishing a more caring national ethos. Ross's study of the New Age was an excellent example of eclectic thick description mixed with a smattering of historical contextualization. He aligned the New Age with anti-Enlightenment movements like mesmerism and drew out its relationship to hermeticism, mysticism, and alchemy, but he did not belabor his readings with a demanding intellectual genealogy for any of those concepts. Directed against the repressive and ascetic authoritarianism associated with the abstract notion of "universal reason," Ross's arguments were not meant to demonize Western science or philosophy. Ross was, however, extremely optimistic about alternative forms of apprehending the world. Against the Enlightenment claims of disembodied and scientific objectivity, he offered a self-consciously autobiographical concept of the incarnate "scholar" grounded in his own body and its particularities and desires.

Ross had been struggling on the front lines of redefining cultural politics since his arrival in the United States from the U.K. in the 1980s. In *No Respect* he worked tirelessly to demystify the Old Left's hostility toward middlebrow and petit bourgeois culture. In *Strange Weather* he went so far as to suggest that intellectuals and academics found New Age culture embarrassing and petit bourgeois. They were repelled by "the more contiguous field of middlebrow culture."[18] New Age cultural critique aimed too close to the intellectual and academic middle class's social and cultural investments; its critique of the healing professions, including doctors, social workers, and psychotherapists, was alleged to be deeply disturbing to a Left that could praise the working class but feared its own intimacy with petit bourgeois cultural forms. Ross seemed to be recapitulating Freud's theory of the narcissism of small differences: intellectuals and academics were simply embarrassed by their middle-class brethren, striving for autonomy and self-determination. Ross seemed to suggest that middle-class academics had an easier time embracing working-class violence and rebellion as embodied by punk, but in the face of New Age cultures, they clung stubbornly to their sense of cultural and intellectual superiority in order to differentiate themselves from people with whom they had too much in common. If intellectuals and academics only were able to embrace solidarity with the New Age community, they would have learned important lessons from its challenges to the "institutions of science and religion."

According to Ross, "One of the undeniable strengths of cultural studies has lain in its willingness to explain the significance of such subcultures. Their practices offer less articulate, less pure, and less overtly political kinds of cultural critique than the left has traditionally felt comfortable endorsing." The New Age also represented a complex and eclectic attempt at "linking subjectivity with larger social or structural change." Where "conservative left patricians" like Christopher Lasch, Daniel Bell, and Russell Jacoby saw an orgiastic picture of countercultural "narcissism," Ross saw a healthy, subjectivist response to the ideological "bankruptcy of state socialist, capitalist and scientific materialism."[19] Although Ross claimed that he did not want to practice "class-reductionist" criticism, he reserved his sharpest class-oriented critique for traditional Left critics, tarring them with the labels of "elitist" and "patrician" in one paragraph. Lasch, Bell, and Jacoby practiced a traditional form of what Ross called "polemical" criticism, making interventions at a safe distance "from the lived experience of culture." Ross was making a powerful argument against the fundamental irrelevance of traditional education. In *The Culture of Narcissism*, Christopher Lasch accused "radicals" of colluding with university administrators in the instrumentalization of higher education. For Lasch, the radical cultural studies scholar and the administrator were equally anti-intellectual. The insistence on relevance in education dovetailed neatly with the service mission of "the multiversity." He continued, "Even when seriously advanced in opposition to sterile academic pedantry, the slogan of relevance embodied an underlying antagonism to education itself—an inability to take an interest in anything beyond immediate experience. . . . Instead of trying to hold the university to a more modest set of objectives, radical critics of higher education accepted the premise that education could solve every sort of social problem."[20]

According to Ross, Lasch was simply trying to dominate public opinion about the critical debates of the day. Critics like Lasch took advantage of their "elitist" access to "media and intellectual opinion" in order to cajole, coerce, and persuade their readers to accept and agree with their positions, but cultural studies was doing something very different. Ross argued that he and other scholars of alternative cultural forms were in fact successfully practicing a kind of academic scholarship that was boots on the ground, implicated and involved with the most urgent problems of the world, squarely situated on the side of "lived experience," and opposed to the reproduction of lofty ideas. Unlike the work of traditional Left critics who hectored the people from their aeries of privilege and presumption, this new, more relevant, and less negative form of cultural critique was poised to draw out all the subtle political implications of the most obscure and eccentric subcultures.[21]

"A Kinder, Gentler Science" opened with an account of Ross's 1989 visit to the Whole Life Expo for Body Mind and Spirit in New York City. At the Expo he was attracted to the conspiracy theory preoccupation with the damaging effects of low frequency electricity. Ross also marveled at New Age obsessions with expanding the capacities of the human mind through brain stimulation, neural enhancement, and technological synchrony of left/right brain action. After a visit to the "science seminar" on the topic of extra low frequency (ELF) electromagnetic radiation (sponsored by ELF Cocoon International, a company that offered consumers protection from these emissions), Ross took in the Expo as a whole, a dizzying collection of spiritual and countercultural adepts and aspirants. He made lists of the featured speakers, which included Timothy Leary, Marilyn Ferguson, Kevin Ryerson, and Deepak Chopra. He confessed that he flocked with others who had attended the science panel to a "free joyride on wild brain machines," of which he offered a tantalizing list: the "Synchro-Energizer, the Alpha Stim, the RelaxPak, the Graham Potentializer." These gadgets embodied the New Age's enthusiasm for technological forms of cognitive enhancement, expanded consciousness, and self-transformation. The dream of mind expansion harked back to Ken Kesey's vision of the post-LSD superman wearing an "electrified second skin," as recounted by Tom Wolfe. The psychedelic superhuman was being realized as a gadget-enhanced, fully wired, New Age cyborg. The entrepreneurs, vendors, and participants at the Whole Life Expo wanted to expand human capacities for experience while reforming medical and scientific research for nonprofessional publics. The Expo was an organized, marketable, 1980s version of the mind expansion Ken Kesey and the Merry Pranksters found in LSD. In a primal act of appropriation and *détournement*, Kesey had taken the drug as part of a military experiment and turned the table on the experimenters: "The White Smocks were supposedly using them. Instead the White Smocks had handed them the very key itself. . . . [W]ith these drugs your perception is altered enough that you find yourself looking out of completely strange eyeholes."[22] The Whole Life Expo, however, seemed bent on lowering the bar of entry into Kesey's altered states and alternative collectivities. At the Expo, Kesey's altered vision could be attained by those who purchased the right gadget or drug. The Merry Pranksters themselves underwent grueling initiations: some were rejected because they could not keep up with the group's constant emotional confrontations, some couldn't stand the squalor, and some could not ingest the necessary amount of acid without lapsing into clinical states of paranoia or psychosis. It was not easy to get on Kesey's bus, and it was even harder to stay there; by the 1980s, however, a wild joy ride with a select and enlightened inner circle seemed a flip of a switch away. Dropping out and tuning in never seemed easier. Even though the commodification and routinization of mind expansion was the last thing Ross would find desirable, he did not condemn the New Age experiments with "brain machines." Nor did he comment on the eminently American hard sell of the many small-scale entrepreneurs staging the Whole Life Expo's exhibits and speeches.

Ross predicted that the New Age was on its way to producing a "personalized" scientific humanism. New Agers combined an embrace of small-scale technologies with a healthy skepticism about mainstream science. According to Ross, the "New Age has assumed a virtuoso experimental role in reconstructing a humanistic personality for science—science with a human face. A kinder, gentler science. Appeals to personalism aggravates deeply rooted in popular distrust of authority and the desire for self-control: it cannot be dismissed as a 'petty-bourgeois' obsession."[23] Crystal healing, spirit channeling, astrology, and Reiki massage presented just the tip of the iceberg when it came to spiritual innovation that would have outraged cultural elitists of the Left and Right. For Ross, the New Age represented one of the most powerful, antiauthoritarian movements that came out of the 1960s counterculture, whose larger projects and goals had been preserved in the entrepreneurial, small-scale technophilia of the late 1980s. Aimed at securing self-determination and sovereignty for ordinary people in a technocratic society where science and scientists had been unquestioningly worshiped, the New Age subculture believed in the coevolution of human beings and their technology. Coevolution was good because it was natural. If "mainstream" science lay claim to God-like authority, the New Age and the counterculture represented a compelling form of heresy.

Ross described the messages of a wide range of channelers as a complex "celebration of the [New Age's] ability to resolve technical problems of communication."[24] He presented himself as a participant/observer fundamentally in sympathy with the New Age project to democratize science and scientific experimentation in keeping with the intuitions of popular "lived experience." Ross insisted that the New Age was aligned with the demands for social justice and civil rights coming from new social movements. For the New Age, intuitive personalism was valued over professional neutrality. Ross urged academics to take the New Age's appeal to the personal sphere very seriously; "personalizing" our relationship to objects of study would allow us to surmount the constraints of specialization and objectivity that had inhibited and deformed the academic mind. The New Age kept adding to its arsenal of spiritual technologies—feng shui, karma, Kabbalah, and Kundalini became subjects of fascination for sophisticated spiritual seekers. In a nonsystematic, non-class-reductionist way, Ross focused on a device sold by Welles Enterprises called the Welles step. It resembled an ergonomically correct prayer bench or pedestal upon which the subject could rest knees and shins while sitting on the toilet. Ross took Dr. Welles's paper, "The Hidden Crime of the Porcelain Throne," as a prime example of "fringe" alternative healing methods. The step was supposed to provide a more natural and healthy posture for human excretory functions, which had been damaged by the hegemony of the Western toilet. Because porcelain toilets forced us to sit rather than squat while performing our daily bowel movement, they had compromised all our bodily functions. Dr. Welles's step promised a cure for a myriad of ills from hemorrhoids to indigestion because it restored the human being to a natural defecatory squat. Ross was fascinated by the Welles step, but he could not hold back from sarcasm in describing the doctor's attribution of a satanic aura to anything that resembled "Western" medicine. He refrained, however, from direct criticism of Welles Enterprises and cautioned his academic colleagues against leaping to judgment about how alternative healing methods were being marketed. As in most cultural studies analyses of this period, the dominant/marginalized paradigm implied scholarly sympathy for every allegedly nondominant form of life and culture. The Welles step was a critique of the dominant ethos of Western medicine, and it therefore demanded a provisional sympathy and respect from progressive observers.

Ross encouraged an expansion of academic capacities and sensitivities with regard to relations of power. By providing an academic frame in which to understand cultural critique as a forceful break with the hegemonic forces of reason and rationality, he "problematized" universal reason while affirming cultural studies' antiliberal, antirational, anti-Enlightenment positions. Ross urged his readers to use his "rules of thumb for constructing a more popular, less guilt-ridden, cultural politics for our time" and fingered cultural condescension as one of the sins of Left elitism. Like John and Barbara Ehrenreich in their article "The Professional-Managerial Class," Ross seemed to be engaged with various post-1960s failures of the American Left.[25] For the Ehrenreichs, one of the New Left's most tragic and pressing failures was its utter inability to mobilize or connect with popular political movements. They saw, however, in the ashes of failure intimations of a possible reconciliation between the working class and a radicalized middle class: this new solidarity would be purged of resentment, guilt, and condescension.

The professional-managerial class (PMC) emerged full force in the United States between 1890 and 1920. It came to consciousness of itself as a newly empowered group of educated people with specific interests and particularities made up entirely of experts at organizing, digesting, and managing the PMC.[26] According to the Ehrenreichs, an authentic third class had emerged during the Progressive Era and a new politics of triangulation along with it. Traditional Marxism had focused exclusively on the antagonism between two classes—the working class and the capitalists. The professionals, doctors, engineers, and social workers who made up the PMC were salaried employees whose credentials were guaranteed by institutions of higher education. They were not, however, sympathetic to capitalists or capitalism. According to sociologist Steven Brint, the explosive growth of the modern professions actually took place over a much longer period, that is, between 1860 and 1960, a century during which "a great many white-collar occupations—from engineers to social workers—sought collective mobility through efforts to emulate the 'established pro-

fessions' of medicine, law, theology and the professoriat."[27] Despite their increasing power and numbers within American society, Brint argued that as the
professions became more powerful, they also became more polarized: while
"social trustee professionals" believed that their role was to protect "socially
important knowledge" often identified with the humanities and the qualitative social sciences, "expert professionals" such as engineers believed that they
possessed the most valuable forms of special knowledge, which could be immediately translatable into profits in a market economy. Roosevelt recruited
freely from the class of professionally trained experts in order to address the
economic and cultural misery of the Depression era United States, while the
professions themselves represented a powerful core of middle-class interests
and investments in American social cohesion.

The PMC may have seen an internal rupture between social trustee professionals and expert professionals, but for Barbara Ehrenreich by the 1980s, the
split between the working class and working poor and the PMC was much more
significant. Of the social movements, the women's movement was probably
the most deeply linked to the PMC, and Ehrenreich offers as unsentimental a
view of middle-class women's lib as Joan Didion in her essay "The Women's
Movement." Didion's essay described middle-class radicals' disappointment
with ordinary Americans: "One oppressed class after another seemed to have
missed the point."[28] From the point of view of middle-class feminists, women
who did not have the famous "ah ha" experience about the patriarchy were being infuriatingly obtuse.

Middle-class feminism justified an important side effect of 1960s hedonistic consumerism: a professional man could justify his reluctance to marry a
woman who might "cramp his style." Men and women became more conscious
of their partner's "earning potential."[29] Professional, credentialed, ambitious,
middle-class singles shunned economic and educational miscegenation: their
bonds and vows were advertised with their impeccable pedigrees on the pages
of the New York Times wedding section. David Brooks was inspired by the Times
wedding pages advertising the vows of the "Résumé Gods" to write an entire
book criticizing the emergence of a new, "upscale" American, out of touch
with the real, blue-collar worker over whom conservatives always seem fawn-
ing.[30] Insofar as she might agree with Brooks, Ehrenreich would concur that the
country was indeed becoming more and more economically and culturally polarized, but she would not tolerate Brooks's definition of a "new upper class."
Credentialed, hardworking professionals and their alleged sophistication have
done double duty for conservatives by maintaining meritocratic barriers to real

social mobility while drawing popular ire away from plutocrats and their political minions and enablers.

In 1979 the Ehrenreichs were not content to identify and analyze the PMC: they thought a thorough critique of its special features could lead to the overcoming of the failures of American Leftism. The PMC became the supervisors of labor and were inspired by an antitraditional and a well-intentioned fervor to intervene in working-class culture. The PMC prized education; they tended to be highly rational and technocratic in orientation. These educated professionals played critical roles in the expansion of social work and meritocracy that came out of progressive ideas of social service and economic mobility. As a class, the PMC held a firm set of beliefs in expertise and organizational solutions to large social problems. Taking shape in the institutions and aspirations of the Progressive Era, the professional-managerial class emerged as a vexed force for social change in a country with no mass working-class political party. Members of the PMC would repudiate social Darwinism even as they embraced the principles of selection by meritocracy. The PMC could be openly critical of capitalism, but it was also protective of professional training and expertise. The PMC was never a natural ally of the working class, who saw quite correctly that professionals and managers would act as their adversaries in labor disputes. White-collar professionals were associated with the implementation of scientific management and other policies that were meant to break up the labor process and de-skill the laborer. Fortuitously for the American rich, the PMC and the working class never managed to forge a strong alliance. The PMC was the site of a particularly contradictory form of anticapitalist, professional-managerial radicalism. In *Fear of Falling*, Barbara Ehrenreich observed that Reagan's war against the poor and working classes had increased a sense of economic insecurity for the PMC; hence, "fear of falling" was one of the primary examples of a middle-class anxiety that marked the rise of the cultural and political obsessions of the 1980s. The PMC started to feel the effects of the social safety net's unraveling, and as a group it clung to by now familiar forms of class reproduction (high-stakes testing and advanced degrees). For Ehrenreich, "the nervous, uphill financial climb of the professional middle class accelerates the downward spiral of the society as a whole."[31] Middle-class power couples were afflicted by anxiety about their children's education. For Ehrenreich, this fear was linked to the dark side of 1980s consumerism—middle-class children, it was always feared, would go soft, lose motivation, and only live for the moment, mindlessly pursuing pleasure and satisfaction.

As we saw in chapter 1, the promotion of testing and regimes of measurement as a means of producing social justice were implemented by experts and professionals: the meritocracy was their invention. In 1979, in the eyes of the Ehrenreichs, members of the PMC were distinguished by their deep belief in the reforming powers of expertise and their enthusiasm for expert "advice" about the most ordinary of everyday activities such as child-rearing and housekeeping. There were deep and disturbing contradictions about American middle-class consciousness: with the rise of the New Left, a kind of radical self-loathing took hold of activists who were faced with the relative comfort of their middle-class lives in the face of entrenched inequality, suffering, and deprivation.

In the Ehrenreichs' account of class history, the New Left broke with the values and interests of its own class when it turned against the university itself. The university was the place where the professional-managerial class had been reproducing itself with the help of the meritocracy and its modern instruments of selection. During the Vietnam War protests, however, university administration and hierarchies appeared to be allied with the government, the military-industrial complex, and powerful corporate interests. It did not help matters that the older generation of the PMC rejected the tactics of the young radicals. The Ehrenreichs observed that "college administrators and sometimes faculty cooperated with the police and the FBI during the violent repression which began in 1968. For their part, student radicals often turned on the University, not in order to 'free' it from complicity with imperialism, but to destroy it."[32] For progressive sociologist Magali Sarfatti Larson, the authoritarian pedagogy of "mystified" and "mass" education inculcated in students an "epistemological deference" as "generalized audience response" to the personal power of the expert. Education itself had become the problem. From the point of view of critics of the military-industrial complex, the 1950s and 1960s university was unequivocally complicit with the state. The university worked hand in glove with its agencies to strengthen mechanisms by which the authority of science and objectivity was cemented in the minds of an ambitious, anxious, but compliant public.[33]

For the Ehrenreichs, Left intellectuals should not be content with rejecting universities and their own expertise as a sign of solidarity with oppressed peoples. Historically confined within the dialectic of middle-class radicalism and middle-class guilt, the Left had to perform the hard work of what the Ehrenreichs called "incipient critique of the PMC" in order to forge authentic bonds of solidarity with the working classes it had once tried to dominate. Only after its self-critique had been performed could the Left and the PMC reinvent their relationship with the working class. In short, the American Left had to come to grips with its particular middle-class, professional identity. The American Left had to address the unequal distribution of "knowledge, skills and culture" by engaging in a transformation of the relationships between professionals and the people and communities they served. In short, the American Left,

> which is now predominantly drawn from the PMC, must address itself to the subjective and cultural aspects of class oppression as well as to material inequalities: it must commit itself to uprooting its own ingrained and often subtle attitudes of condescension and elitism. The tensions between PMC leftists and the working class can only be dealt with by starting with a clear analytical perception of their origins and nature. Guilty self-effacement on the part of PMC radicals and/or simplistic glorification of the working class simply perpetuates the class roles forged in capitalist society.[34]

Andrew Ross concurred with the Ehrenreichs' analysis: he too urged Left academics and professionals to engage in a period of self-criticism and self-evaluation. "Ingrained" and "subtle" forms of cultural condescension were subjective elements of PMC thinking and middle-class Left pretension that had to be "uprooted." Moreover, radicalizing the Ehrenreichs' call for a cultural revolution on the Left, Andrew Ross soundly condemned Old Left condescension toward middle-class petit bourgeois culture and forms of life. In so doing, he identified Left idealization of working-class sufferings as a symptom of its guilt and bad conscience.

By the end of the 1960s, the American SDS (Students for a Democratic Society) was so repelled by its own activities that it held back from participating in any mass antiwar movements. The Ehrenreichs cited Mark Rudd, national secretary of the SDS, when he dismissed student activism and the SDS itself as "a weird pile of liberal shit." Philip Roth's Merry Levov, virtuoso of middle-class self-loathing, might have said something very similar. Merry's self-destructive animus became historically and socially legible in light of New Left self-hatred. Whereas the Ehrenreichs hoped for a rational and collective way out of the affective impasse of the all-consuming self-loathing that tore through *American Pastoral* like a biblical affliction, Roth construed its force as a matter of personal tragedy, embodied by Merry's aggression against the loving, long-suffering, and helpless Seymour Levov, Jewish American golden boy brought low. The Ehrenreichs observed that the New Left had splintered into two groups—the first they called the "radicals in the professions" and the second the "new communists." While radical doctors, social workers, psychiatrists, and lawyers tried to demystify their own expertise, young Communist sympathizers tried to proletarianize themselves by taking up blue-collar jobs and working within a new labor movement. The second strategy seemed to the Ehrenreichs to be regressive and nostalgic. The path of the radicals in the professions seemed much more promising.

The Ehrenreichs overlooked another group of countercultural players from the 1960s who were not of the classical Left. Fred Turner called them New Communalists and saw their activities as critical to the development of new media and new technologies. Libertarian and anarchistic in their political orientation, neither radical nor professional, movement visionaries like Stewart Brand paid scant attention to organized politics. Their most ardent desire was to be autonomous, self-sufficient, creative, and sovereign players in shaping the small-scale technologies and experiences that would allow for new kinds of freedom from routine and bureaucracy. New Communalists based their countercultural projections of a better world on the fusion of technophilia and spiritual enlightenment: their understanding of expanded consciousness and connectivity would set the stage for the emergence of a new countercultural elite. The nonpolitical counterculture brought an experimental ethos of anarchy and experimentation into a culture of entrepreneurialism. In his groundbreaking study of Stewart Brand and the counterculture's hand in shaping cyberculture, Turner proposed that the countercultural rejection of technocratic, mainstream values was directly related to the apocalyptic vision of the future evoked in the everyday life of the Cold War: "If nuclear weapons and the Vietnam War, and perhaps even the urban riots that had plagued the last decade, were the products of a technocratic bureaucracy, then small-scale tools, the pursuit of higher consciousness, and the development of rural collaboratives might undermine the bureaucracy itself and, in the process, forecast a new, more harmonious future."[35] Turner's work has helped to place one critical piece of the countercultural puzzle in a richly significant genealogy of twentieth-century American ideas about the shape of the future.

The New Communalists emphasized small-scale technologies and intuitive togetherness. Nonreligious communes such as Drop City, "a cluster of geodesic domes in Colorado," emphasized the use of LSD, other hallucinogens, and music in forging new forms of collective harmony. Stewart Brand was Turner's emblematic counterculturalist. The creator of *The Whole Earth Catalog*, Brand was an artist, business visionary, entrepreneur, and futurist all wrapped up in one dynamic personality. *The Whole Earth Catalog* was conceived as an interactive and more informative Sears, Roebuck catalog of essential items for commune dwellers, with each edition revised and expanded by its subscribers. For Turner, Brand's catalog became a prototype for the network forum. At first glance, it was simply a list of useful items available to an emerging, geographically far-flung network of communes. Eventually, the catalog morphed into "a textual forum" where information could be shared and academics, artists, and technologists could engage in interdisciplinary collaborations. From its modest beginnings, the catalog projected a mobile, independent reader who wanted to be connected to others in antihierarchical, systems-oriented projects. Brand's vision of the countercultural network presaged forward-looking ideas (especially in online communities such as the WELL [Whole Earth 'Lectronic Link], a pioneering network of scientists, engineers, artists, and writers who shared software code) about art and literature, techniques for living self-sufficiently, as well as sheer enthusiasm for the early days of Internet connectivity. These computing subcultures gave shape to technological advances and innovation in personal computing culture. By 1971 the catalog had sold a million copies. It listed books by Buckminster Fuller as well as a gigantic Hewlett Packard desktop calculator that sold for $4,900; it also included a one-man sawmill "alongside a chronicle of kibbutz life and a catalog of art prints."[36] In Turner's analysis, New Communalism was more than simply a reappropriation of Eastern spirituality: it was a vast, networked experiment that channeled entrepreneurial and technological creative energies to remake the world as we knew it. Its highly individualized, systems-oriented, antibureaucratic spiritual and technological utopianism would unlock the secrets of a truly classless American society, free from the soul-killing competitiveness of the Cold War and its infernal institutions.

The New Age obviously had its roots in New Communalist forms of counterculture. For Sarah Pike, "countercultural people" merged the teachings of nineteenth-century American movements like "New Thought" with "new self-improvement technologies like meditation and yoga" to produce forms of expanded consciousness that would heal the ravages of civilization and allopathic medicine.[37] Following in the tracks left by Kesey and the Merry Pranksters but armed with bigger bank accounts and better technology, 1980s countercultural activists believed that they were poised to access the full range of human experience denied to modern man. Tom Wolfe's account of Kesey's own primitivism still resonated deeply with their fondest dreams of cognitive emancipation: "We're shut off from our own world. Primitive man once experienced the rich and sparkling flood of the senses fully. . . . Somehow, Huxley had said, the drugs opened these ancient doors."[38] If psychedelics opened doors, networks and small-scale technologies could keep them open by allowing the initiates to remain connected to each other within the labyrinth of the new Enlightenment. Philip Roth seemed to have named Merry Levov after the Merry Pranksters: her not-so-merry rejection of middle-class values and her embrace of Jainism led her through doors opened up by the ecstasies of self-deprivation. Asceticism became her drug of choice and spiritual purification her atonement for the sins of the American middle class.

What radicals in the professions and the new communists shared with the New Communalists was a deep hostility against bureaucracy, hierarchy, and centralized control. According to the Ehrenreichs:

> The radicals in the professions took a dramatic step beyond traditional PMC class in- terests. . . . [They] challenged the PMC not for its lack of autonomy (as the student movement had in the early sixties), but for its very claims to autonomy—objectivity, commitment to public service and expertise itself. "Demystification" was the catch- word. Radical doctors wanted not only to free their profession from the grip of the "medical industrial complex," but to demystify medicine. . . . Radical psychiatrists would lead the assault on psychiatric mythology and show that any sensitive commu- nity member could easily replace professionals in therapeutic interventions. Radical teachers would expose the capitalist functions of education. And so on. Credential- ing barriers would tumble. The rule of the experts would be abolished—by a new generation of young experts.[39]

Indeed, during most of the 1980s and 1990s, Ross and a new cohort of young experts were hard at work debunking the cultural prejudices of old experts. Demystifying the biases of a cultural elite was considered the most important task at hand. The more marginal or degraded one's object of study, the more profoundly political one's commitment. For the cultural studies scholar, the New Age represented a particularly important challenge. Despised by both the mainstream media and the Old Left, the New Age represented for Ross a particu- larly engrossing object of study. The New Age was also a reflection of cultural studies' own antitraditionalism. It represented a radical break with the past that traditional ministers, doctors, and intellectuals simply could not recog- nize. In this radically different order of things, the "personal experience" of the sacred was deemed more important than any form of "codified belief."[40] The anti-institutionality and spiritual restlessness of the New Age and New Commu- nalism tapped a deep tradition of American spiritual insurgency. Ross praised "ordinary people," that is, New Age people, for expressing "popular distrust of authority and desire for self-control"; he celebrated popular claims on autono- my and saw the New Age as a vital participant in an intensive phase of spiritual Reformation in the United States. For New Age adherents, "personal experi- ence" of the divine represented the natural resources of antiauthoritarianism. Evangelical Christianity fit into this scheme of spiritual insurgency as well, but it garnered little attention from cultural studies scholarship of the period of its ascendancy.

For Ross, the real enemy of the people and popular experience was CSICOP, or the Committee for Scientific Investigation of Claims of the Paranormal. Its debunking activities he described as witch-hunting: CSICOP's members were "ghost-busters" and "rationalists" who had taken upon themselves the task of initiating a new Inquisition against popular belief. Scientific truth was its orthodoxy. In its own words, CSICOP "encourages the critical investigation of paranormal and fringe-science claims from a responsible, scientific point of view and disseminates factual information about the results of such inquiries to the scientific community and the public. It also promotes science and scientific inquiry, critical thinking, science education, and the use of reason in examining important issues."[41] CSICOP has been historically one of the most vocal opponents of creationism and, more recently, of Intelligent Design. Its strategies of reasoned debate may have seemed literal-minded and lacking in social or psychological analyses of irrationality, but Ross went further and condemned its attempts to debunk the claims of junk and pseudoscience as disciplinary exercises in policing the boundaries protecting legitimate scientific research from usurpers and intruders.

In his arguments against mainstream science, Ross relied on French sociologist and one of the founding thinkers of the field of science and technology studies Bruno Latour's critique of scientific rationality to defend the "irrationality" of New Age science. First of all, according to Ross, the quantum revolution had "relaxed" the difference between the rational and the irrational. In addition, Ross pointed out that Latour had observed that "'irrationality' [was] always an accusation made by someone who wants someone else out of the way."[42] The mainstream critique of irrationality was imbued with a disciplinary function: scientists criticized alternative forms of knowing as irrational even as their own embeddedness in irrational institutions shaped their understanding of what was and was not objectively true. As a progressive historian of science, Latour was a relentless critic of the *social constructedness* of scientific authority and scientific objectivity. According to Latour's critique, "science" and "technology" were contested terms, fought over by "experts" hoping to secure more power and funding for themselves.[43] Even more politically significant, the boundary between "scientific facts" and "pseudo-scientific *beliefs*" was carefully protected by a biased scientific establishment. From Latour's point of view, skepticism should be directed at the institutional contingency of scientific fact.[44]

Less interested in the New Age's relationship with religion than with its ob-

sessions with mainstream science, Ross insisted that the New Age's relationship to "mainstream" science was analogous to the struggles of the working
class against high culture. Although Ross never cited Herbert J. Gans, Gans
would have agreed with Ross's condemnation of high culture as essentially oppressive. Ross attributed to scientific culture an analogous cultural hierarchy:
"mainstream" science shared the qualities of "highbrow" culture. Ross attacked
scientists for being "elitist" about scientific truth. In his version of the historical
struggle between scientific inquiry and professional hegemony, Ross declared
himself, not unpredictably, on the side of the "people" who were excluded from
the mainstream scientific community.[45] In Ross's investigation of meteorology
and the popular experience of weather, he discovered that weather was measured by meteorologists but experienced on the ground by ordinary people. He
concluded that science needed to be opened up to nonscientists, specifically,
progressive and radical social scientists who represented the interests of a diverse array of popular interests spanning race, gender, and class. A democratic
science would empower the alternative and plural visions of the world while
rendering the claims of so-called real scientists contingent and "unstable."

Under the second Bush administration, the U.S. government participated in
cultural studies–style denunciations of "mainstream" global warming science
and evolutionary biology. In response to Bush administration skepticism about
climate science, Latour had to rethink his own antiobjective, anti-Enlightenment positions. He tried to take back some of the more radical claims he made
in his critique of science in his article "Why Has Critique Run Out of Steam?
From Matters of Fact to Matters of Concern."[46] In it, Latour confronted the Republican strategist Frank Luntz's pointed use of scientific uncertainty about
"the facts" to argue against the reality of global warming and the greenhouse
effect. By trying to shake the foundations of scientific fact and by trying to provide more room for "interpretation," Latour later realized that he had to bear
some responsibility for adding fuel to the fire that was ignited by right-wing
global warming skeptics against the Kyoto Protocols. Environmental physicist
and critic of the Kyoto Protocol Fred Singer's case against global warming mim-
icked the rhetoric of science studies skepticism about so-called mainstream
science. "The problem for policymakers is that no one knows what constitutes
a 'dangerous' concentration of greenhouse gases. There exists, as yet, no scientific basis for defining such a concentration, or even for knowing whether it is
more or *less* than current levels."[47] If Right-wing policy makers had wanted more
fuel for their anti–global warming arguments, they would have found Andrew
Ross's critique of meteorology as science even more useful: "Global warming

theory is nothing if not a high cultural expression of Western science, dominant in the field of interpretation of the climactic economy."[48] Strange weather, indeed. Ross later insisted that he was not disputing the scientific theory of global warming, although he did want to point out that "these theories draw their power in the world from an elite culture peopled by those accustomed, by education and an inherited sense of entitlement, to see the globe as part of their *dominion*." Science was elitist, and he was merely underlining, for those of his readers too obtuse to perceive it themselves, the prejudicial conditions under which scientific "'common sense' was shaped in the public mind."[49] If we were to take him at his slippery word, global warming skeptics would be on the side of the carnivalesque, populist, transgressive, and contestatory low culture that opposed itself to the findings of preening "high culture" elitists such as global warming scientists.

The cultural studies critique of science finally attracted the attention of a few angry scientists who decided to respond to attacks on the scientific establishment in print and in person. Paul R. Gross and Norman Levitt's backlash book, *A Higher Superstition: The Academic Left and Its Quarrels with Science*, was published in the early 1990s. Gross was a biologist and Levitt a mathematician who decided to take on "radical science studies with its do-it-yourself epistemologies."[50] Ross's work on the New Age was singled out for special attention. In response, Andrew Ross and Bruce Robbins decided to coedit a special issue of *Social Text* on the emerging interdisciplinary field of critical science studies. In the introduction, Ross explained that the special issue was addressed directly at *A Higher Superstition*. According to Ross's introduction, Gross and Levitt were merely "stalking horses" for their conservative counterparts in the culture wars: they attacked progressive forms of academic work because they saw this new scholarship as dangerous and threatening.[51] For their own part, Gross and Levitt argued that the academic Left emerged from "the legacy of activism of the 1960s and early 1970s, a time when it was assumed that the intellectual, as well as moral authority of victims is beyond challenge." *A Higher Superstition* may have been condescending, but it rarely achieved true shrillness: Gross and Levitt were Enlightenment liberals, not Old Left certainly, but comfortable members of the professional elites. They believed in clarity and clear writing: one of their major objections to the antiscience Left was its "muddle-headedness."[52] For Gross and Levitt, the academic Left had become a "subculture" within the ranks of humanists and social scientists who displayed an "open hostility toward the actual content of scientific knowledge and toward the assumption, which one might have supposed universal among educated people, that scientific knowledge is reasonably reliable and rests on a sound methodology."[53] For science skeptics, scientific method was seen as defined and determined by the "culture" of scientific institutions. Gross and Levitt flatly asserted that a purely culturalist understanding of scientific method was deeply flawed.

Ross referred to Gross and Levitt as "science boosters" and "patriots" who he predicted were going to publish op-eds with "asinine anecdotes about feminist algebra, queer quantum physics and Afrocentric molecular biology."[54] In their critique, Gross and Levitt did not go so far as to offer satire: they simply asserted that Left sociologist of labor Stanley Aronowitz had little understanding of physics or mathematics when discussing the epistemological ramifications of quantum mechanics. Aronowitz was a founding editor of *Social Text* and is director of the Center for the Study of Culture, Technology and Work at the City University of New York. Gross and Levitt remarked, "It undoubtedly seems snobbish to say so, but this is a field of speculation notoriously unkind to amateurs."[55] For Ross, however, critique of amateurism was simply a sign of how defensive experts were about their fields of knowledge. Ross understood the backlash of "conservative" scientists as fundamentally psychological: they were on the hunt for antiscience scapegoats after Congress voted to defund the Supercollider in 1993. For Ross, scientists felt especially defensive because the cancellation of the American initiative to build the Supercollider signaled the end of Cold War confidence in scientific research. After the Cold War, both the U.S. government and the American people no longer assumed that technoscience led to social progress. According to science studies scholar Dorothy Nelkin's article in *Social Text*, "the superconducting super collider became a model of the inefficiency of megascience and an example of the difficulty of managing scientific projects."[56] For Ross, scientists had been deeply shaken by "their loss of standing in the public eye and the decline of public funding from the public purse." As a consequence, the conservatives among them joined "the backlash against the usual suspects—pinkos, feminists and multiculturalists of all stripes."[57]

A new era of amateur empowerment had dawned on the academic Left, and Gross and Levitt simply missed its political significance. For Ross, "self-critical skepticism is not counter-Enlightenment but rather a result of the triumph of the rationality by which scientific inquiry is turned upon its own foundations and methods." Cultural studies scholarship was at the forefront of a normalization of technoskepticism: it gave academic and social science legitimacy to a popular and everyday refusal to defer to scientific authority. Ross called upon nonconservative scientists to speak out in favor of science studies. In expanding the frame of our understanding of the limitations of the "Western laboratory scientist," who was constrained by her own institutional rules, Ross alluded to the Chinese barefoot doctor and rainforest shaman who functioned "logically" in their own "cultural environments."[58] A quick sketch of a Third World idyll of doctors was presented as a strong counterexample to the "technocratic expertise" that dominated the practice of healing medicine in the industrialized West.

The *Social Text* special issue on science studies included sober articles by science and technology studies scholars Dorothy Nelkin, Langdon Winner, Richard Levin, and Steven Fuller as well as an article by pioneering feminist science studies scholar Sandra Harding. Stanley Aronowitz's article, "The Politics of the Science Wars," represented an eloquent and succinct summary of what was at stake for the adversaries in a battle over scientific objectivity and, to some degree, professional identity. According to Aronowitz, the scientific community sought to protect itself from outside criticism by closing its ranks and discrediting its attackers. Aronowitz acknowledged that, historically, external pressures (Nazi, Soviet, and American Cold War politics) on the direction of scientific research might have made scientists defensive about external incursions into their research communities and networks. This historical condition notwithstanding, cultural critics could no longer leave science to scientists: "Behind scientificity stands the awesome and the once unassailable edifice of natural science. Together with the similarly God-like house of medicine, it presents itself as both the guarantor of the Enlightenment and the measure of reason." Furthermore, what passed for scientific truth was shaped by scientific elites: "Rejected or marginal sciences such as parapsychology, the study of clairvoyance, and in the wake of the triumph of molecular biology, ecological and evolutionary biology, are just a few examples of the evidence that the scientific 'community' as a site of power determines what counts as legitimate intellectual knowledge."[59] For Aronowitz, a war against the technocratic idolators had been enjoined. Military applications of scientific research belied the barbarity of the science establishment. For the New Left, scientists had to repent for their complicity with the military-industrial-educational complex. There was a consensus among all the authors that progressive causes, whether feminist, environmental, or economic, would be well served if the material and social conditions surrounding scientific objectivity could be studied and eventually modified. This would lead either to Ross's "kinder, gentler" science or at least to solutions to pressing environmental and social problems. In a sense, the articles in *Social Text* confirmed Gross and Levitt's finding that the academic Left held the conviction that "fundamental political change is urgently needed and can be achieved only through revolutionary processes rooted in a wholesale revision of cultural categories."[60]

Toward the end of the journal an article appeared with a baffling title: "Transgressing the Boundaries: Towards a Transformative Hermeneutics of Quantum Gravity." Written by Alan Sokal, an NYU physics professor, the article contained more hard science than the others while making aggressive claims for the relationship between science and postmodernism. Sokal claimed that deep conceptual shifts within twentieth-century science had undermined "Cartesian-Newtonian metaphysics; revisionist studies in the history and philosophy of science have cast further doubt on its credibility; and, most recently, feminist and poststructuralist critiques have demystified the substantive content of mainstream Western scientific practice, revealing an ideology of domination concealed behind the façade of 'objectivity.'"[61] Sokal celebrated the fact that "postmodern" theories of culture, text, and experience were confirmed by the latest findings and research in quantum mechanics. In "A Kinder, Gentler Science," Ross had written: "Theoretical science, in the wake of quantum physics, has shattered the intellectual security of the mechanical picture of discontinuous time, space, matter and objectivity. . . . In addition, the Heisenberg principle has established that the measuring observer inevitably becomes part of the experiment itself: objectivity and subjectivity are then emptied-out categories since there is no quarantine space for testers or their measuring instruments."[62] Sokal obediently echoed Ross's findings: "The postmodern sciences deconstruct and transcend the Cartesian metaphysical distinctions between humankind and Nature, observer and observed, Subject and Object. Already quantum mechanics, earlier in this century, shattered the ingenuous Newtonian faith in an objective, prelinguistic world of material objects. . . . Finally, postmodern science provides a powerful refutation of the authoritarianism and elitism inherent in traditional science."[63]

Immediately following the appearance of his article in *Social Text*, Sokal published "A Physicist Experiments with Cultural Studies" in *Lingua Franca*.[64] In that article, he revealed that his *Social Text* article was a hoax: having suspected that science and cultural studies operated as pure ideology, he had set out to prove that these radicals in the professions cared nothing for scientific truth or intellectual integrity and were willing to publish scientifically laughable theories as long as they seemed to flatter the editors' ideological biases. Sokal pointed to the following particularly egregious statement in his hoax article: "It has thus become increasingly apparent that physical 'reality,' no less than social 'reality,' is at bottom a social and linguistic construct; that scientific 'knowledge,' far from being objective, reflects and encodes the dominant ideologies and power relations of the culture that produced it."[65] For Sokal, any rational reader would have been repelled by the idea that reality could be reduced to a "social and linguistic construct." Sokal was struck by the editors' utter blindness to a ridiculous claim that physical reality—and not a theory of physical reality—could be described in any way as a purely social construct. In short, Sokal's theory that cultural and science studies had no proper methodological tools by which to judge scientific research seemed to have been proven. The editors confirmed his assumption that they would publish the most egregious falsehoods if the author of those falsehoods paid lip service to cultural studies pieties about emancipation from objectivity, transgression, and scientific bias.

Bruce Robbins and Andrew Ross responded immediately to Sokal's hoax as well as his denunciation of their editorial policies and methods. They admitted to making a tactical mistake in publishing the article. They apologized to their colleagues for any damage the hoax might have done to their work. They admitted to having found Sokal's article "hokey" and his attitude "naïve," but they refused to admit to more serious errors of judgment or method. In one sense, Sokal's hoax only hardened his adversaries' positions. In fact, Ross and Robbins admitted to being so impressed with Sokal's apparently sincere attempts to grapple with endless "self-problematization" that they wanted to encourage him to overcome his somewhat amateurish attempts at doing cultural studies. They also insisted that Social Text was not a peer-reviewed journal. They condemned Sokal's hoax as a breach of professional behavior and a sign of scientific defensiveness against the nagging questions raised by nonexperts regarding the direction of scientific research after centuries of "scientific racism, scientific sexism and scientific domination of nature."[66] Every scientist, including Sokal, it would seem, would have to be accountable for centuries of scientific wrongdoing and scientific biases. Concurring with Sokal that postmodern obscurantism was to be condemned, Robbins and Ross went on to deplore the fact that only credentialed scientists were allowed to address the questions of scientific truth. They appealed to an idea of "popular participation" in setting scientific research priorities. The cultural studies scholars acted as Steven Brint's "social trustee professionals" and denounced, much to the consternation of their scientist colleagues, the kinds of "applied formal knowledge" that could be deployed to nefarious and exploitative ends.[67]

The cultural studies revolution precipitated a populist insurgency within academia. The war was waged on many fronts: social scientists and humanists against scientists, conservatives and liberals against radicals, humanists against theorists, but, most important, Old against New Left. Sokal himself un-abashedly claimed allegiance with Old Left commitments to objectivity and its communicability. The intellectual controversy that Sokal's hoax launched has been well documented and should be understood in the context of the rise to power of a countercultural Left.[68] The academic Left, as Gross and Levitt called it, was a countercultural power. It had world-transformative ambitions, and it was based on the solidarity of networks rather than the politics of rational persuasion. Like-minded young scholars were producing new forms of politics, critique, and solidarity that were despised by their enemies, the Old Left and conservatives alike. They were not simply an academic New Left, they were aca-demic populists, armed with a powerful set of tools to take down "dominant" and "mainstream" social and cultural forms in the name of alternative reason, alternative Utopias, alternative Enlightenments, and alternative science. They saw the world in a fundamentally agonistic way: they took up arms against expertise within the very walls of the modern American university. They saw a moral divide between self-interested experts and abused amateurs. In Brint's analysis, however, even the most radical ideas of the social trustee professional were expressed in rather conventional and conservative venues—academic journals published by universities. The Sokal affair, as it was later to be called, seemed to have little consequence on the shape of debates about the "two cul-tures" and even less effect on the reputations or careers of its adversaries: no one's reputation was tarnished, just no new directions in interdisciplinary re-search or reconciliation presented themselves.

In response to *Social Text*'s response to his hoax, Sokal published "Trans-gressing the Boundaries: An Afterword" in which he cited with dismay a 1993 Gallup poll that found that 47 percent of Americans believed in creationism, or that God created human beings in their present form.[69] For Sokal, attacks on scientific reason had concrete, deleterious political effects. The attacks were so broad and simplistic that they discouraged popular engagement with sci-entific method and scientific research while aggravating popular resentment and misunderstanding of the scientific enterprise. From Ross's point of view, the popular refusal of scientific truth could be interpreted as a positive sign of popular protest against the elitism of scientists and against modernity's ratio-nalizing, depersonalized ethos. Finally, indifference to scientific truth could be justified as resistance against the logic of Cold War technocrats who had draped themselves in the scientific prestige of "mega–research projects" that were underwritten by public deference and public fear. Aronowitz asked his readers to "imagine a polity capable of challenging the use and truth claims of scientific and technological research. Imagine a new scientific citizenship in which democratic forms of decision making were shared between the scientific community and the public."[70] Aronowitz may have thought he was leading the way to a Utopian laboratory of popular participation in scientific research, but his critique, according to Sokal, would lead to the embrace of irrationality rather than the exercise of dissent and argument. In 2007 Gallup found that 39 percent of Americans felt that creationism was definitely true, with 27 percent responding that it was "probably true"; the polling numbers about creationism have remained relatively stable from 1982 to 2007, with between 43 and 47 percent of Americans polled affirming their belief that God created human beings "as they are."[71] What has been most striking about the numerous polls and studies dealing with American public opinion on religion and science is the huge gap between scientists and college graduates, on the one hand, and the rest of the public, on the other. The poor, working-class, and rural communities have consistently rejected scientific findings on evolution at much higher percentages than urban elites. The education and culture gap between country and city that the Populists wanted to bridge in the 1890s seemed a geologically formed abyss that defied the physics of logic and reason.[72]

The analogy that Ross drew between the gap that separated "high" culture and popular culture, on the one hand, and scientific elites and nonspecialists, on the other, suggested that popular contestation of scientific authoritarianism could produce the same "progressive" and democratizing social effects that were expected when the boundaries between high and popular cultures were broken down. Science stood accused of mystifying the truth about its racism, its sexism, and its domination of nature. Ross and Aronowitz chose to target the science specialist as an abuser of popular and public trust. Could the repudiation of experts lead to the reconciliation between middle-class professionals of the New Left and working classes described by the Ehrenreichs? Yes, or so it seemed to Robbins, Ross, and Aronowitz, who together represented a segment of the radical PMC that assiduously cultivated all forms of solidarity with those excluded from mainstream science and high culture; they seemed to anticipate the imminent mobilization of outraged ordinary people. They believed that they were addressing inequities in distribution of prestige and authority, that they were attacking standardization of cognitive capacity, that they were connected to the countercultures and alternative truths directly opposed to the demands of reason and objectivity touted by Sokal and the Old Left. Shared radical beliefs held together new networks of the like-minded. The countercultural New Left was electrified by a passion for transgression: they saw themselves as a populist vanguard that had infiltrated the ivy-covered walls of the academy. Their ideas and their language were founded on the principles of a transmissive intensity: a shared experience and vision of contested realities and Utopic forms of participation bound them together. Whereas Sokal appealed naively to common sense and the public sphere, the radicals saw those ideas about communication and persuasion as outdated. New generations of cultural studies scholars and other radicals in the professions have been hard at work pointing to normative biases and exclusionary policies, from racism to homophobia, in all areas of culture. As a result, the culturalist aspirations and subcultural preoccupations of academic populism have carved out important niches in academia. Unfortunately, Sokal's broad caricature of postmodernism failed to differentiate between cultural studies and what he derided as "lit crit." His hasty dismissal of a set of uneasy and incompatible allies—cultural studies and literary criticism, for example—made it easier for scholars in the human and interpretive social sciences to dismiss him as someone who had not done his own homework on the differences among various schools of humanities and social science thinking. He rushed to tar and feather humanities scholars and social scientists with the derogatory label "postmodernist," a moniker from which Ross, Robbins, and Aronowitz had indeed sought to distance themselves.

Stuart Hall saw the rise of cultural studies as directly related to the crisis of legitimacy that allegedly plagued the humanities. Ross had pointed an accusatory finger at "close textual reading" and was quickly performing a purge of literature from within its own ranks. Cultural studies scholars were also quick to abandon, subvert, and undermine the humanities as an academic enterprise. Like system making or any form of negative criticality, close textual analysis itself was guilty by association with a set of exclusionary and, yes, elitist academic theories and practices. What cultural studies wanted most of all was to be innocent of the past and of collusion or collaboration with any form of organized power. It yearned to be innocent of its institutional and disciplinary limits. It wanted to be free of the past. It wanted to be new. In its own words, cultural studies had to be vigilant about its fundamental difference from older forms of scholarship. In the introduction to the *Cultural Studies* anthology of 1992, Grossberg, Nelson, and Treichler argued suggestively that "it is problematic for cultural studies simply to adopt, uncritically, any of the formalized disciplinary practices of the academy. . . . [A]lthough there is no prohibition against close textual readings in cultural studies, they are also not required. Moreover, textual analysis in literary studies carries a history of convictions that texts are properly understood as wholly self-determined and independent objects as well as a bias about which kinds of texts are worthy of analysis. That burden of associations cannot be ignored."[73] This proscriptive statement was quite ominous: cultural studies did not want to enter into complicity with the political and social damage wreaked by the Western literary critical traditions of "formalized," "close textual reading." "Textual analysis in literary studies" suffered "a burden of associations" that could be ignored only by the politically uninformed.

Sokal, Gross, and Levitt seemed to be unaware that there already was a critique within the humanities of cultural studies methodologies and principles. Gerald Graff had demonstrated that the struggle between amateurs and specialists had a long history in the formation of the American research university. At the end of the nineteenth century, as the modern American university was taking shape, amateurs came from old American elites: they were brilliant, mercurial scholars who found the narrow specialization of modern disciplines to be a turn toward callowness and venality in a profession that should have been reserved to disinterested gentlemen.[74] Graff and English professor John Guillory both criticized cultural studies critique. In their accounts, canon formation and close reading were ambiguous, contingent historical practices, embedded in the social and political contest over the proper place of literature and educational institutions in a larger body politic. Guillory argued against the imaginary politics of representation that permeated cultural studies critique and its purposeful confusion of canon making and canon breaking with political domination and political emancipation. If we were to summarize and simplify his argument, the critique of the canon projected a radically pluralist Utopia where sanctioned objects of study would actually represent an image of a society of diverse makers and writers. The exclusion of a work from this body would be equivalent to the oppression and domination of the minority to which its author/maker belonged; inclusion of such work would be essentially progressive and ameliorative. Any attempt to judge, criticize, or put cultural and literary works in any aesthetic order would run the risk of replicating systems of political domination and exploitation.[75]

Cultural studies scholarship and methodology assiduously distinguished itself from critical paradigms of the past: it stressed innovation and newness, both markers of its freedom from historical biases and error. Max Horkheimer called the desire for newness and the impatience with history a distinctively modern form of absolutism, arising out of Enlightenment philosophy's attitudes about its own past. Enlightenment, he claims, never did justice to the past. The French Enlightenment had condemned medieval thought as "fraud and stupidity" and neglected its indebtedness to the inquiry of the Scholastics.

Our most anti-Enlightenment, and therefore the most enlightened, cultural studies scholars were then resolutely modern, and traditionally so when they heaped contempt on their own historical and intellectual predecessors, mocking Freud's everyday sexism, Richard Hofstadter's political liberalism, Adorno's musical elitism, or C. Wright Mills's alleged lack of sympathy for worker creativity. Presumably, a new age had dawned, and a nonsystematic but extremely self-critical crew of young scholars had, in the process of problematizing everything, freed themselves from all the "biases" of the past. Just as modern astrological history and New Age religion divided temporality into the old and the new, so cultural studies saw itself as making a highly consequential historical break with the past. A clear division was drawn between the age of the benighted and the enlightened, the age of Pisces and the age of Aquarius. What Sokal and the Old Left who came to his defense saw as the "ideological" and jargon-ridden aspect of cultural studies language was for its adherents a sign of their insider initiation into new forms of knowledge and critique that did not have to communicate with an "elitist" notion of a smoothly functioning public sphere.

Cultural studies reflected and embodied a countercultural emphasis on alternative forms of interactivity on the margins of large organizations. Countercultural style and subcultural networks found themselves uneasily installed within the university system. Their fundamental dependence on higher education produced a professionalization of radicalism that earned these scholars the approbation of conservatives, the Old Left, and liberals alike. This development should not have been surprising to readers of the Ehrenreichs. These cultural studies scholars were following the itinerary mapped out for them by the PMC's "radicals in the professions." Cultural studies' antielitist, antihierarchical aspirations resembled the dreams of the alternative forms of connectivity and creativity that were being tested by Fred Turner's New Communalists. As Turner put it, "The concept of building a peer-to-peer information network and the idea that individuals needed to gain control over information and information systems had been features of both the New Communalist movement and the New Left for some time. . . . For those who hoped to turn computing machines toward populist ends, the religion of technology espoused by the Whole Earth Catalog offered an important conceptual framework and source of legitimization."[76] Social Text and science studies survived the Sokal hoax because of the rise of these "networks of legitimization": the durability of cultural studies scholarship proved that science and scientific truth could not and would not have the last word in a world of peer-to-peer networks and associations. The public sphere and its old media supports were indeed being supplanted by peer-to-peer networks and new forms of solidarity that guaranteed cultural and science studies a certain kind of immunity from public opprobrium after the Sokal hoax. There was no substantive and informed listening to the scornful scientists. Cultural studies shook off the scorn of both the Old Left and the scientific establishment. *Social Text* went on to publish excellent work by important scholars on the Left. Nor did the scandal tarnish Bruce Robbins's or Andrew Ross's reputation. Each of them has enjoyed a prolific academic career in outstanding institutions of higher education, Columbia University and NYU, respectively. Leading scholars of cultural studies began to turn their attention to the institutional problems that were plaguing the universities in which they worked, the legacy of the scandal and of cultural studies' hubristic early years in the United States largely ignored or forgotten by a new generation of graduate students attracted to cultural studies critique. Aronowitz returned to his earlier work on class and labor relations. He also became interested in education and its institutional limitations. Nelson and Ross began to address the casualization of academic labor: Ross looked at New Economy "sweatshops" and Chinese labor practices, and Nelson examined the protection of academic freedom. In 2006 Nelson was elected president of AAUP (American Association of University Professors), where he took up a much more activist role in defense of the academic professions. In this turn toward academic freedom and the conditions of labor, these scholars seemed to be returning to certain Old Left preoccupations. Meanwhile, a Cultural Studies Association was formed in 2003. Its annual conference promotes the establishment of professional networks to help young scholars negotiate their careers. The association publishes a journal that reflects the most pressing areas of research and the unexpected combinations characteristic of the field, from queer and transgender identity and youth to sports and new media, from video games and war to torture and music. The range of topics conveys a dizzying array of objects of study, but the scholarly methodologies can be identified by a distinctive synthesis of British cultural studies and Foucauldian, biopower paradigms of research and analysis. It has also become quite apparent that cultural studies has become very comfortable not engaging with either mainstream or elite old media and Old Left debates. The nature of new media networks has allowed cultural studies debates to remain highly localized and niche-marketed. In the years since the Sokal hoax, cultural studies may have lost some of its messianic allure, but many of its intellectual assumptions have become routinized in the methodology of certain departments and institutes within the academy. The New Left dream of a radical reevaluation of the place of the intellectual in American society still remains as a backlash against research and autonomy. American society, as a wide range of observers and commentators from Paul Krugman to Kevin Phillips to Richard Sennett to Barbara Ehrenreich concur, has become more polarized. Economic inequality has grown more entrenched. The new forms of cultural and political solidarity imagined by cultural studies scholars with the working class have receded from the horizon even as entire segments of the teaching profession in higher education have become proletarianized. In fact, because the fate of the PMC was always linked to the power of embedded liberalism and the social democratic ethos of the Progressive state, the PMC has, if anything, seen its powers wane due to external political and economic conditions.

:: :: ::

In the 1990s legal scholar and public policy advocate Wendy Kaminer published a brace of books engaged with the New Age cultures of recovery and self-help. She represented an Old Left perspective on new superstition, and although she was of the same generation as the cultural studies scholars, she did exactly what Andrew Ross warned academics and elites against. She criticized the middlebrow, therapeutic culture of self-help for undermining critical thinking in popular discourse. She encouraged the debunking of superstition, deplored public professions of piety. Her books were polemical and public interventions that were addressed to the maligned liberal and more or less thoughtful reader who took an interest in the issues of the day. In some ways, her writing was a popularization of some of psychoanalytic theory scholar, sociologist, and cultural critic Philip Rieff's and Richard Hofstadter's critiques of a therapeutic culture of anti-intellectualism.[77] She speculated that the decline of secular values in the political sphere was linked to the rise of a culture of recovery and self-help that had come out of the popularization of New Age, countercultural beliefs and practices. In both *I'm Dysfunctional, You're Dysfunctional: The Recovery Movement and Other Self-Help Fashions* and *Sleeping with Extra-Terrestrials: The Rise of Irrationalism and the Perils of Piety*, Kaminer publicly denounced the decline of secular culture and the rise of a therapeutic culture of testimony and self-victimization that brooked no dissent while demanding unprecedented leaps of faith from its adherents.[78] Kaminer's work combined a belief in Habermasian rational communication with an uncompromising skepticism about the ubiquity of piety that for her was shared by both conservatives and liberals.

For Kaminer, argument and persuasion could no longer be operative when belief and subjective experience became the baseline proofs that underwrote public and private assertions. No speaker or writer was under any obligation to answer his or her critics because argument and testimony were fatefully blurred. When reasoned impiety was slowly being banished from public dialogue, political responsibility would inevitably wane. In the warm bath of generalized piety and radical plurality, everyone could assert a point of view, an opinion, and different beliefs, but no one was under any obligation to defend them. Whereas cultural studies scholars saw themselves contesting dominant forms of discourse and hegemonic forms of thinking, Kaminer saw them participating in a popular embrace of an irrational Counter-Enlightenment. Like Andrew Ross, Kaminer cited Franz Mesmer as an important eighteenth-century pioneer of twentieth-century alternative healing techniques. Mesmer's personal charisma and his powers of psychic healing and invocation of "animal magnetism" entranced the European courts of the late eighteenth century. Mesmer performed miracle cures and attracted a devoted, wealthy following. Despite scandals that plagued his European career, the American middle class was eager to embrace his hybrid of folk practices and scientific-sounding proofs. Mesmerism projected an alternative mystical cosmology based upon magnets and invisible flows of energy. Mesmer, who was said to control the invisible magnetic flow of forces that operated upon human and animal bodies, built upon a network of wealthy patrons who were devoted to the powers of a charismatic leader, Mesmer himself. Mesmer's manipulation of magnets and hands-on healing evoked for the French court the ancient arts of folk healing while it had recourse to ostensibly modern scientific proofs. Historian of the French eighteenth century Robert Darnton insisted that mesmerism could not be dismissed as mere quackery or charlatanism but represented a transitional worldview, one that bridged the Enlightenment and the particular forms of nineteenth-century Romanticism that followed.[79]

Kaminer attended seminars by the popular, modern-day equivalents of Franz Mesmer: New Age healers, channelers, and gurus. Undercover at a variety of New Age seminars, she witnessed fellow attendees unanimously accept Kevin Ryerson's claim that he was channeling "an entity" from ancient Egypt. She participated in past-life regression with New Age psychiatrist Brian Weiss. She paid $299 (not adjusted for inflation) to attend a seminar on angels given by Matthew Fox, who asserted that "angels move at the speed of light." In her observations of the seminars and weekend retreats, Kaminer was particularly disturbed by the general acceptance of Ryerson's, Weiss's, and Fox's diverse claims of knowledge of the supernatural. Kaminer observed, "When as an anonymous member of the audience, I have respectfully argued with the experts, they have almost always reacted with anger and surprise. . . . The arrogance underlying the gestures of humility typically offered by gurus is evident in their hostility to challenges."[80] When Kaminer appeared critical or skeptical of a teacher or guru, she was shunned not only by the teacher but also by other attendees for her disrespectful attitude.

Kaminer's description of intellectual quietism provided a sharp contrast with Andrew Ross's perspective. Ross seemed to be observing an entirely different New Age culture when he wrote, "New Age addresses its adherents as active participants, with a measure of control over their everyday lives and not as passive subjects, even victims of larger, objective forces."[81] In Kaminer's view, the "follower had to suspend any critical or ambivalent feelings she may have had about the guru's or leader's statements, or else be threatened with group ostracism and a sense of being left behind." Kaminer also argued that "gurus always confirm our essential godliness. They lead by flattery."[82]

Andrew Ross recognized in New Age Utopianism a "deeply felt response of New Age humanism to large-scale technological organization, especially those organizations of political rationality whose explanatory social models exclude the politics of everyday life and subjectivity."[83] Ross saw no leaders or followers in the New Age movement, only adherents and equals who all sought a collective experience distinct from the ones offered by political rationality. For Kaminer, the most successful New Age leaders often preached vague, simplistic homilies like celebrity New Age teacher and lecturer Marianne Williamson's analysis of economic theory, "What goes around comes around." Williamson, like Deepak Chopra, maintained in Kaminer's eye a false intimacy with countless followers: "The submissiveness expected of New Age consumers is often cloaked in a show of camaraderie by the expert who consistently reminds her fans that they are close to god as she."[84] While Kaminer argued that the guru preached a false message, Ross affirmed that the New Age could lead to spaces of redemption and revelation directly connected with the countercultural rejection of technocratic, political rationality. Whereas Kaminer argued that gurus harmed democratic culture because they encouraged their adherents to surrender their capacities for critical thinking, Ross claimed that these teachers facilitated a rejection of the oppressive forms of political rationality foisted upon ordinary people by hectoring elites. Ross himself could ignore Kaminer as a hectoring Old Left elitist who worshiped at the altar of mainstream science and whose writing aimed at reproducing "elitist access to media and intellectual opinion."[85] While Kaminer published with Vintage, a division of Random House, Ross published with university presses. Ross could argue that Kaminer was a part of mainstream culture, and her liberal condescension gained her the attention of the mainstream media because she still believed in communicative and political rationality. He did not, and his dissenting viewpoint could only find an editorial and publishing home in "alternative" venues. Ross was arguing for something entirely unrecognizable to the "establishment" and could only find a sympathetic hearing in "alternative" spaces and presses. For cultural studies scholars of the early 1990s, faith in "mainstream" liberal institutions was the greatest if not highest superstition of them all.

According to religious studies scholar Olav Hammer, "New Age texts can present experience as a democratic road to spiritual insight. . . . The democratization of religious experience within the Esoteric Tradition has gone hand in hand with the psychologization of religion. Not only is truth to be found within each other, the very locus of spirituality is our own Self."[86] The New Age self was a critical node in a countercultural network, and the network represented an alternative form of politics, community, and communication that Kaminer would not have been able to recognize. The New Age was governed by the sign of Aquarius, ruler of technology, telecommunication, and electricity: if enough selves were networked to other like-minded, Enlightened "selves," social change would be precipitated by this critical, communicative mass. New Age visionary and founder of the Association of Humanistic Psychology Marilyn Ferguson's *The Aquarian Conspiracy: Personal and Social Transformation in Our Time* promoted just such a magical idea of social networks without the theoretical and rhetorical resources upon which to base her particular authority. For Ferguson, astrological calculation predicted that positive global transformation was going to be not just effortless but inevitable in the age of Aquarius, since New Age people were reaching enlightenment while finding each other on the astral network.[87] The political processes, wars, conflicts, and struggles for legitimacy that used to bring about social change in the age of Pisces could be literally short-circuited in favor of the anarchic precipitation of a better, more interconnected world. The concept of contradiction was so last millennium! As each of us found our individual paths to the better, more personal Enlightenment, we were contributing to the accumulation of a critical mass of spiritual redemption.

The New Age shaped many different cultural studies investigations of selfhood and experience. In the 1992 *Cultural Studies* anthology, Elspeth Probyn's "Technologies of the Self" suggested that a performative politics of autobiography had emerged, giving academics permission to be "selves."[88] Self-transformation and self-discovery would emancipate them from the various impasses of social theory and identity politics. Academics could finally exit the community of scholars to enter a "community of caring." Probyn's ambitions for cultural studies and identity politics aimed at nothing less than the total transformation of intellectual operations and associations. In the New Age of academia forecast by cultural studies, she believed that the practice of disciplined and virtuous self-transformation created an ethical foundation for new forms of academic work. Just as the New Age was going to make a radical break with religious tradition by steering spiritual practices away from "codified belief" toward "personal experience" of the sacred, so cultural studies scholars were going to steer students and readers away from traditional forms of objectivity toward a deeper engagement with the stormy and suppressed academic self.[89]

Probyn seemed to claim that anguished academic battles over identity politics could be avoided because self-representation constituted a process and technique that would release us into a world of harmonious mutual recognition. Since Foucault had endowed the self with so much historico-politico-epistemological importance, the "self" had to be mobilized for politics, for action, for fantasy, for pleasure, and, last but not least, for theory. Somehow all of this was linked in Probyn's article to her feelings about the 1989 massacre of fourteen young women at the University of Montreal by a shooter named Mark Lepine, a deeply disturbed young man who allegedly asserted that "he hated feminists." Probyn could not bear to speak of the massacre for a long time, but when she was able to, she insisted that she had to speak as a feminist and a woman, even though it seemed for a long time that the fourteen dead women would not want their deaths made part of a public discussion about backlash politics. Although none of what Probyn declared in her essay was in the least bit controversial, at least in a cultural studies context or a progressive yoga studio (some of it was quite anodyne, even clichéd), she defiantly argued "for the positivity of experience and the possibilities of using the self in theory." She wanted to articulate the deep question, "'who am I?' and 'who is she?'" Moreover, she insisted that her "elaboration of theoretical selves is . . . not a reinscription of authorial centrality." Instead, she wanted to "emphasize the urgency of constructing enunciatory selves." The self did not reify knowledge; the self defied normativity; the self was the site of radical potentiality; the self, most important, was "not an end in itself."[90]

Probyn understood self-transformation as one of the most important new forms of work, and she believed that while the value of this labor was entirely self-evident, it was entirely innovative and had no relation to historical forms of self-discipline and self-reflection like Daniel Bell's liberal, modernized version of Friedrich Schiller's aesthetic education.[91] According to Probyn, "Simply put, we need to consider the work of the self, to refigure identity and difference as images that enable alternative articulations of the non discursive to the discursive which then play back again into the non discursive." It was hard work to be a self; it was, at times, very confusing: your self could never "stand on difference," whatever that state of supine laziness might have entailed. According to Probyn, "Instead of standing on our difference and wearing our identities as slogans, we need to put the images of our selves to work epistemologically and ontologically."[92] This work of self-transformation promised almost effortless, conflict-free social change (selves would have to struggle to actualize themselves, but they seemed essentially peaceful and even hardworking).

Probyn's assertions resonated with a "deeply felt" optimism about what could be accomplished in the future when our bodies had been mobilized by our—selves. Once networks of like-minded people connected with each other, massive social change would be the inevitable outcome of such magical connectivity. Although it would be tempting to indulge in a furious bout of noncaring, nonloving, noncommunitarian mockery at this kind of mindless, antiintellectual wishful thinking, it would be entirely futile. In any case, Christopher Lasch already articulated what was at stake in countercultural narcissism. Even in the most painfully unreadable, convoluted cultural studies text, the shape of countercultural Utopias could be identified: Probyn's shape-shifting, hierarchy-breaking, flexible, queer, performative, liberated, networked, alternative, and counterculture self was just the kind of entity who could live happily online. These "selves" were poised to preside over the counterculture's marriage of spiritual miracles with digital Utopias. In this kind of networked world, Wendy Kaminer's arguments in defense of critical thinking would fall on deaf ears, especially within the most radical segments of academia itself. Andrew Ross emphasized that the New Age was "a response to the so-called Enlightenment 'project of modernity.' . . . In principle, New Age proposes a continuation of this project, but in the name of a different human rationality."[93] Ross went so far as to argue that the New Age's "antiauthoritarian populism" was a vanguardist form of practical and critical activism that intellectuals would do well to emulate.

New Age populism? Was this a grotesque oxymoron, a miscegenation of the esoteric with the popular, the spiritual with the insurgent? Was this cultural political formation Ross's answer to the Ehrenreichs' dream of a true alliance between the middle-class radicalism of the PMC and the antiauthoritarianism of working people? Was this the Second Coming, the rough beast, the widening gyre? Was this how Joan Didion's countercultural falling apart would reconstitute itself, a scant twenty years after Haight-Ashbury, as a grown-up movement, composed of ever-rebellious, wide-eyed children, just stretching their by now slightly arthritic limbs to assume their full capacities, attaining their majority, connecting with their deepest Kundalini, tripping out on their profound understanding of a world that escaped the rest of us? Any contradiction between New Age esotericism and academic populism dissolved when their adversary appeared on the horizon. Who was the enemy of the spiritual adept and outraged ordinary person? The traditional intellectual, of course. The professor, the scientist, the expert, the elitist, and the skeptic. The one who did not give herself over easily to piety or drugs, the one who remained skeptical of mind expansion and alternative cures. These people were not of the people. They held themselves back, perhaps perversely, to some other notion of value: perhaps they believed in negative ideas of critical complexity, whether theoretical, aesthetic, literary, or scientific. They could not get on the bus.

Haight-Ashbury in 1967 was a hotbed of "political potential" beyond political rationality. The actors in this drama were, according to Didion, "less in rebellion against the society than ignorant of it, able only to feed back certain of its most publicized self-doubts, Vietnam, Saran-Wrap, diet pills, the Bomb." Didion was betraying her interlocutors by pointing to everything they lacked: a sense of place, real stories, some sense of the rules (even when they were breaking them), family, and even an adequate vocabulary for describing their experiences of all of the above. She was also doing what Andrew Ross warned against: she was being critical, she held herself back, she withdrew to writing, to language, to words, to discourse or at least to the give and take of articulated conversation, which the "children" distrusted most of all: "They feed back exactly what is given them. Because they do not believe in words—words are for 'typeheads.'" Hare Krishna was not a word, it was a chant, and because it lacked meaning, it was on its way to becoming an "international movement." If everybody chanted, "then there wouldn't be any problem with the police or anybody. . . . You can get high on mantra."[94] Mantras, chants, and words emptied of meaning became pure phonemic intensity: the end to social contradiction imagined in Haight-Ashbury would come painlessly, as a worldwide, collective high. Only "typeheads" and people with what Kesey's group called "intellectual hang-ups" would demand coherence and intelligibility, persuasion, and reason. Words emptied of meaning could facilitate and even precipitate the destruction and re-creation of all forms of life and connectedness, the immolation of the intellect by the intellect in the name of an inchoate and radicalized political and cultural potential. The rough beast was slouching toward

Bethlehem to be born. We wanted this Second Coming to remake our very inability to use words correctly, to render historical and conceptual connections
legible again. In 1967 people may have been missing. Some of them turned up
in Haight-Ashbury, having run away to the counterculture's crucible in order to
be reborn. In 1987 Fredric Jameson saw that consummation of the 1960s in the
aesthetic, theoretical, and political aspirations of that moment. At the end of
the 1980s, the people and the public that they were thought to constitute were
again missing, but a cultural and New Age antielitism emerged to take on the
identities and institutions that remained invested in Arthur Schlesinger's political center. The people's will and their desires were redeemed within academia
in specialized practices of transgression and subversion. New Age populism was
a spiritual and intellectual movement for those who dreamed of myriad alternatives to the present: liberal humanism and its public sphere would give way
to networks, affects, animals, and cyborgs. A brave new world, stripped of tradition and aesthetics, antimodernist and defiantly antiliterary, would defy the
discipline and constraints of signification itself. Typeheads would be defeated
by flower children, and what was wrong would be made right.

conclusion

the farm, the fortress, and the mirror

Richard Hofstadter thought of populism as a fundamentally unstable and American political isotope: in his view, whatever liberal or progressive impulses populism might contain, its politics would eventually break down into nativist aggression. He thought that there was something conceptually and critically limited in its idealization of the "plain people," its idealization of agrarian life. He deplored the leveraging of the American pastoral into political and cultural capital and denounced the narrow provincialism, defensive ignorance of the world, and fundamentally anti-intellectual orientation that accompanied the idealization of farm life. Hofstadter's history has been roundly criticized for its inability to understand the populists and their initiatives for popular cooperation and education. Despite the weaknesses of some parts of his arguments, his position represented an authentically dissenting view of "ordinary Americans." In fact, Charles Postel's recent history could have given Hofstadter's views archival support: for Postel, the People's Party was full of modernizers, discontented with the gap between urban and rural life. They did not romanticize the bleakness of provincial life, they strained for rural modernization and reform. The Farmers' Alliance hoped to push through radical economic transformations in the name of rural improvement. Hofstadter emphasized the political progress made by rural states when he pointed to the many advantages secured by their legislative power (especially in the Senate) and their relentless and successful demands for federal farm subsidies.

At the end of the twentieth century, history and historiography seemed to be fading from public and academic consciousness. Large chunks of historical conflict had broken free of their chronological, historical, social, and economic contexts: they now floated in the cold waters of semiology. The past itself was reduced to a cool, streaming medium of disassociated, rapidly apprehensible, seductive images that made history melt altogether into an ethereal, weightless collection of eclectic styles, signs, and signifiers. The rhetorical style of an unglamorous populist insurgency came in handy for angry political protagonists. At first, the backlash politicians of the 1960s and 1970s, angry men like George Wallace and Spiro Agnew, were able to appeal to working-class resentments by conflating "experts" and "eggheads" with "phonies" and liberal elites who were trying to undermine the working man's dignity. Circulating in the semiotic matrix of late capitalism, populism had by the 1980s and 1990s become "a fashion statement," according to Michael Kazin.[1] A deeply felt hostility against experts found public and political expression in ubiquitous and inescapable denunciations of both liberalism and elitism. In this semiotic maelstrom, populism and its folksy, down-to-earth "style" migrated mind-bending distances from the dusty prairies and run-down sharecropping farms of historical Populism to the popular imagination of postmodernism and the New Economy. Kazin identified two print advertisements from the early 1990s that bore witness to the advertising industry's embrace of populist style as branding strategy: the first was for a Hewlett-Packard printer that was described as neither "'liberal' nor 'conservative' but 'Populist' . . . the perfect printer for the masses." The second was for Banana Republic's "Men's 100% Cotton Twill POPULIST pants . . . steeped in grass-roots sensibility and simple good sense of solid workmanship. . . . No-nonsense pants for the individual in everyman."[2] Populism had morphed from a cultural politics of economic insurgency into an irresistible style for the self-effacing entrepreneur as hardworking Everyman. Khakis were the ultimate fashion statement for ordinary billionaires like Bill Gates, as was coming into work with rolled-up sleeves on a casual Friday. New Economy entrepreneurs made strenuous allusion to the creativity and self-sufficiency of the American yeoman even as they demanded more freedom from government regulation, taxes, and bureaucracy. Counterculture and geekiness had found a way of expressing themselves through the modest utility of khakis and personal inkjet printers: every billionaire a revolutionary Everyman, every desktop computer a publishing enterprise.

The intoxicating mixing of high and low culture that was the trademark of the late 1980s could be found in Anna Wintour's first cover for the November 1988 issue of American *Vogue*. *Vogue* was the flagship magazine of haute couture and high society in the United States, but its understanding of fashion and the New York social world was disrupted by the arrival of Anna Wintour, child of London's swinging sixties. Her sensibilities were shaped by the celebrity-driven bohemian hedonism that dominated the London of her own youth. Wintour revitalized the style and feel of the American magazine by being simultaneously more irreverent about couture and more worshipful of new-money celebrity. Wintour's first cover for American *Vogue* featured a model named Michaela wearing a ten-thousand-dollar (not adjusted for inflation) jewel-encrusted Christian Lacroix jacket and fifty-dollar Georges Marciano jeans, a slight swell of her belly visible between the top of her pants and the bottom of her top. She smiled radiantly at the camera, her hair freely blowing in the wind. Working-class denim paired with bejeweled haute couture represented the hierarchy-busting ethos of the Zeitgeist. Wintour's pop sensibility embraced new money and old, debutantes and movie stars in New York's fast-changing social scene. Her editorial trademark exuded a *Social Text*–compatible desire for transgression: she was leading her own cultural revolution against the unwritten laws of fashion propriety.

Cultural revolution was invoked as the one form of political struggle that would shake the foundations of liberal, progressive, and conservative establishmentarianism: a cultural revolution would finally unleash popular desires to be free from hierarchy, technocracy, expertise, and administered solutions. Although Fredric Jameson opened *The Political Unconscious* with the famous injunction to his readers to "always historicize," he seemed increasingly fascinated with historical erasure in Lawrence Kasdan's *Body Heat* (1981), a film that was able to disguise all signs of its temporal provenance, novels like E. L. Doctorow's stylized historical narrative *Ragtime* (1975), and buildings like the Westin Bonaventure, a fusion of medieval fortress and glass-clad skyscraper.[3] In "Periodizing the 60s," Jameson's attempt to frame the history of the decade identified Maoism as the animating intellectual force behind the most important political struggles linking the 1980s with the 1960s. Like many on the academic Left, in the waning days of the Cold War, Jameson still understood Maoist cultural politics as a way out of the dilemmas posed by existing socialism. Maoism provided a refuge for Left thinkers (think of Andrew Ross's barefoot doctors), and Mao still seemed to be the master thinker of Left insurgency. His thought sanctioned antielitist revolt, autonomy, and self-education.

In Mao's China, the revolt against liberalism and technocratic modernity targeted culture and intellectual life. The extreme Left adopted the enemy of authoritarian personality. Intellectuals would come to represent feudal privilege and "tradition," which had to be eliminated in order to achieve the perpetually self-renewing revolution envisaged by Mao. Imposing a reign of terror on the intellectuals and the bourgeoisie became a strategy through which the Chinese Communist Party could avoid the ossification of bureaucracy. The critical question is how revolt against "administered life" became a weapon for the absolute suppression of dissent and debate and had redounding influence beyond China's borders. Mao had captured the imagination of the New Left when he encouraged the young Red Guard to question, if not overthrow, their elders. In China, radical student movements that sprang up on urban campuses in the late 1960s were encouraged by Mao and his wife, Jiang Qing, to rebel against their oppressors, to rid themselves of centuries-old deference to teachers and scholars. If teachers were naturally on the side of the oppressors, students were naturally on the side of the oppressed: this was Mao's precious lesson to radicalism. The radicalism of the young expanded the potential of the revolutionary moment. In the 1970s and 1980s, from a Western Left point of view, Mao's promotion of the cultural revolutionary agent against the bourgeoisie and the technocrats pointed the way toward a politics of the future. Influenced as he was by French theory and its particular embrace of Maoism, Jameson showed that class struggle could be and should be transformed into intensive forms of cultural struggle.

In fact, in a gesture as stylized and radical as any that Anna Wintour performed, Jameson juxtaposed the "impregnability" of the politics of second-wave feminism in the United States with the strategic regrouping of the Chinese Communist Party at Yenan, a bleak retreat in Northwest China, and the destination of the Long March. For second-wave feminism, "the personal is the political."[4] It was at Yenan, a natural fortress or mountain stronghold, that Mao consolidated his vision of peasant revolution and guerilla warfare. In the cave-homes carved out of the loess hills, the Chinese Communist Party grasped that the reinvention of Chinese folk culture as Communist revolutionary culture could create lasting images of political solidarity that could both unite and mobilize a nation fractured by civil war, regional warlordism, and Japanese military aggression. For the CCP, Yenan was a mythical site of cultural rebirth and political reinvention. Did Jameson mean that for the Left, feminism was a comparable site of radical Left retreat and then redemption? What kind of cryptic historicizing analogy was he making about radicalism and Leftism? Despite the notorious difficulty of his writings, Jameson did articulate a minimal but critical point of agreement among the most strident adversaries of the culture wars: political struggles were now to be fought on the cultural field with images, styles, and allusiveness that his own heuristic gestures at perpetual historicization put into action.

Both politics and culture had lost their distinctness: as culture and politics suffused each other, new forms of struggle emerged in unexpected places. As the idea of aesthetic autonomy lost intellectual appeal and social prestige, the elevation of ordinary tastes, popular culture, and a critique of all forms of cultural elitism and exclusivity was initiated by the Left and ended up serving conservative and reactionary purposes just as well. By the late 1980s and early 1990s, George Wallace's and George Gilder's antielitist chestnuts animated cultural criticism across the political spectrum. Adversaries in the culture wars shared a deep conviction that the sphere of culture could no longer lay claim to any kind of autonomy. Right and Left alike believed that the political potential of liberal thought had been exhausted, on the one hand, as overweening secularism and, on the other, as hegemonic universalism. In the meantime, culture warriors of all allegiances could not praise the ordinary people enough.

Populism was evolving into a style, shaped by practices of consumption and self-presentation, sundered from historical condition and economic circumstance. "The people" in American political rhetoric still resonated with grievance and rhymed with trauma. Unfortunately, the stylization of populism could never quite dissolve the residual anger and resentment that came out of the people's struggle for what Thomas Frank called "economic democracy."[5] Populism came with a significant amount of historical baggage that was difficult to leave behind with impunity. As a result, an unpredictable and resurgent historical anger seemed to animate appropriations of populist rhetoric. By the 1990s it seemed that everyone—from management gurus to progressive professors—was rushing to embrace cultural antielitism in all its forms. The unstinting flattery of ordinary people could not, however, completely dissolve the bitterness of the populist legacy. The more the adjective "populist" has been used, the more confused it has become with "popular." Philologically and etymologically, the adjective "populist" was first used to describe the politics of the agrarian revolt organized by the Farmers' Alliance and People's Party in the American West and South.[6] For Michael Kazin, the late twentieth-century arsenal of populist rhetoric drew upon powerful figures of speech that were forged alongside the very conception of Americanness itself. From the earliest years of the young Republic, the American people understood themselves as eminently capable of both reason and self-rule. In their attempts to wrest from the people their freedom and capacity for self-determination, tyrants might try to encourage ignorance and superstition, but the yeoman would think for himself, just as he farmed for himself and crafted with his own hands the necessities of survival for his family and kin. It was with a fervent belief in the power of self-education that the Farmers' Alliance and the People's Party mobilized an economic education initiative designed to provide isolated farmers and ranchers access to fundamental financial and economic information.

By the end of the nineteenth century, the struggle between people and tyrants had taken on an increasingly moralizing cast. The tyrant was not only power hungry but essentially corrupt and parasitic. As economic inequality increased during the Gilded Age, Enlightenment and evangelical strains of populist insurgency were united by their animosity toward economic elites. Many of the

People's Party's demands for intervention in reckless speculation and robber baronism were taken up by William McKinley's 1896 campaign against William Jennings Bryan, the Democratic–People's Party fusion candidate. Bryan's defeat was engineered by a well-financed Republican campaign waged in the name of "progressive politics."[7] Mark Hanna, a brilliant political tactician and industrialist, was William McKinley's presidential campaign manager, and he succeeded in using progressive politics against Bryan. In historian Lawrence Goodwyn's analysis, this campaign was critical in setting the terms of all political struggles that followed. Hanna was a tireless fund-raiser. With large amounts of cash, he managed to use mass media in unprecedented ways. He scared law-and-order Republicans who believed that Bryan and the agrarian insurgency were about to bring "anarchy" to the land. He used the American flag as the emblem of the Republican Party itself, thereby purloining Bryan's and the People's Party's patriotic credentials. Bryan's electoral defeat was resounding and had enormous consequences for American politics. The People's Party fell apart after Bryan's trouncing. McKinley's campaign used concentrated mass advertising "aimed at organizing the minds of the American people on the subject of political power, who should have it and how."[8] Hanna was able to associate McKinley's candidacy with the American flag itself: any critique of McKinley seemed to be an attack on the national interest. In Goodwyn's account, the campaign of 1896 saw the emergence of a yawning gap between the interests of an authentic and popular grassroots movement and the implementation of state-sponsored progressive social reforms: "A great testing was in process, centering on two competing political concepts—that of 'the people' on the one hand and of the 'progressive society' on the other."[9] Henceforth, "progress" was no longer good for the people. A particular experience of powerlessness was bred by the innovations of the "progressive society": populist Utopias presented themselves as alternatives to progressive ones. In the populist Utopia, self-determining citizens and pioneers shared one language and a similar culture: they lived in a state of deep distrust of the federal government, its administrative solutions, and its expert-driven social policies.

In 1892, during the previous election, the People's Party was able to overcome regional differences and attract indebted and outraged farmers from across regions that had once fought on either side of the Civil War. At its first convention, the People's Party nominated James Baird Weaver, former Union general, as its first presidential candidate. Farmers and their families gathered in large numbers in Omaha to listen to Minnesota firebrand Ignatius Donnelly's fiery rhetoric. The Omaha platform opened with these still-resonant phrases:

The conditions which surround us best justify our co-operation; we meet in the midst of a nation brought to the verge of moral, political, and material ruin. Corruption dominates the ballot box, the Legislatures, the Congress, and touches even the ermine of the bench. The people are demoralized; most of the States have been compelled to isolate the voters at the polling places to prevent universal intimidation and bribery. The newspapers are largely subsidized or muzzled, public opinion silenced, business prostrated, homes covered with mortgages, labor impoverished, and the land concentrating in the hands of capitalists.[10]

How did such an inspiring revolt against cultural and economic monopoly at the end of the nineteenth century turn into a conspiracy-minded, racist, and reactionary politics by the second half of the twentieth century? Why did so many of the movement leaders retreat behind religious fundamentalism and white supremacy? Why did they turn against their African American fellow farmers and newly arrived immigrants when they saw their own movement and interests appropriated and distorted by both Republicans and Democrats? Is there anything of the populist insurgency that can be redeemed?

In the late 1970s, we saw that Stuart Hall coined the term "populist authoritarianism" as a way of describing Margaret Thatcher's reactionary, antisocial democratic politics. Barbara Ehrenreich evoked right-wing populism as a politics of resentment and reaction that fed upon white middle-class anxieties about an increasingly polarized society. Right-wing politicians and media moguls were skillfully positioning themselves in alliance with outraged working people against a "New Class" of experts and elites who colluded with government and bureaucracy to pander to the poor. Populism had become distorted, but its enemies and a sense of perpetual outrage continued to animate its many revivals and reappropriations.

At the end of the twentieth century, one could be a populist in habits of consumption and image only: ordinariness became apotheosized as the space of true innovation and creativity. Within the humanities and in the contested interdisciplinary areas of cultural studies and communications, cultural populism came to represent the ways in which scholars and intellectuals thought of themselves in relationship to the world around them. Emerging out of a passionate desire to close the distance between intellectuals and ordinary people, cultural and academic populism was also a response to the theoretical appropriation by a new elite of ordinariness itself. Academic populism allowed for increasingly complex expressions of solidarity with popular hostility against the reign and the "authority" of experts. Its idealization of "extra-academic" experiences of fandom, the body, unreason, subcultures, and the New Age were used as rhetorical weapons against specialization and professionalization. This movement has generated hybrid forms of writing and criticism that rejected academic norms and standards in favor of the cultivation of autobiographical and confessional essays, thought to be less daunting than scholarly forms of writing to a general readership who was also interested in breaking down barriers between ordinary people and the elites. Academics, demagogues, and campaign managers alike have been able to aggravate a popular sense of grievance and plead the people's cause even when working against popular interests. The ordinary student, like the average American, has found herself flattered and stymied all at the same time. While purloining the emotions of populist rhetoric, American elites, both corporate and academic, have tried to harness its awesome power.

An animus against formal knowledge and "tradition" has actually always played a critical role in the American intellectual tradition: pragmatism and its philosophical gambit on industrial democracy were deeply antihierarchical and antiacademic in spirit and form. Stuart Hall's ideas resonated more than he could know with his American readers. John Dewey projected and envisioned a philosophy steeped in the problems of ordinary people and everyday life in industrial democracy. The wide-ranging experimentalism of Dewey's thought, alongside his rejection of academic disciplinarity, formed the core of American Progressive educational reforms. It does not, therefore, seem surprising that in the United States, cultural studies found enthusiastic institutional support for its intellectual innovations. During the very moment of cultural studies' triumphant emergence as institutional critique within academia, the Christian Right inaugurated a movement in favor of conservative cultural critique. Right-wing culture warriors believed as fervently as their Left counterparts that they too were defending the cause of ordinary people against dishonest and corrupt elites.

Early in 1989 the Reverend Donald Wildmon, a United Methodist minister and then executive director of the American Family Association, went public in his annual fund-raising letter about his feelings toward contemporary art. He was particularly disturbed by Andres Serrano's *Piss Christ* (1987), a large-format, luridly orange and red photograph of a plastic and wood crucifix submerged in urine. Partially funded by the National Endowment for the Arts, the Southeastern Contemporary Arts Center in Winston-Salem, North Carolina, had given Serrano the prize in visual arts that year. Wildmon raised the example of Serrano's artwork with his parishioners because he wanted to draw their attention to the cultural and moral decay of contemporary American culture. North

Carolina senator Jesse Helms got a copy of Wildmon's letter. Helms inaugurated his attack on the arts by denouncing the National Endowment for the Arts on the Senate floor. Instead of defending the great works of Western civilization against the barbarism of liberal/Left professors, Helms took on the National Endowment for the Arts in the name of outraged ordinary Americans. The NEA and its sister organization, the National Endowment for the Humanities, were created by acts of Congress in 1965 as footnotes to Lyndon B. Johnson's Great Society. While Helms and the Republicans had a bead on the Civil Rights Act and the expansion of federal programs and powers to address poverty and education, the NEA and the NEH represented the soft underbelly of the liberal agenda, allegedly unloved and unwanted by the people. Reagan had tried to close the agencies in 1981, but moderate Republicans who believed in cultural trustee-ship and support of the arts as legitimate parts of a national endeavor blocked his efforts. Privatizing Social Security and getting rid of Medicare were the primary objectives: discrediting and defunding the NEA and the NEH were strategic moves made to soften the enemy's resistance to the conservative war on government itself.

In 1989 Helms saw a strategic opportunity to exploit the connection between liberal elites and a decadent, America-hating avant-garde. In opening a new front in the culture war, he did not hesitate to invoke his common man credentials. Armed with Wildmon's letter and descriptions of Serrano's photographs, Helms, aided by Senator Alphonse D'Amato of New York, was able to pass an amendment on the floor of the Senate forbidding the federal funding of "offensive" works of art that denigrated religion or represented obscene subjects. In his long career in the Senate, Helms represented an aggrieved southern conservatism that came into its own in the late 1980s. In the *Wall Street Journal* obituary of Helms, John Fund wrote: "One liberal consultant told me he learned from Helms's ability to distill complicated ideas to a level that connected with ordinary people."[11] Was it possible to consider Helms a Deweyan when it came to aesthetic judgment, since he believed, or so he professed, that Everyman was an art critic and that no privileges should be given to specialization to restrict aesthetic judgment?

Helms wounded the NEA, but not fatally. More important, his campaign rallied conservatives, many of them southern and Evangelical, around a new and defiant form of cultural populism. The *National Review* immediately endorsed Helms's position and gleefully pointed to the disarray of their liberal adversaries, cornered into defending artists who soaked crucifixes in urine and photographed these objects in order to call blasphemy art. Freedom of speech seemed a weak line of defense against the force of moral and righteous outrage. Senator Slade Gordon, a relatively moderate Republican from Washington, evoked the ordinary person in his statement to the Senate on May 31, 1989, regarding the Serrano case, showing that even moderates would speak out against bad contemporary art. Gordon described his own reaction to the alleged excesses of installation and performance by giving voice to the common man's perspective: "I believe I speak for the common man and the uncommon intellectual when I confess my indifference, at best, to these heroics."[12] Helms had no intellectual aspirations, common or uncommon: he claimed his place right next to ordinary Americans and Christians who, if we were to believe Wildmon, were facing a new age of martyrdom and religious persecution.

In June 1989 the Corcoran Art Gallery canceled the Robert Mapplethorpe exhibit *The Perfect Moment*, curated by Janet Kardon, which was traveling from the Institute for Contemporary Art in Philadelphia and which featured his exquisitely crafted photographs of orchids, lilies, tumescent penises, and celebrities.[13] The art world attacked Corcoran director Christine Orr-Cahill for caving in to outside pressures, but she insisted that her decision was based on an attempt to protect the appropriations bill upon which the National Endowment for the Arts depended. Republican members of Congress continued to press their tactical advantage. "Throughout July, 1989, the NEA appropriations bill is debated by Congress. Proposals to abolish the NEA or cut its funding dramatically abound. Representative . . . Rohrabacher rose to urge Congress to eliminate the agency's entire budget, 'Mr. Chairman, my amendment would save the taxpayers $171 million in one year by striking funds for the National Endowment for the Arts,' he said."[14] The Right successfully reframed public debate about cultural affairs and the federal government by flexing its culture war muscles during the NEA controversies of 1989–90.[15] Politicians were able to use with great effectiveness conservative cultural critique to redefine the parameters of discussion when it came to public policy and arts administration. Although Republicans were once again unable to shut down the NEA, this legislative defeat seemed minor compared to the publicity garnered by D'Amato, Helms, and freshman California Republican representative Dana Rohrabacher. Helms managed to forever associate the federal arts agency with the excesses of hubristic elites and a corrupt avant-garde. He forced arts agencies around the country to rush to rethink their missions and programming.

In an editorial for the *New York Times* published in the summer of 1989, art critic Hilton Kramer would join his critical voice in an antielitist campaign against art experts, declaring that "professional opinion in the art world can no longer be trusted to make wise decisions."[16] In the spring of 1990, hours after the opening of the Robert Mapplethorpe show at the Contemporary Art Center in Cincinnati, Dennis Barrie, then director of the center, was arrested for pandering obscenity: he was indicted by a grand jury, but after a six-month trial during which art critics and historians were able to convince a jury that Mapplethorpe's photographs of homosexual and sadomasochistic practices were art and not pornography, Barrie was acquitted. In a sense, formalism and expertise had triumphed in the courts. Testimony from art critics, curators, and experts about the formal integrity of the photographs convinced jurors that Mapplethorpe was not simply a purveyor of pornography.

Meanwhile, in New York City, on March 15, 1989, Richard Serra's *Tilted Arc* was dismantled, cut into three pieces, and dumped in a scrap-metal yard. William Diamond, appointed the regional administrator of the General Services Administration in 1985, wanted the public sculpture removed from Lower Manhattan's Federal Plaza. In public hearings about Richard Serra's public sculpture, the "art world" defended the 120-foot arc of raw steel. A federal judge ordered the work dismantled and moved; Serra insisted that it was a site-specific sculpture and refused to agree to alternative locations. When the GSA Arts in Architecture commissioned the public sculpture in 1979, there was strong federal support for the arts. That year, funding levels for the NEH and the NEA reached historic heights never to be attained again. A decade later, Richard Serra's public sculpture seemed to be turned against the public itself: its self-rusting surface and threatening angle appeared to represent the nihilistic and postapocalyptic fantasies of a pampered art world elite who were far removed from the difficulties of everyday life for federal employees who had to cross the plaza to get in and out of the massive office blocks.[17] Polls showed that "public opinion" was fairly evenly divided on the subject of Serra's sculpture. William Diamond and the presiding judge, Edward D. Re, however, were virulently opposed to the sculpture and the alleged arrogance and insularity of the New York art world.

In 1939 Clement Greenberg criticized Norman Rockwell and kitsch in order to praise the values of a leftist avant-garde; by 1999 kitsch had few critics and many admirers. In 2009, when asked what she would do if she ran the National Endowment of the Arts, right-wing pundit Ann Coulter claimed that she would sponsor only "bourgeois art," including a major Norman Rockwell retrospective, and then, after having enraged "liberals and other half-brights," she would close down the federal arts agency. She issued a correction about her proposal wherein she mockingly pointed out that the Guggenheim had already offered a Rockwell retrospective.[18] Not only had love of kitsch become a badge of conservative honor, it was displayed conspicuously as a sign of solidarity with populist cultural values that allowed everyone to feel on the "right" side of the culture wars. The ordinary American taxpayer and his kitschy tastes had become the beleaguered victim of a conspiracy between the federal government and art experts to despoil the public treasure in the name of aesthetic autonomy.

The first phase of the culture wars was waged by conservative thinkers like Irving Kristol, William Buckley, Hilton Kramer, Allan Bloom, and Roger Kimball, who thought that out-of-control left-wing professors had dumbed down the curriculum and were hell-bent on destroying the Western canon while promoting immoral art and culture. These thinkers argued for academic freedom from leftist ideologues; more specifically, they argued for great literature and great art that were neither easily accessible nor available to ordinary people. After 1989, these right-wing culture warriors changed tactics, enfolding market populism in a warm embrace.[19] In the second phase of the culture wars, the Christian Right had become the vanguard. The Right was able to mobilize its rank and file against a cultural Left that found itself on the defensive, making dark allusion, as Robert Brustein did, to the Ayatollah Khomeini and his fatwa on Salman Rushdie's *Satanic Verses*.[20] While the NEA was not shut down, as many conservatives would have liked, its budget was frozen for the next two decades. It stopped giving out grants to individual artists. Arts institutions were forced to spend more and more of their time fund-raising from private donors and private foundations. The federal arts agency played a purely defensive game for its survival. The decline of federal funding for arts agencies made contemporary art a much more lucrative and speculative field for collectors, philanthropists, and donors. Museum patrons, who were more often than not also private collectors, suddenly found themselves with more influence in shaping arts programming. In 2002 Chin-tao Wu hailed speculative philanthropy as "corporate art intervention."[21]

The old cultural conservatives made their peace with the philistinism of the Christian Right by attacking universities and research programs. With the Christian Right as the vanguard in this cultural struggle, the National Endowment for the Arts was never to recover its budget or its prestige. But the Right demonstrated a remarkable quasi-Maoist ability to take the class struggle into classrooms, museums, and other notoriously elite enclaves. It hailed its congressional victories in 1994 as a full-fledged cultural revolution. When Newt Gingrich rode triumphantly into Washington, D.C., in 1994 after disastrous midterm elections for the Democrats, he declared himself at the forefront of a right-wing insurgency against elitists of all stripes. Ironically, campus radicals had prepared his cultural revolution for him. The plebeian revenge was at hand, but what, in the end, did the ordinary person achieve after all the efforts on her behalf? The Right evoked with great efficacy the cause of the ordinary person in a struggle over aesthetic value at a time when Americans, like their populist predecessors, were trying to come to grips with the intractable economic polarization of a country whose national identity was linked to a distinctive and revolutionary commitment to radical egalitarianism. Extreme expressions of thinly veiled racist and anti-immigrant sentiment periodically explode upon the national stage: insurgent defenders of American integrity mash up the language of the People's Party while imitating heroes from the early republic. These extremists may eagerly give voice to conspiracy theories about foreign pretenders usurping the sovereignty of the people, but they are unable to do justice to populist demands for massive reform of the economic structures of exploitation. Anger and fear cast a pall over a thwarted critique of the real problem of finance capital and its increasing power over the distribution of the national treasure.

Hofstadter's denunciation of populism's irrational and reactionary qualities seems as resonant today as Ignatius Donnelly's century-old attack on the money power. Popular suspicion about experts and the abuse of expertise, however, cannot replace critique of economic forms of exploitation. Populist cultural critique has provided a politically legitimate but conceptually incomplete critique of progressive society's reengineering of American education into a tool of social sorting. Academic populism, on the other hand, has been content to celebrate an affective, personalist irrationalism: its ingrained antielitism does irreparable damage to the role that theory, reason, and history have to play in establishing authentic forms of solidarity between popular discontent and the life of the mind.

In the humanities, and this includes the by now established subfield of cultural studies, academics and intellectuals have been hyperbolic as well as melodramatic about the heroic agonies of scholarly struggles and the glory of intellectual successes. For Edward Said, the intellectual was a dynamic figure engaged in epic battles: she was "an exile and a marginal," "an amateur," as well as "an author who speaks truth to power." For him, the intellectual must be engaged in "dissent against the status quo at a time when the struggle against underrepresented and disadvantaged groups seems so unfairly weighted against them."[22] In 1984 Fredric Jameson called dramatically for a new understanding of the social and political conditions of criticism. According to Jameson, it was during the 1960s that culture lost its privilege as "an autonomous space or sphere." In fact, "culture itself falls into the world, and the result is not its disappearance, but its prodigious expansion, to the point where culture becomes co-terminous with social life in general; now all the levels become 'acculturated,' and in the society of the spectacle, the image or the simulacrum, everything has at length become cultural."[23] If everything, including social life, had become cultural, then nothing was more political than the practice of cultural studies itself. Putting his 1984 theory into practice, in 1991 Jameson published *Postmodernism, or, The Cultural Logic of Late Capitalism*, a work of daunting significance for theoretical engagements with cultural populism and postmodernist aesthetics and experience.[24] Following the lead of Robert Venturi and Denise Scott Brown's peripatetic affirmations of Las Vegas and its architectural vernacular, Jameson suggested that postmodernist architecture's "commercial kinship" with a heterogeneous landscape should serve as a positive model for aesthetic and intellectual interventions. He urged us to shed no tears for the downfall of the high modernist genius—the charismatic guru who represented "an entrepreneurial and inner-directed individualism." Instead, for Jameson, we were all plebeian wage laborers now, sharing information in a more socially and culturally democratic milieu: a critical material change had erased heretofore fixed boundaries between high and low art. Jameson's book was a Promethean attempt to deal with his historical moment, which he described as marked by a congenital inability to think historically in the first place. Multinational or late capitalism was "baleful," but it should also make us "hold to a positive or 'progressive' evaluation of its emergence."[25]

When Russell Jacoby excoriated a generation of New Left American academics for refusing to participate in wider public debates outside the university, he was directing his comments at such ambiguous Jamesonian formulations, which were notoriously equivocal and difficult to pin down. Jacoby pointed to the unreadability of Jameson's New Left writing as a damning sign of this generation's willful insularity.[26] While the style of theory may have been esoteric, its "positionality" was more often antielitist than not: Jameson's virtuoso analysis of the architect and developer John Portman's Westin Bonaventure hotel, built in 1979 in downtown Los Angeles, was one of the most striking examples of a highly theoretical and ambivalent embrace of "popularity" as "populism." It was here that Fredric Jameson most famously and scandalously theorized populism's relationship to postmodernism. When Jameson commented equivocally on the Bonaventure's "populist" insertion into the commercial vernacular of downtown Los Angeles's urban fabric, he emphasized the way in which its glass-clad exterior enigmatically reflected the cityscape around it. In the Bonaventure, Jameson saw the populist, antimodernist impulses of the new architecture. The Bonaventure gave flesh to a postmodernism that refused the "elevated, Utopian language" of the elitist and modernist masterworks. If Le Corbusier's ambitious housing projects were defined by their negative relationship to the "tawdriness" of urban development, then Portman's hotel "aspire[d] to being a total space" that literally supplanted the city surrounding it. The Bonaventure aspired to be the equivalent of a miniature city in the middle of a city: it was a "substitute" and a simulacrum of urban space itself.[27] More importantly, Jameson hailed the radicalism of its powers of decontextualization: the hotel was fortresslike and wrapped in a reflective glass skin. Its inner spaces were fluid and capacious. John Portman was an expert at creating mall/hotel hybrids as part of urban renewal projects that abjured any relationship to existing city streets. His hotel complexes turned in on themselves, demonstrating a new aspiration for self-contained built environments in urban settings. Jameson's analysis of the Bonaventure was like the Bonaventure itself: the theory of postmodernity was less an intervention than a studiously enigmatic, flatly reflective insertion into the eclectic, commercial, postmodern culture in which the critic himself was immersed. Furthermore, the Westin Bonaventure represented the demise of the modern city and the extinction of its peripatetic, skeptical, libidinous, and choleric inhabitant, the modern intellectual as amateur and provocateur.

In Russell Jacoby's account of recent American intellectual life, the demise of "nonacademic intellectuals" has been hastened by the rise of the professional academic, a decidedly nonheroic figure who polishes his résumé while keeping an eye on his bank account. Jacoby's professional intellectual is contemptuous of vernacular language and pragmatic engagements. He indulges in obscure theories and tendentious radicalism that are in fact protected by the fortresslike university, where the new academic is consigned to a comfortable life of obsolescence and inconsequentiality. For Jacoby, an independent class of freethinkers is "an endangered species: industrial development and urban blight have devastated their environment."[28] Jacoby had particular venom for Fredric Jameson's version of New Left postmodernism, and he reviled Jameson's reading of the Westin Bonaventure. Jacoby pointed to Jameson's analysis of postmodern architecture as an example of theoretical obscurantism masquerading as radical thought. In Jameson's argument, the messy pedestrian life of the modern city was disappearing into a self-contained, simulacral space where the intellectual or cultural critic could no longer afford "the luxury of old-fashioned ideological critique." According to Jameson, criticism is immersed in the space of postmodernism: here, "the indignant moral denunciation of the other becomes unavailable."[29] In the early 1990s, the Utopian aspect of the critical act had to be renounced for cognitive and corporeal immersion in modernism's "other"—the commercial, ugly, mass-produced kitschiness of popular and populist culture. Theory itself could be a mimetic and reflective surface, stealthily inserting itself into the geography of popular culture and popular practices. Jacoby denounced postmodern jargon for its veneer of pseudoexpertise. He longed for the authentic and organic forms of language and experience embodied by the "vernacular": he, like generations of Americans, looked toward the ordinary people and their problems for moral guidance. And yet it was with this selfsame ordinariness that postmodernism claimed its own special form of intimacy. In the digital age, intellectuals play a more ambiguous and more modest role than either Edward Said or Russell Jacoby would like to admit. In fact, intellectuals, like experts, reinforce and perpetuate the "status quo," sometimes in their very attempts to provide dissenting points of view.[30] As Richard Hofstadter has shown, intellectuals and academics are no better equipped than ordinary people at escaping the consensus of their historical moments. The neopopulist, culture-centric antielitist consensus of the past twenty years has perhaps finally run out of steam: it is time for a better and more convincing critique of the objective situation. The ideal of a classless society—a place where ruthless competition and economic polarization are abolished in the name of cooperation and collaboration—is, according to historian of American intellectual and social life Howard Brick, a deeply American vision.[31] For Brick, there is a distinctly American interpretation of social collectivism and political economy that persisted in liberal thinking well after World War II. To achieve this unattained but desirable American idyll, Barbara Ehrenreich asserts that we should aspire to be a nation of one class—an educated middle class.

Despite the fact that the PMC has an unfortunate tendency to get into a defensive institutional crouch when it feels itself threatened, it also believes in the "hedonism of work" and values skill, expertise, and service in a way that the rich do not. In the wake of the recessions of the early 1980s and the 1987 stock market crash, Ehrenreich remarked that, "compared to the world as seen by middle-class intellectuals at mid-century, ours is a world of scarcity."[32] If Ehrenreich found the professional middle class anxiously clinging to its relative privilege in the 1980s, she was dismayed by its raw desperation after the convulsive fraying social safety nets and corporate downsizing of the past two decades. We are even further from that sense of midcentury intellectual confidence today— rewarding, remunerative work has become even scarcer. The PMC should not be looking up to the rich or accepting the pseudopopulism of the new plutocrats with their worship of quick fixes, kitsch, ignorance, and greed. The PMC should not accept a spurious cultural populism that has allowed conservatives to veil policies that have exacerbated increasingly grotesque economic polarization of the past twenty years with a mask of "down-to-earthness." In 2007 Walter Benn Michaels offered a controversial argument that diversity initiatives within educational and academic institutions also functioned as pseudoprogressive fig leaves designed to disguise a lack of will to address entrenched economic inequality. He is correct to point out that economic inequality is the last thing diversity initiatives are able to deal with.[33] The meritocracy was designed to embrace high-scoring, entitled elites of all races and ethnicities while keeping class difference intact.

The PMC should be the first to reject the meritocracy and high-stakes testing. In fact, one of the original supporters of conservative 1980s educational reforms, Diane Ravitch, has renounced standardized testing and is offering a robust defense of teachers and the autonomy of the educational process.[34] The PMC can choose to follow Barbara Ehrenreich's exhortation that the professional class rediscover and reaffirm "its own tacit rebuttal of capitalism" in its commitment to "the pleasure of work," a pleasure that cannot be easily "commodified or marketed."[35] In his *Unmaking the Public University*, Christopher Newfield framed the budget cuts to public education as a war of the financial elites on an increasingly beleaguered middle class. Newfield points to the defunding of the University of California system during the height of the New Economy bubble as an example of the political logic of austerity measures: in good economic times, as in bad, a public university is seen as an entity that the state no longer needs to support. The more beleaguered the middle class, the more it seeks to secure its privileges through the meritocratic institutions choking off dreams of social mobility for millions of poor students all over the country.[36] For Newfield, as for Ehrenreich, the American middle class has all the makings of a progressive social force, but its anxieties about its own prospects have almost entirely crippled its political imagination. For Benn Michaels, administrators and educators need a renewed understanding of equality in terms of political economy.

Better than mind-expanding gadgets or pseudoreligious rituals, pleasurable work would truly set us free from the soul-sapping drudgery of totally administered life and exhaustively instrumentalized human capacities. For Ehrenreich, middle-class and working-class solidarity could be strengthened on the basis of shared attitudes about work and its value. Middle-class intellectuals have special skills and capacities that should not be renounced or disparaged in the name of pseudopopulist sympathies or esoteric radicalism: intellectuals and professionals should be the first to refuse to compromise their training and their skills for profits and short-term advantages. The PMC class is uniquely gifted with a set of objective skills to resist the rapacity and narrow-mindedness of the corporate profit motive. It is also a class increasingly beleaguered and besieged: its interests are the interests of ordinary Americans, its problems the problems of the working classes. We need, however, experts and expertise at every level to perform the work of reframing and refashioning cultural, historical, and scientific knowledge to deal with the social contradictions of living in a deeply troubled world. Just as social, cultural, and economic polarization is not overcome when academics celebrate the popular, the amateur, and the fan, the powers that be are not threatened at all when we criticize the expert or the professional as a living avatar of the unholy elites. Fleeing from the iron cage of professional identity, academic populists found themselves in an unexpectedly intimate embrace with the cultural consensus of the neoliberal era: having rejected and transgressed the embedded liberalism that had once protected universities, they found themselves caught in a mirrored tower, making history behind their own backs.

notes

Introduction

1 See the work of Henry Jenkins, especially *Textual Poachers: Television Fans and Partici-patory Culture* (New York: Routledge, 1992), and *Convergence Culture: Where Old and New Media Collide*, rev. ed. (New York: New York University Press, 2008).

2 Andrew Ross, *No Respect: Intellectuals and Popular Culture* (New York: Routledge, 1989).

3 Ibid., 243.

4 Ernesto Laclau, *On Populist Reason* (London: Verso, 2005).

5 Ernesto Laclau, "Towards a Theory of Populism," in *Politics and Ideology in Marxist Theory: Capitalism—Fascism—Populism* (London: New Left, 1977), 143–98.

6 Michael Hardt and Antonio Negri, *Empire* (Cambridge, Mass.: Harvard University Press, 2001).

7 Laclau, *On Populist Reason*.

8 Slavoj Žižek, "Against the Populist Temptation," *Critical Inquiry* 32 (Spring 2006): 551–74.

9 Christopher Lasch called this rejection of democracy "the revolt of the elites" (*The Revolt of the Elites and the Betrayal of Democracy* [New York: W. W. Norton, 1995]).

10 See François Cusset, *French Theory: How Foucault, Derrida and Company Transformed the Intellectual Life of the United States* (Minneapolis: University of Minnesota Press, 2008), for an excellent account of the Anglo-American reception of "French theory."

11 Rick Perlstein, *Nixonland: The Rise of a President and the Fracturing of America* (New York: Scribner, 2008).

12 Thomas Frank, *One Market under God: Extreme Capitalism, Market Populism and the End of Economic Democracy* (New York: Anchor Books, 2001).

13 See Walter Wriston, *The Twilight of Sovereignty: How Information Technology Is Trans-forming Our World* (New York: Scribner, 2002), for a primer of 1990s free market technopopulism, as well as George Gilder on the necessity of belief for business success in *The Spirit of Enterprise* (New York: Simon and Schuster, 1984).

14 Frank, *One Market under God*, 55.

15 Fred Turner, *From Counterculture to Cyberculture: Steward Brand, Whole Earth Network and the Rise of Digital Utopianism* (Chicago: University of Chicago Press, 2008).

16 Kevin Kelly, interview with George, "When Bandwidth Is Free," *Wired* 1.04 (Sep-tember–October 1993), http://www.wired.com/wired/archive/1.04/gilder.html.

17   David Harvey, *A Brief History of Neoliberalism* (Oxford: Oxford University Press, 2005), 42.

18   Raymond Williams, *Keywords: A Vocabulary of Culture and Society* (New York: Oxford University Press, 1985).

19   Lawrence Grossberg, *Dancing in Spite of Myself* (Durham, N.C.: Duke University Press, 1997), 172.

20   Gerald Graff, *Professing Literature: An Institutional History* (Chicago: University of Chicago Press, 1987), 99–100.

21   Richard Hofstadter, *Anti-intellectualism in American Life* (1963; New York: Vintage Books, 1966).

22   Angela McRobbie, "Post-Marxism and Cultural Studies: A Post-Script," in *Cultural Studies*, ed. Lawrence Grossberg, Cary Nelson, and Paula Treichler (New York: Routledge, 1992), 719–30, quote at 721.

23   Christopher Lasch, *True and Only Heaven* (New York: W. W. Norton, 1991).

24   Ibid., 507–8.

25   Ibid., 531.

26   Michael Kazin, *The Populist Persuasion: An American History* (Ithaca, N.Y.: Cornell University Press, 1998).

27   Mark Fenster, *Conspiracy Theories: Secrecy and Power in American Culture* (1999; Minneapolis: University of Minnesota Press, 2008). For a revisiting of conspiracy theory from a point of view critical of classical liberalism in political philosophy, see the work of political science professor Jodi Dean, especially *Aliens in America: Conspiracy Cultures from Outerspace to Cyberspace* (Ithaca, N.Y.: Cornell University Press, 1998).

28   Richard Hofstadter, *The Paranoid Style in American Politics and Other Essays* (Cambridge, Mass.: Harvard University Press, 1965).

29   Fenster, *Conspiracy Theories*, 38.

30   Ibid., 28.

31   David S. Brown, *Richard Hofstadter: An Intellectual Biography* (Chicago: University of Chicago Press, 2006).

32   T. W. Adorno, Else Frenkel-Brunswick, Daniel J. Levinson, and R. Nevitt Sanford, *The Authoritarian Personality* (1950; New York: W. W. Norton, 1969).

33   Charles Postel, *The Populist Vision* (New York: Oxford University Press, 2010).

34   Thomas Frank, *The Conquest of Cool* (Chicago: University of Chicago Press, 1998).

35   Thomas Frank, *What's the Matter with Kansas?* (New York: Henry Holt, 2004).

36   Kevin Phillips, *Wealth and Democracy: A Political History of the American Rich* (New York: Broadway Books, 2002).

37   Barbara Ehrenreich, *Fear of Falling: The Inner Life of the Middle Class* (New York: HarperCollins, 1989), 202.

38 Teresa Sullivan, Elizabeth Warren, and Jay Westbrook, *The Fragile Middle Class: Americans in Debt* (New Haven, Conn.: Yale University Press, 2001).

39 Phillips, *Wealth and Democracy*, 131–32.

40 Richard Sennett, *The Culture of the New Capitalism* (New Haven, Conn.: Yale University Press, 2006), 54.

41 Richard Arum and Josipa Roksa, *Academically Adrift: Limited Learning on College Campuses* (Chicago: University of Chicago Press, 2011), 37. I have not been able to fully assimilate the findings in this book in my arguments, but Arum and Roksa's empirical findings seem to support Hofstadter's double-edged thesis (which I will expand upon in greater detail in what follows)—that American educational leaders invest in a fantasy of educational reforms as a remedy for social inequity while actual academic content in secondary and higher education has been deeply compromised, if not nullified.

42 See Wendy Kaminer, *Sleeping with Extra-Terrestrials: The Rise of Irrationalism and the Perils of Piety* (New York: Vintage, 2000), and, more recently, Susan Jacoby, *The Age of American Unreason* (New York: Pantheon, 2008).

Chapter One. The Problem with the Meritocracy

1 Hofstadter, *Anti-intellectualism*, 299.

2 Henry M. Kliebard, *The Struggle for the American Curriculum (1893–1958)* (New York: Routledge, 1986), 12.

3 Graff, *Professing Literature*, 32.

4 Ibid., 83.

5 G. Stanley Hall was the first president of the American Psychological Association. A specialist in the developmental psychology of children and adolescents, he also hosted Sigmund Freud's 1909 visit to Clark University, where he was president. Joseph Mayer Rice was trained as a physician: he went to Germany to study the educational system and returned to the United States to publish his most influential work, a series of muckraking articles that appeared in the *Forum* between 1892 and 1893 in which he documented the lamentable state of American public schools.

6 Kliebard, *Struggle*, 77.

7 John Dewey, *Democracy and Education* (1916; New York: Macmillan, 1944), 119.

8 Ibid., 120.

9 Horace Mann, *Twelfth Annual Report of the Board of Education, Together with the Twelfth Annual Report of the Secretary of the Board* (Boston, 1849), 84, cited in Lawrence A. Cremin, *The Transformation of the School: Progressivism in American Education 1876–1957* (New York: Alfred A. Knopf, 1962), 9.

10 Cremin, *Transformation*, 10.

11 Joseph Mayer Rice, *The Public School System of the United States* (New York: Century Company, 1893).

12 Ibid., 64.

13 John Dewey, "The Recovery of Philosophy," in *Democracy and Education*, 23.

14 Rice, *Public School System*, 52.

15 Cremin, *Transformation*, 193.

16 Ibid., 192.

17 *The Cardinal Principles of Secondary Education* was published in 1918 as a U.S. government publication. In 2008 the California Digital Archive made accessible a digitized and downloadable version of the original 1918 publication at http://www.archive.org/details/cardinalprinciploonatirich.

18 Ibid.

19 Cited in Hofstadter, *Anti-intellectualism*, 336–37.

20 Judith Sealander, *The Failed Century of the Child: Governing America's Young in the Twentieth Century* (Cambridge: Cambridge University Press, 2003), 193–94.

21 Cremin, *Transformation*, 56.

22 Ibid., 57.

23 Frederick W. Taylor, *The Principles of Scientific Management*, digitized and archived by the National Humanities Center, in downloadable PDF format at http://nationalhumanitiescenter.org/pds/gilded/progress/text3/taylor.pdf.

24 Diane Ravitch, *Left Back: A Century of Failed School Reforms* (New York: Simon and Schuster, 2000), 324.

25 Ibid.

26 Michael Young, *The Rise of the Meritocracy* (London: Thames and Hudson, 1958).

27 Ibid., 92.

28 Michael Young, "Down with the Meritocracy," *Guardian*, June 29, 2001, http://www.guardian.co.uk/politics/2001/jun/29/comment.

29 Ibid.

30 Lawrence Goodwyn, *Democratic Promise: The Populist Movement in America* (New York: Oxford University Press, 1976).

31 Paula S. Fass, "The IQ: A Cultural and Historical Framework," *American Journal of Education* 88, no. 4 (1980): 431–58.

32 Thorstein Veblen, *Theory of the Leisure Class* (New York: Oxford University Press, 2008).

33 Stephen Jay Gould, *The Mismeasure of Man* (1981; New York: W. W. Norton, 1996), 30–31.

34 Richard Herrnstein, "IQ," *Atlantic Monthly* 228, no. 3 (1971): 43–64.

35 Lasch, *Revolt*, 41.

36 Ibid., 45.

37 Ibid., 47.

38 Christopher Lasch, *The Culture of Narcissism: American Life in an Age of Diminishing Expectations* (1978; New York: W. W. Norton, 1991), 62–63.

39 Ibid., 235.

40 Ibid., 222.

41 David Brooks, *Bobos in Paradise: The New Upper Class and How They Got There* (New York: Simon and Schuster, 2001).

42 Nicholas Lemann, *The Big Test: The Secret History of the American Meritocracy* (New York: Farrar, Strauss and Giroux, 1999).

43 Allan Nairn and Ralph Nader, *The Reign of ETS: The Corporation that Makes Up Minds* (Washington, D.C.: Learning Research Project, 1980).

44 David Owen and Marilyn Doerr, *None of the Above: The Truth behind the SAT's*, rev. and updated (1985; Lanham, N.Y.: Rowman, Littlefield, 1999), 15.

45 Nairn and Nader, *Reign of ETS*.

46 Owen and Doerr, *None of the Above*, 193.

47 Daniel Bell, *The Reforming of General Education: The Columbia College Experience in a National Setting* (New York: Columbia University Press, 1966), 129–41.

48 Peter Sacks, *Standardized Minds: The High Price of America's Testing Culture and What We Can Do to Change It* (New York: Perseus Books, 1999); *A Nation at Risk: The Imperative for Educational Reform*, National Commission on Excellence in Education, April 1983, http://www.ed.gov/pubs/NatAtRisk/risk.html.

49 Lemann, *The Big Test*.

50 Sacks, *Standardized Minds*.

51 See Hofstadter's *Anti-intellectualism* and its affinity with Theodor Adorno's critique of administered life in *The Culture Industry* (1991; New York: Routledge, 2001).

52 See Joseph Mayer Rice, *The Public School System of the United States* (New York: Century Company, 1893).

53 Samuel Bowles and Herbert Gintis, *Schooling in Capitalist America: Educational Reform and the Contradictions of Economic Life* (New York: Basic Books, 1976).

54 Sacks, *Standardized Minds*, 155–57.

55 For a Christian account of the harm that standardized testing and the principle of ubiquitous competition have on adolescents, see Chap Clark, *Hurt: Inside the World of Today's Teenagers* (Grand Rapids, Mich.: Baker Book House, 2004).

56 The New York State Regents Credential is granted after students have passed a Regents Exam in specific subject areas. The exam was imposed after the Civil War to normalize standards in New York public schools and is developed by New York State teachers to test student mastery of specific disciplines, including English, foreign languages, sciences, math, and history. Ambitious working-class and immigrant students could "test" into academic tracks.

57 Lionel Trilling, "Van Amringe and Keppel Eras," in *A History of Columbia College on Morningside* (New York: Columbia University Press, 1954), 36–37.

58 James Crouse and Dale Trusheim, *The Case against the SAT's* (Chicago: University of Chicago Press, 1988), 20–21.

59 John Wechsler quoted in Paula S. Fass, "The IQ: A Cultural and Historical Framework," *American Journal of Education* 88, no. 4 (1980): 431–58, quote at 432.

60 "Episcopacy" was Lemann's shorthand for the American ruling classes: he married *Episcopalian* and *aristocracy* in order to describe the social and cultural sensibilities of Ivy League presidents and social reformers.

61 Crouse and Trusheim, *The Case*, 17.

62 John Wechsler, *The Qualified Student* (New York: John Wiley and Sons, 1977).

63 Lemann, *The Big Test*, 5.

64 James Bryant Conant, "Education for a Classless Society: The Jeffersonian Tradition," *Atlantic Monthly* 165, no. 5 (1940): 593–602.

65 Report of the Harvard Committee, *General Education in a Free Society*, with an introduction by James Bryant Conant (1945; Cambridge, Mass.: Harvard University Press, 1962).

66 Conant, introduction to ibid., ix.

67 Carl Campbell Brigham, *A Study of American Intelligence* (Princeton, N.J.: Princeton University Press, 1922).

68 Walter Lippmann, "The Mental Age of Americans," *New Republic*, October 25, 1922, 213–15.

69 Gould, *Mismeasure of Man*, 230.

70 Brigham, *Study of American Intelligence*, 210.

71 Owen and Doerr, *None of the Above*, xvi, 61, 178.

72 Crouse and Trusheim, *The Case*, 35.

73 Ibid., 31.

74 Ibid., 33–34.

75 Lemann, *The Big Test*, 344.

76 Owen and Doerr, *None of the Above*, 180.

77 Gould, *Mismeasure of Man*, 262–63.

78 Ibid.

79 Lemann, *The Big Test*, 345.

80 Stephen J. McNamee and Robert K. Miller, Jr., *The Meritocracy Myth* (Oxford: Rowman and Littlefield, 2004), 102.

81 Bell, *Reforming of General Education*, 8.

82 Dewey, *Democracy and Education*, 306.

83 Ibid., 87–88.

Chapter Two. Ordinary Americans, Average Students

1   Hofstadter, *Anti-intellectualism*, 326. It is outside of the purview of this study to address the school systems in the European Union and Great Britain, not to mention the rest of the world. I follow Hofstadter's arguments while considering the significance of his conclusions in the contemporary intellectual and academic context.

2   Sealander, *Failed Century*, 187.

3   Harry Braverman, *Labor and Monopoly Capital: The Degradation of Work in the Twentieth Century* (1974; New York: Monthly Review Press, 1998), 96.

4   Ibid., 99. Aptitude tests for workers proved unreliable in the long run as predictors of worker performance and were abandoned during the labor crises of the 1930s; but, as we have seen, the aptitude test would leave an indelible mark upon the managerial imagination. Industrial psychology believed that it could find new instruments of calibration to promote worker-management harmony.

5   Sealander, *Failed Century*, 201–3.

6   Ibid., 207.

7   David Riesman, *The Lonely Crowd* (New Haven, Conn.: Yale University Press, 2001), 59.

8   Ibid., 63.

9   Michel Foucault and Gilles Deleuze would have described the evolution of pedagogical method as one that moved from a society of discipline to a society of control.

10 Arthur E. Bestor, *Educational Wastelands: The Retreat from Learning in Our Public Schools* (Urbana: University of Illinois Press, 1953), 121.

11 Cremin, *Transformation*, 55.

12 Evan Watkins, *Class Degrees: Smart Work, Managed Choices and the Transformation of Higher Education* (New York: Fordham University Press, 2008), 3.

13 U.S. Office of Education, *Life-Adjustment Education for Every Youth* (Washington, D.C.: U.S. Government Printing Office, 1948).

14 Cited in Kliebard, *Struggle*, 213.

15 Hofstadter, *Anti-intellectualism*, 344.

16 Dewey, *Democracy and Education*, 369.

17 Sealander, *Failed Century*, 156–57.

18 Franklin Roosevelt, *The Public Papers and Addresses of Franklin Roosevelt*, vol. 2, *The Year of Crisis, 1933* (New York, 1938), 80, cited in Sealander, *Failed Century*, 156.

19 Charles Prosser and Charles A. Allen, *Vocational Education in a Democracy* (New York: Century, 1925).

20 Watkins, *Class Degrees*, 18.

21 Taylor, *Principles*, 61–62.

22 Hofstadter, *Anti-intellectualism*, 346.

23 Bestor, *Educational Wastelands*, 82–83.

24 Cited in Hofstadter, *Anti-intellectualism*, 344.

25 Graff, *Professing Literature*, 162–63.

26 Kliebard, *Struggle*, 90.

27 Hofstadter, *Anti-intellectualism*, 345.

28 "From Here to There: The Road to Reform of American High Schools," http://www.ed.gov/about/offices/list/ovae/pi/hsinit/papers/history.pdf, 2.

29 Braverman, *Labor and Monopoly Capital*.

30 Sealander, *Failed Century*, 192.

31 Hofstadter, *Anti-intellectualism*, 327.

32 Quoted in Louis Menand, *The Metaphysical Club: The Story of Ideas in America* (New York: Farrar, Strauss and Giroux, 2001), 188. From Adolphe Quetelet, *A Treatise on Man and the Development of His Faculties*, trans. R. Knox (Edinburgh, 1842), 96. Many twentieth-century historians and theorists have dealt with the nineteenth century's attempts to represent and measure deviance, the most thorough and rigorous of which must be the work of Alan Sekula on photography's role in the definition of criminality.

33 Menand, *Metaphysical Club*, 187.

34 Sarah Igo, *The Averaged American* (Cambridge, Mass.: Harvard University Press, 2007).

35 Robert S. Lynd and Helen Merrell Lynd, *Middletown: A Study in Modern American Culture* (New York: Harcourt Brace and Company, 1929).

36 Igo, *The Averaged American*, 12.

37 Ibid., 110.

38 Watkins, *Class Degrees*, 3–4.

39 Martin Jay, *Permanent Exiles: Essays on the Intellectual Migration from Germany to America* (New York: Columbia University Press, 1985), 121.

40 Theodor Adorno, *The Psychological Technique of Martin Luther Thomas' Radio Addresses* (Stanford, Calif.: Stanford University Press, 2000).

41 Theodor Adorno, *Negative Dialectics* (1973; London: Routledge and Kegan Paul, 2004), 14.

42 Detlev Claussen, *Theodor W. Adorno: One Last Genius*, trans. Rodney Livingstone (Cambridge, Mass.: Harvard University Press, 2008), 183.

43 Max Horkheimer and Theodor Adorno, *The Dialectic of Enlightenment*, trans. Edmund Jephcott (1969; Stanford, Calif.: Stanford University Press, 1997).

44 See David Jenemann, *Adorno in America* (Minneapolis: University of Minnesota Press, 2007), and Anthony Heilbut, *Exiled in Paradise: German Refugee Artists and Intel-*

lectuals from the 1930s to the Present (Berkeley: University of California Press, 1997) for accounts of this period.

45 Dewey, *Democracy and Education*, 39–40.

46 Eli Zaretsky, *Capitalism, the Family and Personal Life* (New York: Harper & Row, 1976) and *Secrets of the Soul: A Social and Cultural History of Psychoanalysis* (New York: Vintage, 2004).

47 Hofstadter, *Anti-intellectualism*, 388, 389.

48 Dewey, *Democracy and Education*, 47.

49 Ibid., 390.

50 See the work of Richard Shusterman for a contemporary expansion of this idea, especially *Pragmatist Aesthetics: Living Beauty, Rethinking Art* (New York: Rowman and Littlefield, 2000), with its predictable attacks on "highbrow" culture and its antidemocratic ambitions.

51 Dewey, *Democracy and Education*, 115.

52 Hofstadter, *Anti-intellectualism*, 340.

53 Dewey, *Democracy and Education*, 51.

54 Brown, *Richard Hofstadter*, 138.

55 Peter Gay, *A Godless Jew: Freud, Atheism and the Making of Psychoanalysis* (New Haven, Conn.: Yale University Press, 1987), 49.

56 Ibid.

57 Sigmund Freud, *Civilization and Its Discontents*, Standard Edition of the Complete Psychological Works, ed. James Strachey (London: Hogarth Press, 1961), 21:59–145, quote at 75.

58 C. Wright Mills, *White Collar: The American Middle Classes* (1951; New York: Oxford University Press, 2001), 224–25.

59 Ibid., 227.

60 Freud, *Civilization and Its Discontents*, 21:84.

61 Ibid., 21:84.

62 Mills, *White Collar*, 226.

63 Sigmund Freud, *Future of an Illusion*, Standard Edition of the Complete Psychological Works, ed. James Strachey (New York: W. W. Norton, 1976), 21:53.

64 Ibid., 21:28.

65 One of the most nuanced pleas for a rethinking of traditional Leftism was made by Mark Poster in his essay "Words without Things: The Mode of Information," in "The Humanities as Social Technology," special issue, *October* 53 (Summer 1990): 62–77.

66 Hofstadter, *Anti-intellectualism*, 360–61.

Chapter Three. The Curious Cult of Religious Practicality

1   Brooks, *Bobos in Paradise*, 186–87.

2   Ross, *No Respect*, 56.

3   Ibid., 50.

4   Hofstadter, *Anti-intellectualism*, 222–23.

5   Arthur Schlesinger, Jr., "The Highbrow in Politics," *Partisan Review* 20 (March–April 1953): 156–65.

6   Editorial, "The Nation: The Will of the People," *Time*, November 10, 1952, 21–28, quote at 21.

7   Schlesinger, "The Highbrow in Politics," 159.

8   Adorno et al., *The Authoritarian Personality*.

9   Rolf Wiggershaus, *The Frankfurt School in History, Theories, and Political Significance*, trans. Michael Robertson (Cambridge, Mass.: MIT Press, 1995), 409.

10 William Leuchtenberg quoted in Brown, *Hofstadter*, 93.

11 Hofstadter, *Anti-intellectualism*, 224.

12 Ibid., 5.

13 Joan Didion, *Slouching towards Bethlehem* (New York: Farrar, Straus and Giroux, 1968).

14 Ross, *No Respect*, 64.

15 Hofstadter, *Anti-intellectualism*, 145–46.

16 Ibid., 264–65.

17 Philip Roth's *American Pastoral* (New York: Vintage, 1998), a novel about the degradation of the American dream, pits a successful entrepreneur against his daughter's antipatriarchal antiradicalism. Merry, Roth's mythic, countercultural monster, participates in this ecstasy of destruction, which seems to be directed against her father's business success and dreams of assimilation.

18 Max Weber, *The Sociology of Religion*, trans. Ephraim Fischoff (Boston: Beacon Press, 1956).

19 Louis Schneider and Sanford Dornbusch, *Popular Religion: Inspirational Books in America* (Chicago: University of Chicago Press, 1958), 37.

20 Ibid., 49.

21 Hofstadter, *Anti-intellectualism*, 253–71.

22 Ibid., 268.

23 Cited in ibid., 269. See also Henry C. Link, *The Return to Religion* (1936; New York: Pocket Book, 1943).

24 Link, *Return to Religion*, 34.

25 Mills, *White Collar*, 282.

26   "American Rhetoric," an online "speech bank" collecting famous American oratorical performances and texts, has audio and print versions of Conwell's speech online at http://www.americanrhetoric.com/speeches /rconwellacresofdiamonds.htm.

27   Schneider and Dornbusch, *Popular Religion*, 92.

28   Mills, *White Collar*, 110.

29   Hofstadter, *Anti-intellectualism*, 266.

30   Ibid., 266–67.

31   Norman Vincent Peale, *The Power of Positive Thinking* (New York: Prentice Hall, 1952).

32   Quoted in Hofstadter, *Anti-intellectualism*, 269.

33   Anson Rabinbach, *The Human Motor: Energy, Fatigue, and the Origins of Modernity* (New York: Basic Books, 1997).

34   In *The Human Motor* Rabinbach shows that Helmholtz's ideas had enormous cultural significance, especially in the bourgeois theorization of power as labor power.

35   Mills, *White Collar*, 111.

36   Ibid., 271.

37   Adorno et al., *The Authoritarian Personality*.

38   Theodor Adorno, *The Stars Down to Earth and Other Essays on the Irrational in Culture*, ed. Stephen Crook (1994; London: Routledge, 2001), 48.

39   Adorno, *The Psychological Technique*, 41.

40   Moreover, as science studies would go on to show in the pioneering work of Bruno Latour, laboratory conditions could be shaped by social pressures and institutional biases. Both Adorno and Hofstadter emphasized the qualities of detachment and objectivity in the work of critical theory.

41   Claussen, *Theodor W. Adorno*, 204.

42   According to Andrew Ross, before the 1960s American intellectuals bent over backward to worship the German Jewish representatives of high culture. Adorno and Horkheimer should have been the clear beneficiaries of such adulation, but neither their own accounts nor accounts given by their biographers give any evidence that this was actually their experience of their place in the United States.

43   Martin Jay, *The Dialectical Imagination: A History of the Frankfurt School and the Institute of Social Research 1923–1950* (Berkeley: University of California Press, 1973), 5–6.

44   Max Pensky, introduction to *The Actuality of Adorno: Critical Essays on Adorno and the Postmodern*, ed. Max Pensky (Albany: SUNY Press, 1997), 4.

45   Theodor W. Adorno, "The Actuality of Philosophy," *Telos* 31 (Spring 1977): 120–33, quote at 127.

46   Matthew Rampley, "Mimesis and Allegory: On Aby Warburg and Walter Benjamin," in *Art History as Cultural History*, ed. Richard Woodfield (Amsterdam: OPA, 2001), 121–50.

47 After Warburg became incapacitated and could no longer work on the project, Fritz Saxl, his student and director of the Warburg Institute in London, completed the work of the collection and had it published. The original collection, housed in the Warburg Library in London, was published with Fritz Saxl and Aby Warburg as coauthors in English and called *Catalogue of Astrological and Mythological Illuminated Manuscripts of the Latin Middle Ages* (London: Warburg Institute, 1966).

48 Marian Green, *Magic for the Aquarian Age: A Contemporary Textbook of Practical Magical Techniques* (Los Angeles: J. P. Tarcher, 1980), 19.

49 Walter Benjamin, "On Astrology," in *Selected Writings*, vol. 2, *1931–1934*, ed. Michael W. Jennings, Howard Eiland, and Gary Smith (1999; Cambridge, Mass.: Harvard University Press, 2005), 684–85, quote at 685.

50 Walter Benjamin, "On the Mimetic Faculty," in *Selected Writings*, 2:719–22, quote on 719.

51 Theodor W. Adorno, *Aesthetic Theory*, trans. Robert Hullot-Kentor (Minneapolis: University of Minnesota Press, 1996), 84.

52 Benjamin, "On the Mimetic Faculty," 719.

53 Adorno, *Aesthetic Theory*.

54 Robert Kaufman, "Lyric's Expression: Musicality, Conceptuality, Critical Agency," *Cultural Critique*, no. 60 (Spring 2005): 197–216, quote at 200.

55 Benjamin, "On the Mimetic Faculty," 722.

56 Roger Caillois, "Mimicry and Legendary Psychasthenia," trans. John Shepley, *October* 31 (Winter 1984): 16–32.

57 Theodor Adorno, *Minima Moralia*, trans. E. F. N. Jephcott (London: Verso, 1999), 154.

58 Jürgen Habermas, *The Theory of Communicative Action*, vol. 1, *Reason and the Rationalization of Society* (Boston: Beacon Press, 1981), 380–83.

59 Albrecht Wellmer's proposed method of reading Adorno proves very apt here, as he proposes that we read the works as a multidimensional and shifting series of constellations. Albrecht Wellmer, "Adorno, Modernity and the Sublime," in Pensky, *The Actuality of Adorno*, 112–34, quote on 115.

60 Jack Lindsay, *Origins of Astrology* (London: Frederick Muller, 1971), 419.

61 Adorno, *Stars Down to Earth*, 164.

62 Ibid., 58.

63 http://www.nytimes.com/1988/05/04/obituaries/carroll-righter-dies-hollywood-astrologer.html.

64 Adorno, *Stars Down to Earth*, 51.

65 Stephen Crook, "Introduction: Adorno and Authoritarian Irrationalism," in Adorno, *Stars Down to Earth*.

66 Carroll Righter, *Dollar Signs* (New York: G. P. Putnam, 1975), 30–31.

67   It would seem that in his analysis of the two kinds of popular astrology, Adorno
      tried to offer a more nuanced version of culture industry that even sympathetic
      assessments of his cultural criticism would find lacking in his analyses. See,
      for example, Richard Wolin, "Utopia, Mimesis, Reconciliation: A Redemptive
      Critique of Adorno's *Aesthetic Theory*," *Representations* 32 (1990): 33–49.

68   Ellic Howe, *Urania's Children: The Strange World of the Astrologers* (London: William
      Kimber, 1967), 68.

69   http://www.astrology-world.com/kim.

70   Adorno, *Stars Down to Earth*, 51.

71   Ibid., 54.

72   Ibid., 61.

73   Ibid.

74   Horkheimer and Adorno, *Dialectic of Enlightenment*.

75   Adorno, "Adjustment and Individuality," in *Stars Down to Earth*, 105–27.

76   For a more recent discussion of craftsmanship and labor, see Richard Sennett,
      The Craftsman (New Haven, Conn.: Yale University Press, 2008).

77   Ibid., 161.

78   Adorno, *Stars Down to Earth*.

79   Ibid., 42.

80   Herbert Marcuse, *One Dimensional Man: Studies in the Ideology of Advanced Industrial
      Society* (New York: Beacon Press, 1991).

81   Kevin Phillips, *American Theocracy: The Peril and Politics of Oil, Radical Religion and Bor-
      rowed Money in the 21st Century* (New York: Penguin, 2007).

82   J. M. Bernstein, introduction to Adorno, *The Culture Industry*, 13.

83   Lorenz Jäger, *Adorno: A Political Biography*, trans. Stewart Spencer (New Haven,
      Conn.: Yale University Press, 2004), 151.

84   Adorno, *Stars Down to Earth*, 63.

85   Jäger, *Adorno*; Jenemann, *Adorno in America*; and Claussen, *Theodor Adorno*.

86   Jenemann, *Adorno in America*, cited on 50.

87   Hofstadter, *Anti-intellectualism*, 236.

88   Charles A. Prosser and William F. Sahlin, *How to Get a Job and Win Promotion* (Bloom-
      ington, Ill.: McKnight and McKnight, 1945).

89   Norman Mailer, *Advertisements for Myself* (New York: Putnam, 1959).

90   Dwight Macdonald, "Masscult & Midcult," in *Against the American Grain* (New York:
      Da Capo Press, 1962). Originally published in *Partisan Review* (Spring 1960).

91   Adorno, *Stars Down to Earth*, 71.

92   Riesman, *The Lonely Crowd*, 141.

93   Adorno, *Stars Down to Earth*, 101.

94   Ibid., 102–3.

95   Righter quoted in ibid., 70.

96   Ibid., 102.

97   Ibid., 103.

98   Czech Who Escaped, "An Escapee Warns of Red Menace," *Los Angeles Times*, November 10, 1952.

99   Adorno, *Stars Down to Earth*, 111.

100   Ibid.

101   Wiggershaus, *The Frankfurt School*, 434–35.

102   Paul Apostolidis, *Stations of the Cross: Adorno and Christian Right Radio* (Durham, N.C.: Duke University Press, 2000).

103   See chapter 2 on the inaccessibility of critical thinking for the average student.

104   Adorno, *Stars Down to Earth*, 42.

105   Apostolidis, *Stations of the Cross*.

106   Adorno et al., *The Authoritarian Personality*.

107   Stuart Hall, *The Hard Road to Renewal: Thatcherism and the Crisis of the Left* (London: Verso, 1988).

108   Roth, *American Pastoral*, 12.

109   Nathan Zuckerman is a fictional character who reappears throughout Philip Roth's fiction as an alter ego, as a womanizing novelist in *Zuckerman Unbound* (1981), and in a trilogy of later works, *The American Pastoral* (1997), *I Married a Communist* (1998), and *The Human Stain* (2000), as an aging and reclusive writer who grew up in New Jersey and lives in New England.

110   Ibid., 5.

111   Hofstadter, *Paranoid Style*, 3.

112   Roth, *American Pastoral*, 105.

Chapter Four. Against All Experts

1   "Although the German SDS shares the same initials with the Students for a Democratic Society in the United States, the two organizations are otherwise unconnected." The SDS was associated with the Social Democratic Party until its members rejected German rearmament. "The SDS subsequently provided the breeding ground for the German New Left, including ultimately its anarchist and terrorist tendencies." (Claussen, *Theodor Adorno*, 409n270 [translator's footnote]).

2   Jäger, *Adorno*, 207.

3   Claussen, *Theodor W. Adorno*, 334.

4   Russell Berman, "From 'Left Fascism' to Campus Anti-Semitism," *Dissent*, Summer 2008, 14–30.

5   Theodor Adorno, "The Meaning of Working Through the Past," in *Critical Models:*

Interventions and Catchwords, trans. Henry Pickford (New York: Columbia University Press, 2005), 89–103, quote at 89.

6   Ibid.

7   Ibid., 98–99.

8   Claussen, *Theodor W. Adorno*, 332. "Was bedeutet: Aufarbeiten der Vergangenheit?" was given as a public lecture in Wiesbaden in November 1959 and later published by Deutschen Koordinierungsrat der Gesellschaften für Christlich-Jüdische Zusammenarbeit (Frankfurt: Verlag Moritz Diesterweg, 1960). It was delivered as a radio lecture on Hessicher Rundfunk, February 7, 1960.

9   Jäger, *Adorno*, 206.

10 "In an article that will appear in late May in *Deutschlandarchiv*, a periodical dedicated to the ongoing project of German reunification, Helmut Müller-Enbergs and Cornelia Jabs reveal that documents they found in the Stasi papers show that Kurras began working together with the Stasi in 1955. He had wanted to move to East Berlin to work for the East German police. Instead, he signed an agreement with the Stasi to remain with the West Berlin police force and spy for the communist state" ("Stasi Archive Surprise: East German Spy Shot West German Martyr," *Der Spiegel* online, http://www.spiegel.de/international/germany/ 0,1518,626275,00.html).

11 http://mikeely.wordpress.com/2009/05/27/history-twists-the-killing-of-benno -ohnesorg/.

12 Berman, "From 'Left Fascism,'" 19.

13 Jäger, *Adorno*, 198.

14 Rudi Dutschke quoted in Wolfgang Kraushaar, ed., *Frankfurter Schule und Studentenbewegung: Von der Flaschenpost zum Molotowcocktail, 1946–95* (Hamburg: Rogner & Bernhard, 1998), 259. Cited in Berman, "From 'Left Fascism,'" 16.

15 Berman, "From 'Left Fascism,'" 16.

16 Claussen, *Theodor W. Adorno*, 337.

17 Wiggershaus, *The Frankfurt School*, 633.

18 Jäger, *Adorno*, 203.

19 Fredric Jameson, *Late Marxism: Adorno or the Persistence of the Dialectic* (London: Verso, 1990), 7.

20 Roth, *American Pastoral*, 145.

21 *WACK! Art and the Feminist Revolution*, organized by Cornelia Butler (Cambridge, Mass.: MIT Press, 2007).

22 Peggy Phelan, "The Returns of Touch: Feminist Performances, 1960–1980," in ibid., 346–61, 346.

23 Donald S. Lopez, Jr., *Prisoners of Shangri-La: Tibetan Buddhism and the West* (Chicago: University of Chicago Press, 1998).

24 Theodor Roszak, *The Making of a Counter Culture* (Garden City, N.Y.: Doubleday & Company, 1969), 7.

25 Adorno, "The Meaning of Working Through the Past," 98.

26 Ibid., 89–90.

27 Adorno, *Stars Down to Earth*, 35.

28 Theodor Adorno, *Prisms*, trans. Samuel and Shierry Weber (Cambridge, Mass.: MIT Press, 1997), 236.

29 *Theodor W. Adorno and Walter Benjamin: Complete Correspondence, 1928–1940*, ed. Henri Lonitz, trans. Nicholas Walker (New York: Polity Press, 1999), 131.

30 Roszak, *Making of a Counter Culture*, 252.

31 Hall, *Hard Road to Renewal*, 51.

32 Adorno, "The Meaning of Working Through the Past," 99.

33 Adorno, *Prisms*, 236.

34 Walter Benjamin, "On Astrology," in *Selected Writings*, 2:685.

35 Wolin, "Utopia, Mimesis, Reconciliation."

36 Walter Benjamin, "The Work of Art in the Age of Mechanical Reproducibility," in *Selected Writings*, vol. 3, *1945–1938*, ed. Michael W. Jennings, Howard Eiland, and Gary Smith (Cambridge, Mass.: Belknap Press of Harvard University Press, 2002), 114.

37 Anne Friedberg, *Window Shopping: Cinema and the Postmodern* (Berkeley: University of California Press, 1994).

38 Anson Rabinbach, *In the Shadow of Catastrophe: German Intellectuals between Apocalypse and Enlightenment* (Berkeley: University of California Press, 1997), 46.

39 Susan Buck-Morss, *The Dialectics of Seeing* (Cambridge, Mass.: MIT Press, 1989).

40 Eric Hobsbawm, *The Invention of Tradition* (Cambridge: Cambridge University Press, 1992).

41 Apostolidis, *Stations of the Cross*, 83.

42 Kazin, *Populist Persuasion*, 111.

43 Ibid., 113.

44 Ibid., 123.

45 Theodor Adorno, *The Psychological Technique of Martin Luther Thomas' Radio Addresses* (Stanford, Calif.: Stanford University Press, 2000).

46 Ibid., 1.

47 Martin Luther Thomas, radio broadcast, May 29, 1935, cited in ibid., 34.

48 Ibid., 36.

49 Theodor Adorno and Max Horkheimer, "The Concept of Enlightenment," in Horkheimer and Adorno, *Dialectic of Enlightenment*, 3–42, quote at 12.

50 Theodor Adorno, "Culture and Administration," in Adorno, *The Culture Industry*, 123.

51 Max Weber, *On Charisma and Institution Building*, ed. S. S. N. Eisenstadt (Chicago: University of Chicago Press, 1968).

52 Kazin, *Populist Persuasion*, 131.

53 Steven Brint, *In an Age of Experts: The Changing Role of Professionals in Politics and Public Life* (Princeton, N.J.: Princeton University Press, 1994).

54 Lawrence Levine, *Highbrow, Lowbrow: The Emergence of Cultural Hierarchy* (Cambridge, Mass.: Harvard University Press, 1990).

55 See also Siegfried Kracauer, *The Salaried Masses: Duty and Distraction in Weimar Germany*, trans. Quintin Hoare (London: Verso, 1998).

56 Walter Benjamin, "On Communist Pedagogy," in *Selected Writings*, 2:274.

57 Marc Bousquet's analysis of casual graduate student labor proposed that the university has represented, since the 1970s, a vanguardist model of the use of a flexible labor force, especially in its management of casual employees. The longer you have been a graduate student, the more devalued you are as an employee of your university (Marc Bousquet, *How the University Works: Higher Education and the Low-Wage Nation* [New York: New York University Press, 2008]).

58 Buck-Morss, *Dialectics of Seeing*, 326.

59 Miriam Bratu Hansen, "Room-for-Play: Benjamin's Gamble with Cinema," *October* 109 (Summer 2004): 3–45, 6.

60 Theodor W. Adorno, "Schema of Mass Culture," in Adorno, *Culture Industry*, 77.

61 Hansen, "Room-for-Play," 36n90.

62 Benjamin, "On Communist Pedagogy."

63 See the introduction to Peter Krapp, *Déjà Vu: Aberrations of Memory* (Minneapolis: University of Minnesota Press, 2004).

64 Walter Benjamin, "The Work of Art in the Age of Mechanical Reproducibility," in *Illuminations*, trans. Harry Zohn (New York: Schocken Books, 1968), 234.

65 Jeffrey Mehlman, *Walter Benjamin for Children* (Chicago: University of Chicago Press, 1993), 15–18. Benjamin's radio programs have been published as *Aufklärung für Kinder* (Frankfurt: Suhrkamp, 1985). Later, they were retitled *Fundfunkgeschichten für Kinder* and published in volume 7 of Benjamin's complete works (Frankfurt: Suhrkamp, 1989).

66 Buck-Morss, *Dialectics of Seeing*, 273–79.

67 John Fiske, "Bodies of Knowledge, Panopticism, and Spectatorship," unpublished paper delivered at the 1991 North American Society for the Sociology of Sport (NASSS) conference, Milwaukee. Cited in Eric Dunning, *Sport Matters: Sociological Studies of Sport, Violence and Civilization* (London: Routledge, 1999), 2–3.

68 See Henri Lefebvre, *Critique of Everyday Life*, 3 vols., trans. Gregory Elliot and John Moore (London: Verso, 2008); Raoul Vaneigm, *The Revolution of Everyday Life* (San Francisco: PM Press, 2011), also available online at http://library.nothingness

.org/authors.php3?id=4. See also Raymond Williams, *The Country and the City* (Oxford: Oxford University Press, 1975).

69   Adorno, "Culture and Administration," 128.

70   Ibid., 129.

71   Jim McGuigan, *Cultural Populism* (London: Routledge, 1992), 2.

72   Ibid., 171.

73   Hall, *Hard Road to Renewal*, 53.

74   Jon Savage and Simon Frith, "Pearls and Swine: Intellectuals and the Media," *New Left Review*, no. 198 (1993): 107–16.

75   Dick Hebdige, *Subculture: The Meaning of Style* (New York: Routledge, 1979), 78–80.

76   Chris Rojek, *Cultural Studies* (London: Polity, 2007), 142–43.

77   Introduction to Grossberg, Nelson, and Treichler, *Cultural Studies*, 1–17, quote at 1.

78   Homi K. Bhabha, "Postcolonial Authority and Postmodern Guilt," in Grossberg, Nelson, and Treichler, *Cultural Studies*, 56–68.

79   Jan Zita Grover, "AIDS, Keywords and Cultural Work," in Grossberg, Nelson, and Treichler, *Cultural Studies*, 227–39, quote at 228.

80   "The Sixties without Apology," *Social Text*, nos. 9–10 (Spring–Summer 1984): 1–390; Fredric Jameson, "Postmodernism, or the Cultural Logic of Late Capital," *New Left Review* 1 (July–August 1984): 52–96.

81   Certeau, *The Practice of Everyday Life*.

82   John Fiske, "The Culture of Everyday Life," in Grossberg, Nelson, and Treichler, *Cultural Studies*, 154–65; John Fiske, *Understanding Popular Culture* (New York: Routledge, 1989); Jenkins, *Textual Poachers*.

83   Jon Wiener, "Pop and Circumstance," *Nation*, November 6, 1989, 540; Robert Christgau, "Radical Pluralist: Andrew Ross's 'No Respect,'" *Village Voice*, 1990, archived online at http://www.robertchristgau.com/xg/bkrev/ross-90.php.

84   Wiener, "Pop and Circumstance."

85   Stuart Hall, "The Emergence of Cultural Studies and the Crisis in the Humanities," special issue, "Humanities as a Social Technology," *October* 53 (Summer 1990): 11–23, quote at 12.

86   Jennifer Daryl Slack, in Grossberg, Nelson, and Treichler, *Cultural Studies*, 553; Andrew Ross, *Strange Weather: Culture, Science and Technology in the Age of Limits* (New York: Verso, 1991).

87   Fredric Jameson, "On 'Cultural Studies,'" *Social Text*, no. 34 (1993): 17–52, quote at 24.

88   Fredric Jameson, "Periodizing the 60s," in *The Ideologies of Theory: Essays 1971–1986*, vol. 2, *Syntax of History* (Minneapolis: University of Minnesota Press, 1988), 208.

89   Marshall McLuhan, *Understanding Media* (London: Routledge & Kegan Paul, 1964), 255–56.

Chapter Five. The New Age of Cultural Studies

1   Arthur M. Schlesinger, "Not Right, Not Left, but a Vital Center," *New York Times Magazine*, April 4, 1948.

2   The Port Huron Statement can be accessed at http://www.campusactivism.org/server-new/uploads/porthuron.htm.

3   William Butler Yeats, "The Second Coming": "Turning and turning in the widening gyre / The falcon cannot hear the falconer; / Things fall apart; the centre cannot hold; / Mere anarchy is loosed upon the world, / The blood-dimmed tide is loosed, and everywhere / The ceremony of innocence is drowned; / The best lack all conviction, while the worst / Are full of passionate intensity."

4   Young, *The Rise of the Meritocracy*.

5   Fenster, *Conspiracy Theories*.

6   Joan Didion, *Slouching towards Bethlehem*, in *We Tell Ourselves Stories in Order to Live: Collected Nonfiction* (New York: Alfred A. Knopf, Everyman's Library, 2006), 67; Jacques Derrida, "Mythologie blanche," in *Poétique*, 1971, and in English as "White Mythology: Metaphor in the Text of Philosophy," in *Margins of Philosophy*, trans. Alan Bass (Chicago: University of Chicago Press, 1985), 207–72.

7   Turner, *From Counterculture to Cyberculture*, 66.

8   Ibid.

9   Tom Wolfe, *The Electric Kool-Aid Acid Test* (1969; New York: Picador, 2008), 263.

10 Didion, *Slouching*, 93.

11 Wolfe, *Electric Kool-Aid Acid Test*, 30.

12 Ibid., 29–30.

13 Kazin, *Populist Persuasion*, 279.

14 Lasch, *Culture of Narcissism*, 149.

15 Herbert J. Gans, *Popular Culture and High Culture: An Analysis and Evaluation of Taste* (1974; New York: Perseus Books, 1999), 68.

16 Zygmunt Bauman, *Legislators and Interpreters: On Modernity, Post-modernity and Intellectuals* (Ithaca, N.Y.: Cornell University Press, 1987).

17 Sarah Pike, *New Age and Neopagan Religions in America* (New York: Columbia University Press, 2004), 80.

18 Ross, *Strange Weather*, 26–27.

19 Ibid., 72, 68.

20 Lasch, *Culture of Narcissism*, 149.

21 Ross, *Strange Weather*, 28–29.

22 Wolfe, *Electric Kool-Aid Acid Test*, 44.

23 Ross, *Strange Weather*, 30.

24 Ibid., 37.

25 Barbara and John Ehrenreich, "The Professional-Managerial Class," in *Between Labor and Capital*, ed. Pat Walker (Boston: South End Press, 1979), 5–45.

26 The existence of this class was hotly debated by American socialists; fortunately, we do not have to enter into the arguments that tore the Left apart during the 1970s and 1980s.

27 Brint, *In an Age of Experts*, 5.

28 Joan Didion, "The Women's Movement," in *The White Album* (New York: Simon and Schuster, 1979), 109–19, quote at 110.

29 Ehrenreich, *Fear of Falling*, 218–19.

30 Brooks, *Bobos in Paradise*. Brooks basically stole Barbara Ehrenreich's arguments and refashioned them into a genial, liberal-bashing weapon.

31 Ehrenreich, *Fear of Falling*, 250.

32 Ehrenreich and Ehrenreich, "The Professional-Managerial Class," 37–38.

33 Magali Sarfatti Larson, "Expertise and Expert Power," in *The Authority of Experts*, ed. Thomas L. Haskell (Bloomington: Indiana University Press, 1984), 28–80.

34 Ehrenreich and Ehrenreich, "The Professional-Managerial Class," 45.

35 Turner, *From Counterculture to Cyberculture*, 78.

36 Ibid., 79–80.

37 Pike, *New Age and Neopagan Religions*, 73.

38 Wolfe, *Electric Kool-Aid Acid Test*, 44.

39 Ehrenreich and Ehrenreich, "The Professional-Managerial Class," 39.

40 Pike, *New Age and Neopagan Religions*, 171–72.

41 http://www.csicop.org/.

42 Ross, *Strange Weather*, 15–74, 60.

43 Bruno Latour, *Science in Action: How to Follow Science and Engineers through Society* (Cambridge, Mass.: Harvard University Press, 1988).

44 Ross, *Strange Weather*, 25.

45 Gans, *Popular Culture*, 199.

46 Bruno Latour, "Why Has Critique Run Out of Steam? From Matters of Fact to Matters of Concern," *Critical Inquiry*, Winter 2004, 225–48.

47 S. Fred Singer, "The Scientific Case against the Global Warming Treaty: A Report from the Science & Environmental Policy Project, Arlington, Virginia, July 2001," http://www.sepp.org/, a website promoting a conservative agenda that offers an array of talking points and a series of documents refuting the reality of global warming.

48 Ross, *Strange Weather*, 217.

49 Ibid., 219.

50 "Preface to the 1998 Edition," in Paul R. Gross and Norman Levitt, *A Higher Super-*

stition: The Academic Left and Its Quarrels with Science (Baltimore, Md.: Johns Hopkins University Press, 1994), ix–xiv, quote at xii.

51 Andrew Ross, introduction to "Science Wars," ed. Andrew Ross and Bruce Robbins, special issue, *Social Text* 46–47 (Spring–Summer 1996): 7.

52 Gross and Levitt, *A Higher Superstition*, 40.

53 Ibid., 2.

54 Ross, introduction, 7.

55 Gross and Levitt, *A Higher Superstition*, 52.

56 Dorothy Nelkin, "Responses to a Marriage Failed," in "Science Wars," ed. Andrew Ross and Bruce Robbins, special issue, *Social Text* 46–47 (Spring–Summer 1996): 93–110.

57 Ross, introduction, 6.

58 Ibid., 2, 3.

59 Stanley Aronowitz, "The Politics of the Science Wars," in "Science Wars," ed. Andrew Ross and Bruce Robbins, special issue, *Social Text* 46–47 (Spring–Summer 1996): 177–98, quotes at 178, 191.

60 Gross and Levitt, *A Higher Superstition*, 1–3.

61 Alan Sokal, "Transgressing the Boundaries: Towards a Transformative Hermeneutics of Quantum Gravity," in "Science Wars," ed. Andrew Ross and Bruce Robbins, special issue, *Social Text* 46–47 (Spring–Summer 1996): 217–52.

62 Ross, *Strange Weather*, 42.

63 Sokal, "Transgressing the Boundaries," 21–22.

64 Alan Sokal, "A Physicist Experiments with Cultural Studies," *Lingua Franca*, May–June 1996, accessed at Alan Sokal's site, http://www.physics.nyu.edu/faculty/sokal/lingua_franca_v4/lingua_franca_v4.html. The full text of Sokal's article in *Lingua Franca* and Robbins's and Ross's responses have also been anthologized in *Quick Study: The Best of Lingua Franca*, ed. Alexander Star (New York: Farrar, Strauss and Giroux, 2002).

65 Sokal, "Transgressing the Boundaries," 217–18.

66 Bruce Robbins and Andrew Ross, "Response by Social Text Editors," in July–August issue of *Lingua Franca*, accessed at http://www.physics.nyu.edu/sokal/SocialText_reply_LF.pdf. These broad accusations against scientific transgressions lacked effective specificity, for in the struggles over the pseudoscience of intelligence testing, we saw that scientists and humanists Stephen Jay Gould and Nicholas Lemann could work together to counter the effects of scientific racism and eugenics.

67 Brint, *In an Age of Experts*, 17.

68 Sokal's own collection of material related to the affair is online at http://www.physics.nyu.edu/faculty/sokal/. For more materials relating to the Sokal affair, see http://www.drizzle.com/~jwalsh/sokal/.

69   Alan Sokal, "Transgressing the Boundaries: An Afterword," *Dissent* 43 (Fall 1996): 93–99.

70   Aronowitz, "Politics," 196.

71   http://www.gallup.com/poll/21814/Evolution-Creationism-Intelligent-Design .aspx.

72   See Postel, *Populist Vision*.

73   Introduction to Grossberg, Nelson, and Treichler, *Cultural Studies*, 2.

74   Graff, *Professing Literature*.

75   John Guillory, *Cultural Capital: The Problem of Literary Canon Formation* (Chicago: University of Chicago Press, 1995).

76   Turner, *From Counterculture to Cyberculture*, 115.

77   See Philip Rieff, *Freud: The Mind of a Moralist* (Chicago: University of Chicago Press, 1979) and *The Triumph of the Therapeutic: The Uses of Faith after Freud* (Chicago: University of Chicago Press, 1987).

78   Wendy Kaminer, *I'm Dysfunctional, You're Dysfunctional: The Recovery Movement and Other Self-Help Fashions* (Reading, Mass.: Addison-Wesley, 1992) and *Sleeping with Extra-Terrestrials: The Rise of Irrationalism and the Perils of Piety* (New York: Vintage Books, 2000).

79   Robert Darnton, *Mesmerism and the End of the Enlightenment* (Cambridge, Mass.: Harvard University Press, 1986).

80   Kaminer, *Sleeping with Extraterrestrials*, 149–53.

81   Ross, *Strange Weather* 69.

82   Kaminer, *Sleeping with Extraterrestrials*, 142.

83   Ross, *Strange Weather*, 71.

84   Kaminer, *Sleeping with Extraterrestrials*, 144.

85   Ross, *Strange Weather*, 28.

86   Olav Hammer, *Claiming Knowledge: Strategies of Epistemology from Theosophy to the New Age* (London: Brill Academic Publishers, 2003), 340.

87   Marilyn Ferguson, *The Aquarian Conspiracy: Personal and Social Transformation in Our Time* (New York: J. P. Tarcher, 1987).

88   Elspeth Probyn, "Technologies of the Self," in Grossberg, Nelson, and Treichler, *Cultural Studies*, 501–11, 503.

89   Pike, *New Age and Neopagan Religions*, 171–72.

90   Probyn, "Technologies of the Self," 503, 510.

91   Schiller's foundational ideas on aesthetic education were founded on the practice of an endless series of self-critical and self-problematizing exercises, with the goal of achieving natural detachment and disinterestedness.

92   Probyn, "Technologies of the Self," 505, 511.

93 Ross, *Strange Weather*, 73.

94 Didion, *Slouching*, 93, 91.

Conclusion

1 Kazin, *Populist Persuasion*, 271.

2 The Hewlett-Packard advertisement for the HP Deskjet 1200c appeared in the *New Yorker* in 1993, while the Banana Republic ad dates from 1986 and appeared in a variety of national circulation magazines (ibid., 271, 359n3).

3 Fredric Jameson, *The Political Unconscious: Narrative as Socially Symbolic Act* (Ithaca, N.Y.: Cornell University Press, 1982).

4 Jameson, "Periodizing the 60s," 189.

5 Frank, *One Market under God*.

6 "Populist: n. a member of a political party claiming to represent the common people; especially often capitalized: a member of a United States political party formed in 1891 primarily to represent agrarian interests and to advocate the free coinage of silver and government control of monopolies." The dictionary definition of "populist" is changing: the *Oxford English Dictionary* has recently allowed "popular" to supplant the historical reference of the term. See http://www.merriam-webster.com/dictionary/populist, accessed March 3, 2011.

7 Laclau, *On Populist Reason*, 206.

8 Goodwyn, *Democratic Promise*, 527.

9 Ibid., 523.

10 http://historymatters.gmu.edu/d/5361/

11 http://www.careerjournal.com/article/SB121521073192129407.html?mod=fpa_mostpop.

12 Senator Slade Gordon, "On the Official Funding of Religious Bigotry," statement to the Senate, May 31, 1989, collected in Richard Bolton, *Culture Wars: Documents from the Recent Controversies in the Arts* (New York: New Press, 1992), 33.

13 Robert Mapplethorpe, *The Perfect Moment*, with essays by Janet Kardon, Kay Larson, and David Joselit (Philadelphia: Institute of Contemporary Art, 1988).

14 http://www.publiceye.org/theocrat/Mapplethorpe_Chrono.html.

15 In 1990 four artists (Karen Finely, Holly Hughes, Tim Miller, and John Fleck) were awarded NEA individual artist grants by a peer-review board. John Frohnmayer, chairman of the NEA, subsequently vetoed their awards out of concerns about obscenity. These artists came to be known as the NEA 4, and they sued the agency successfully. Their case was settled in 1993 with the restoration of their grants. In the summer of 1990, Congress did pass a "decency clause" about the NEA grant-making policies, stipulating that the agency had to consider the "general standards of decency . . . of the American public." In 1998 the U.S. Supreme Court heard arguments about the decency clause and decided to uphold it but limited

its proscriptions as advisory. Frohnmayer was forced to resign in 1992. The NEA no longer gives grants to individual artists.

16   Hilton Kramer, "Is Art above the Laws of Decency?," *New York Times*, July 2, 1989.

17   Harriet Senie, *The Tilted Arc Controversy: A Dangerous Precedent* (Minneapolis: University of Minnesota Press, 2002).

18   http://latimesblogs.latimes.com/culturemonster/2009/02/nea-if-i-ran-th.html.

19   Naomi Klein, *Shock Doctrine: The Rise of Disaster Capitalism* (New York: Metropolitan Books, 2008).

20   Robert Brustein, "Don't Punish the Arts," *New York Times*, June 23, 1989.

21   Chin-tao Wu, *Privatising Culture: Corporate Art Intervention since the 1980s* (London: Verso, 2002).

22   Edward Said, *Representations of the Intellectual* (1994; New York: Vintage Books, 1996), xvi–xvii.

23   Jameson, "Periodizing the 60s," 201.

24   Fredric Jameson, *Postmodernism, or, The Cultural Logic of Late Capitalism* (1991; Durham, N.C.: Duke University Press, 2005).

25   Robert Venturi and Denise Scott Brown, *Learning from Las Vegas: The Forgotten Symbolism of Architectural Form* (Cambridge, Mass.: MIT Press, 1977); Jameson, *Postmodernism*, 61, 305–6. See also Charles Jencks, *The New Paradigm in Architecture: Language of Postmodernism* (1977; New Haven, Conn.: Yale University Press, 2002).

26   Russell Jacoby, *The Last Intellectuals: American Culture in the Age of Academe* (New York: Basic Books, 2000), 141.

27   Jameson, *Postmodernism*, 39–41.

28   Jacoby, *The Last Intellectuals*, 7.

29   Jameson, *Postmodernism*, 46.

30   Brint, *In an Age of Experts*.

31   Howard Brick, *Transcending Capitalism: Visions of a New Society in American Thought* (Ithaca, N.Y.: Cornell University Press, 2006).

32   Ehrenreich, *Fear of Falling*, 260.

33   Walter Benn Michaels, *The Trouble with Diversity: How We Learned to Love Identity and Ignore Inequality* (New York: Henry Holt, 2007).

34   Diane Ravitch, *The Death and Life of the Great American School System* (New York: Basic Books, 2010).

35   Ehrenreich, *Fear of Falling*, 260–61.

36   Christopher Newfield, *Unmaking the Public University: The Forty Year Assault on the Middle Class* (Cambridge, Mass.: Harvard University Press, 2008).

index